"A rollicking introduction to the history of a country that, until barely 150 years ago, was not one. Vibrant, admirably clear, and often wryly amusing, Ross King's narrative benefits again and again from his eye for the telling detail—a splendid achievement."
—**John Hooper, author of *The Italians* and Italy correspondent for *The Economist***

"Few have as much insight into the history of Italy as the author of *Brunelleschi's Dome*, and here Ross King offers a masterful and perceptive account of Italian virtues—and sins—from the Romans to Berlusconi, as well as the country's inimitable art and architecture. An ideal handbook for anyone who loves Italy."
—**Richard Owen, author of *Hemingway in Italy***

"Dazzling, instructive, and highly entertaining."
—*The Wall Street Journal*, **on *The Bookseller of Florence***

"Magnificent . . . King's meticulous research provides an immersive reading experience."
—*Booklist*, **starred review, on *The Bookseller of Florence***

"King makes the familiar fresh."
—*Publishers Weekly*, **on *Michelangelo and the Pope's Ceiling***

"King is ever the brilliant docent murmuring the right, telling details and critical backstories in our ear as we move through space and time."
—*Library Journal*, **starred review, on *Mad Enchantment***

"[King is] an exceptional portraitist and craftsman."
—*Booklist*, **starred review, on *Leonardo and the Last Supper***

"King has made a career elucidating crucial episodes in the history of art and architecture."—*Time* **magazine**

THE
SHORTEST
HISTORY
OF
ITALY

3,000 Years from the Romans to the Renaissance to a Modern Republic— A Retelling for Our Times

ROSS KING

THE EXPERIMENT

NEW YORK

THE SHORTEST HISTORY OF ITALY: *3,000 Years from the Romans to the Renaissance to a Modern Republic—A Retelling for Our Times*
Copyright © 2024 by Ross King
Pages 251–52 are a continuation of this copyright page.

Originally published in Australia by Black, Inc. First published in North America in revised form by The Experiment, LLC.

The Experiment, LLC
220 East 23rd Street, Suite 600
New York, NY 10010-4658
theexperimentpublishing.com

The Experiment's books are available at special discounts when purchased in bulk for premiums and sales promotions as well as for fundraising or educational use. For details, contact us at info@theexperimentpublishing.com.

Library of Congress Cataloging-in-Publication Data available upon request

ISBN 978-1-891011-45-0
Ebook ISBN 978-1-891011-46-7

Cover and text design by Jack Dunnington

Manufactured in the United States of America

First printing April 2024
10 9 8 7 6 5 4 3 2 1

To Destine Bradshaw

Contents

Chronology

ARCHAIC PERIOD	**C. 1184 BCE**	Legendary arrival of Aeneas in Italy following the Trojan War
	753 BCE	Legendary founding of Rome
	509 BCE	Founding of the Roman Republic
ROMAN REPUBLIC	**264–41 BCE**	First Punic War
	218 BCE	Hannibal crosses the Alps and invades Italy
	146 BCE	Roman destruction of Carthage and Corinth
	91–87 BCE	Social War
	60 BCE	First Triumvirate founded
	44 BCE	Assassination of Julius Caesar
	30 BCE	Deaths of Antony and Cleopatra
	27 BCE	Octavian proclaimed "Augustus" by the Senate
ROMAN EMPIRE	**14 CE**	Death of Augustus; Tiberius becomes emperor
	64 CE	Great Fire in Rome
	79 CE	Eruption of Vesuvius
	80 CE	Completion of the Colosseum
	117	The Empire reaches its greatest expanse under Trajan
	180	Death of Marcus Aurelius, last of the "Five Good Emperors"
	235–284	"Third Century Crisis"
	293	Diocletian establishes the Tetrarchy
	312	Battle of the Milvian Bridge
	410	Sack of Rome by the Visigoths
	452	Huns under Attila invade Italy
	476	End of the Roman Empire in the West
LATE ANTIQUITY	**493**	Beginning of the Kingdom of the Ostrogoths (until 553)
	568	Lombard invasion of Italy
	800	Charlemagne proclaimed Holy Roman Emperor

MIDDLE AGES	831	Emirate of Sicily established (until 1061)
	1061	Beginning of Norman conquest of Sicily
	1176	Lombard League defeats Frederick Barbarossa at Battle of Legnano
	1209	St. Francis of Assisi gains papal approval for his order
	1302	Dante exiled from Florence; he begins *The Divine Comedy*
	1309	Pope Clement V moves the papal court to Avignon (until 1376)
	1378	Beginning of the Western Schism (until 1417)
RENAISSANCE	1417	Donatello completes his sculpture of St. George in Florence
	1452	Birth of Leonardo da Vinci
	1454	Peace of Lodi
	1492	Birth of Vittoria Colonna
	1494	Invasion of Italy by King Charles VIII of France
	1512	Michelangelo completes his fresco on the vault of the Sistine Chapel
	1527	Sack of Rome by the troops of Holy Roman Emperor Charles V
	1545	The Council of Trent opens (until 1563)
	1593	Birth of Artemesia Gentileschi
	1632	Galileo publishes *Dialogo sopra i massimi sistemi del mondo*; a year later he is forced to abjure his "errors"
ILLUMINISMO	1734	Beginning of Bourbon rule in Naples
	1764	Cesare Beccari publishes *On Crimes and Punishments*
	1796	French forces led by Napoleon invade Italy
	1797	End of the Venetian Republic
	1805	Napoleon crowns himself King of Italy in Milan
RISORGIMENTO	1848	First Italian War of Independence
	1859	Second Italian War of Independence
	1860	Expedition of The Thousand under Giuseppe Garibaldi

KINGDOM OF ITALY	1861	Victor Emmanuel II becomes King of Italy
	1866	Third Italian War of Independence
	1870	Italian troops capture Rome from the papacy
	1900	Assassination in Milan of King Umberto I
	1911	Italian invasion of Libya
	1915	Italy enters the First World War on the side of Britain and France
	1922	The Fascist "March on Rome"; Benito Mussolini becomes prime minister
	1935	Italian invasion of Ethiopia
	1940	Italy enters the Second World War by invading Greece
	1943	Allied invasion of Sicily and then mainland Italy
	1944	Liberation of Rome by the Allies
	1945	Release of Roberto Rossellini's *Rome, Open City*, starring Anna Magnani
REPUBLIC OF ITALY	1946	Italians vote to abolish the monarchy and establish a republic
	1949	Italy joins NATO
	1956	Beginning of Italy's "Economic Miracle" (until 1963)
	1968	Beginning of the *Anni di Piombo* (Years of Lead)
	1986	Beginning of the *Maxiprocesso* (Maxi Trial) against the Mafia (until 1992)
	1992	Assassination of anti-Mafia judges Paolo Borsellino and Giovanni Falcone; the Tangentopoli scandal and investigation
	1994	Media tycoon Silvio Berlusconi becomes prime minister for the first time
	2020	During the COVID-19 pandemic Italy becomes the first country to impose a nationwide lockdown
	2022	Giorgia Meloni becomes the first female prime minister of Italy

CHAPTER 1

"That People in Togas"
Ancient Italy and the Roman Republic

The refugee-laden boats nudge through the choppy waters as the storm blows in: fugitives crossing the Mediterranean in search of asylum. Hungry, exhausted, and fearful, they have been separated from loved ones, or have buried them on the journey with hasty, makeshift rites. The dream of a new land has kept them going through the tense wait on the beach for good weather and the threatening presence of ragged strangers speaking their enemy's tongue. They have been warned that navigation will be difficult, and that passing through the narrow strait is dangerous, if not impossible.

Now, as thunder crashes, the bow of the lead vessel yaws sharply in the swell and the helmsman breaks his oar. Helpless, they slide toward shoals rising from the foam like monstrous spines. The boat spins three times, shipping water and casting men and belongings into the roiling waves. The small fleet strains to make landfall, prows thudding over breakers. Through the lashing rain the men see a cove where they can go ashore: a stretch of calm water between vast cliffs whose tops bristle with trees. "Trojans, ecstatic with joy at regaining the dry land, / Leap from the ships and establish themselves on the sand-covered coastline."[1]

So opens Virgil's great epic, the *Aeneid*, completed in 19 BCE. The poem recounts the legendary tale of Aeneas and his companions fleeing the ruins of Troy and arriving in Italy—after shipwrecks and other mishaps—to become the ancestors of the Romans. Virgil's descriptions of storm-tossed refugees washing ashore on the north coast of Africa eerily presages the European migrant crisis that witnessed hundreds of thousands of refugees from Africa and the Middle East launching inflatable dinghies and other ramshackle craft into the Mediterranean in search of a new life in Europe. Italy was a natural destination given the proximity to Libya and Tunisia at its southernmost border and the islands of Sicily and Lampedusa. In 2015, more than 150,000 migrants arrived on Italian shores, with almost 3,000 more dying en route in shipwrecks and drownings. A year later, more than 180,000 arrived on boats from across the Mediterranean.

The social, political, economic, and cultural effects of the crisis on Italy still remain to be determined. However, the country's most powerful myth of its origins involves, as Virgil shows, migrants from a war-torn land arriving on Italian shores and becoming, thanks to Aeneas's illustrious descendants, "the masters of all in existence," that is, "that people in togas" (as Virgil proudly describes them).[2] The mastery of the Romans is difficult to overestimate. First under the Republic, then during the Imperial period—taken together, a span of almost a thousand years—the Romans were to make the Italian peninsula one of the world's greatest and most influential centers of political and cultural activity. A thousand years later, during the Renaissance of the fifteenth and sixteenth centuries, the peninsula would once again become the seat of a splendid civilization. Finally, Italy has been, for almost two thousand years, the seat of Christianity in the West—something else that has placed it at the epicenter of Western civilization.

This is a history of, in the first place, a geographical entity in which, over the millennia, many different societies and cultures have lived. Certainly, Italy always was, and still is, a well-defined geographical entity (albeit with, as we shall see, some gray areas). Few countries have their borders as clearly marked by natural features. Italy is known for good reason as *Lo Stivale* (The Boot), its distinctive profile shaped by the Alps in the north and the three seas (Adriatic, Ionian, and Ligurian-Tyrrhenian) surrounding it. Few countries, too, can boast the natural beauty and agreeable climate, making it what the poets Dante and Petrarch both called *il bel paese* (the fair country), and what a Greek historian, writing in the first century BCE, called the "country abounding in universal plenty and every charm mankind craves."[3] But Italy has always been much more than its mountains, shores, rivers, and plains. It is defined and shaped more emphatically by the wide and diverse range of people who have been born and lived there, or indeed, like Aeneas and his fellow Trojans, moved there from elsewhere. This is a story that I hope will do justice to at least a few of them, and that will show how identifying "Italy" and the "Italians" is inherently more difficult than spotting the telltale boot on a map of the world.

Virgil's account of the settlement of Italy is not a complete fiction. Parts of Sicily and the southern Italian mainland were indeed settled by Greek immigrants coming across the Ionian Sea. Overpopulation and famine on the Greek mainland and the Aegean Islands meant that by the eighth century BCE successive waves of Greeks, sailing westward on the prevailing currents, began colonizing both Sicily and the southern coastline of peninsular Italy. These Greek newcomers found fertile lands abundant in water and rich in grain and wine, together with a healthy climate. The area where they settled in Sicily and southern Italy became known as Magna Graecia (Greater Greece). Their cities included Neapolis (New City), or present-day Naples, and Tarentum (Taranto), founded by a group of Spartans. According to one tradition that began with Dionysius of Halicarnassus, a Greek-born contemporary of Virgil, the name "Italy" actually derived from these Greek immigrants, specifically from a wise and just leader, King Italus, who ruled in the region of present-day Calabria. Italy therefore originally referred, by this account, not to an indigenous population but rather to Greek colonists occupying the peninsula's southern shores.

King Italus may never have existed, but the Greeks certainly made a deep and lasting impression during their five hundred or so years of political and cultural domination in the South. They introduced, among other things, the alphabet, and their vibrant intellectual and artistic life produced the brilliant scientist Archimedes and philosophers such as Empedocles and Pythagoras. The latter immigrated to Croton from the Aegean island of Samos in about 529 BCE, founding a religious community dedicated to moral and political renewal. The civilization of Magna Graecia also left behind splendid monuments. The magnificent amphitheater of Syracuse—where the playwright Aeschylus staged one of his tragedies in the 450s BCE —remains largely intact. Greek temples at Paestum on the Italian mainland and in the Valley of Temples at Agrigento in Sicily likewise survive, counting among the first of Italy's many architectural treasures.

Italy c. 800 BCE

INSUBRI
VENETI
CENOMANI
LIGURI
PICENI
ETRUSCANS
UMBRI
FALISCI
SABINES
Rome
LATINI
SAMNITES
VOLSCI
IAPYGES
Neapolis
OSCI
Tarentum
SARDI
LUCANI
MAGNA GRAECIA
Croton
BRUTTII
SICULI
MAGNA GRAECIA
Syracuse

In the eighth century BCE, these Greek colonists were only the most recent migrants to Italy.

During the late Bronze Age, roughly from 1150 to 950 BCE, the peninsula's length and breadth became home to a mosaic of ethnic groups. Most were descendants of settlers who came across the Alps during the centuries-long Indo-European migrations, the massive and prolonged influx into Europe from the area north of the Baltic and Caspian seas (present-day Ukraine and southern Russia). Celtic tribes came to occupy large areas in the north between the Po River and the Alps. A patchwork of interlinked people, who for the most part spoke languages of Indo-European origins, pushed further down the peninsula, into parts of central and southern Italy. One of these languages was Oscan, named after the Osci, the ancient inhabitants of the region to the south of what would become Rome. Speakers included tribes such as the Sabines and one of their offshoots, the Samnites.

More mysterious in origin was the civilization to the north of the Oscan tribes: the Etruscans. They occupied ancient Etruria, the beautiful and fertile lands in central Italy that by and large encompass present-day Tuscany. They were unique insofar as they were linguistically different from the other Bronze Age arrivals on the Italian peninsula since, unlike Oscan, Etruscan was not an Indo-European-based language. All of which raises the question of where the Etruscans came from, and when, if not this great migration. Their origins have been a matter of much conjecture and debate, from ancient times to the present, though a recent study of DNA has suggested that the Etruscans did, in fact, migrate from the same Pontic–Caspian steppe as the other Indo-European tribes.[4]

The Etruscans were one of the most dominant political and cultural forces on the Italian peninsula from about 800 to 500 BCE, overlapping with the heyday of the great civilization of Magna Graecia in the South. The Etruscans were skilled artisans, metalworkers, seafarers, and charioteers, a status-conscious people devoted to pleasure and luxury. However, by around 400 BCE, they as well as the Greeks and the Celtic tribes faced competition from a relatively new and increasingly irresistible power on the peninsula.

Sometime during the tenth century BCE or earlier, another tribe known as the Latini (whose name means "people of the plains") came to occupy a region stretching some 50 miles (80 km) south from the lower reaches of the Tiber to present-day Terracina. By the time we reach the eighth century BCE, according to legend, a chunk of this land was ruled by a king named Numitor, whose capital was Alba Longa (the exact site of which is much debated). Fraternal strife—what will become a pervasive theme in Roman history—enters the story when Numitor is usurped by his younger brother Amulius. Although Amulius takes the precaution of forcing Numitor's daughter Rhea Silvia to become a vestal virgin (one of the six priestesses tending the fire in the Temple of Vesta), she soon gives birth to twins. The father, she claims, is none other than Mars, the god of war. Amulius orders the two babies to be drowned in the Tiber, but the men forced to carry out the deed are less than conscientious, merely placing the basket containing the boys into a sluggish stretch of water, which, as it ebbs, leaves them high and dry.

At this point the famous she-wolf appears and, hearing their cries and displaying her maternal instincts, begins suckling them. As these sons of Mars grow to manhood, they prove themselves courageous and strong, ultimately killing Amulius and restoring their grandfather to his rightful place. Leaving Alba Longa in the capable hands of their grandfather, the stout young twins set off to found a new city that will rise along the Tiber near the spot where the she-wolf discovered them.

More fraternal strife. Romulus selects a spot on the Palatine Hill and begins marking the perimeter with a plough pulled by an ox. Remus decides on a different location a short distance to the southwest, on the Aventine Hill. To settle the matter, the twins resort to auguries, a borrowing from

The she-wolf comes to the rescue of Romulus and Remus.

the Etruscans that involves interpreting the will of the gods through various signs in nature such as the behavior of birds. Remus receives his sign first: six birds flapping their way over the Aventine. But then Romulus, on the Palatine, spots a dozen vultures. Which is more favorable: the sign given first or the one with more birds? The will of the gods seems open to dispute. A violent altercation follows in which Romulus kills Remus. Following this deadly skirmish, Romulus finds himself the sole leader of the new city, which, referencing his name, is called Rome. The date, according to the legend, is April 21, 753 BCE.

A new city needs people. Once he had built his walls and other defenses, Romulus set about finding inhabitants. He did so by opening the gates to all comers and, in a short space of time, attracted a ragtag band of runaway slaves and fugitives from justice. Because most of these new residents were male, Romulus needed to find women for them; but because they were such a rough lot, the people in the surrounding area were reluctant to offer their daughters. He therefore hit upon a desperate and brutal strategy—a mass kidnapping. Promising games and other entertainments, he extended an invitation to a nearby tribe, the Sabines, and when the festivities were underway his men drew their swords and began carting off the young women (a scene of half-clad writhing female panic later much beloved of painters such as Nicolas Poussin).

Such, then, were the legendary origins of Rome: a brawl ending in fratricide, a population of bandits, slaves, and renegades, and a mass kidnapping to supply these outcasts with womenfolk and the city with babies. And yet this community of misfits, asylum-seekers, and captives would become the stock for the greatest power the ancient world had ever seen.

Poussin's The Abduction of the Sabine Women *(c. 1633): Romulus surveys the scene from the upper left.*

So much for the myth. Archaeology offers little evidence of anything as dramatic as the founding of the new community of Rome on the Palatine Hill in the middle of the eighth century BCE. If we could transport ourselves back to around 800 or 900 BCE, we would find a number of villages and hamlets already overlooking the Tiber. The hills with their steep sides provided the villagers with natural protection, while the Tiber gave fresh water and access to the sea, some 20 miles (32 km) downstream. The site was situated along natural arteries for trade and travel: both the Tiber—the widest river valley in Italy, featuring forty tributaries—and a series of roads intersecting at the site.

It's a safe assumption that Rome was not named after a dim and distant historical figure named Romulus. In ancient times, there were more than twenty-five different accounts of how Rome was founded, who the founder was, and from whom or what it took its name. The story of the outcast twins suckled by a she-wolf did not actually appear until around 300 BCE—and yet, dubious as it must have seemed, the story somehow stuck.

Romulus became the first of the seven legendary kings of Rome who ruled between 753 and 509 BCE. The last, Lucius Tarquinius Superbus, or Tarquin the Proud, embellished Rome with grand building projects and expanded its territory through an aggressive foreign policy. However, his kingship ended, according to legend, after his son, Sextus Tarquinius, raped a married woman named Lucretia, who then killed herself (a scene likewise much visited by painters). Her death was avenged by her husband's friend Lucius Junius, who had earned the cognomen Brutus, or "stupid," because he feigned idiocy to survive Tarquin's tyrannical rule. Brutus put her corpse on public display and then called on the people of Rome to avenge her death and expel the tyrants. Tarquin was duly toppled and the monarchy abolished. For the next 482 years, Rome would be a republic, with the powers of the kings eventually (by the fourth century BCE) devolving onto, and shared by, a pair of annually elected consuls who could command the army and summon a 300-strong advisory body named the Senate. The name of this institution, which would survive for the better part of a millennium, derived from *senex*, "old man," because it was staffed, in theory at least, by wise, gray heads. Ultimately, the Roman Republic would evolve a system (later widely copied) whereby its government was separated into three branches: the executive (the two consuls), the legislature (the Senate and other assemblies), and the judiciary (the judges and priests).

Most offices, such as that of consul, were elected positions. Our word "candidate" comes from the fact that someone vying for votes would appear in public in a whitened robe, the *toga candidata* (from the Latin *candidus*, "white"—the root of words like incandescent and candle). A political campaign was known as an *ambitio*, from which, naturally, we get "ambitious." The word *ambitio* comes from *ambire*, "to go around," because the white-clad candidates, like today's politicians, engaged in glad-handing walkabouts, often accompanied by a slave whose job it was to remember the names of important voters. Candidates wrote their names in red on the walls of buildings, often proclaiming themselves a *virum bonum*—"good chap." Excavations at Pompeii have shown the fate a would-be politician named Quinctius wished upon his opponents: "Anyone who votes against him should go and sit next to a donkey!"[5]

The institutions of the Roman Republic would soon need to be robust enough to govern large numbers of people spread across wide areas. The Italian peninsula in 509 BCE was still a patchwork of different civilizations: the Celts and Etruscans to the north of Rome, the Samnites and other tribes in the mountains to the south and east, and the Greeks in their settlements hugging the coast to the south. The Roman Republic frequently came into conflict with these various neighbors. Disaster struck around 390 BCE when the city was sacked by a migrating tribe of Celts, necessitating the building of a defensive fortification, the Servian Wall (a stretch of which can still be seen outside Rome's Termini station). Seventy years later, a defeat at the hands of the Samnites witnessed vanquished Roman soldiers forced to march under yokes (*sub iugum*), a ceremony from which we get "subjugate." However, by the middle of the third century BCE, through a series of conquests and alliances, virtually the entire peninsula, including Magna Graecia, would be incorporated into the Roman federation. The peninsula would therefore gradually transform from a land of Greek, Etruscan, and Celtic cities and scattered settlements populated by tribes speaking a variety of dialects, practicing different customs, and forging varying alliances, into more of a political, cultural, and linguistic unity.

One of the great secrets of the success of Roman expansion was how they treated their defeated enemies. Their erstwhile combatants became what were called *socii*, from *socius* (partner), the root of the word "society." The Romans developed a system of alliances with these partners—cities and ethnic communities up and down the peninsula—such that a kind of federation of tribes and city-states existed, with Rome at its head. The main obligation of the *socii* was to provide manpower to Rome in times of warfare, a kind of military conscription for which they received, in turn, protection from Rome and a share of plunder. All were invested, to one extent or another, in the fortunes of Rome.

Rome's dominance soon spread far beyond the Italian peninsula. The years between the middle of the third century BCE and 168 BCE witnessed the Romans fighting the Carthaginians and then the Macedonian kingdoms that had succeeded Alexander the Great, who died in 323 BCE. Their victories in these prolonged and bloody struggles meant that by 168 BCE they had effectively become masters of much of the known world.

The first of the great civilizations to fall to unrelenting Roman pressure was the Carthaginians. Carthage was a colony founded on the north coast of Africa (in present-day Tunisia) in 814 BCE by Phoenicians from Tyre. Quickly becoming one of the wealthiest and most powerful colonies on the Mediterranean, Carthage controlled sea routes to the west and extended its influence along the top of the African continent (across present-day Libya and Morocco) as well as into Sicily, Sardinia, and southern Spain. The Carthaginians maintained good relations with the Romans until the latter's domination of Magna Graecia in the middle of the third century BCE. Between 264 and 146 BCE, the Romans fought three "Punic Wars" against the Carthaginians. (The name comes from the fact that the Romans called Carthaginians the Poeni, from the Greek word for "Phoenician.") The most famous was the Second Punic War during which, beginning in the spring of 218, the great Carthaginian general Hannibal began a 900-mile (1,500 km) march that would take him from southern Spain, through the Pyrenees, and then, via the Alps, into Italy, complete with a battalion of thirty-seven war elephants.

The journey from southern Spain to the Po Valley took five months and came at a cost of many thousands of Hannibal's men: the ancient historian Titus Livius put the toll as high as thirty-six thousand. Hannibal also lost almost all the elephants, primarily due to starvation. The feat is all the more stupefying considering how Hannibal's exhausted and depleted army proceeded to inflict a series of defeats on the Romans that served as preludes to his most famous triumph, at Cannae in Apulia in August 216 BCE, fought against a numerically superior Roman army. In a tactically brilliant maneuver, Hannibal encircled and then mercilessly slaughtered the Romans, whose losses were put by the historian Polybius at seventy thousand—still perhaps the highest casualties in a single day's fighting that any Western army has ever suffered. Such was Roman panic and desperation that the most extraordinary measures were taken to appease the angry gods: two couples, one Greek and the other Celtic, were buried alive in the city's cattle market. It was one of the few occasions on which the Romans practiced human sacrifice.

Yet Rome did not fall. One refrain of Roman history is a devastating and humiliating disaster—such as those against the Gauls and Samnites—followed by an almost miraculous comeback. After Cannae, Hannibal appeared poised to march on Rome, only 250 miles (400 km) away. Posing as the liberator of the Italian peoples from their Roman oppressors, he knew his chances for success depended on the defection of Rome's allies on the peninsula—the *socii* who formed the federation of independent states. However, most of the tribes on which Hannibal pinned his hopes stayed loyal to Rome, resulting in him and his army being confined to the south of Italy for more than a decade. In 203 BCE, with the Romans under Publius Cornelius Scipio taking the fight into Africa, Hannibal was recalled to Carthage. There, a year later, at the Battle of Zama, he suffered a comprehensive defeat at the hands of Scipio, subsequently known because of his famous victory as Scipio Africanus.

Decades later, Rome's final confrontation with the Carthaginians, known as the Third Punic War, concluded with the destruction of Carthage in 146 BCE. That same year, the Romans also sacked and devastated another great and ancient city. In 214 BCE, they had begun a series of wars against the Macedonians following their support of Hannibal in the Second Punic War. The subjugation of Greece was accomplished in a matter of a few decades as the Macedonian phalanxes, so invincible under Alexander the Great, proved no match for the Roman legions, the maneuverability of whose tactical units, the maniples, had been perfected during the long wars against the Samnites. Having defeated the Macedonians, by the middle of the second century BCE, the Romans were battling their own former allies in the Achaean League, a confederation of Greek city-states in the central and northern Peloponnese. In 146, the Romans defeated the League in battle before the walls of Corinth, Greece's wealthiest city. With the Senate having decreed that Corinth should be burned and all valuables taken as booty to Rome, the victorious army sacked the city in a horrifying display of savagery. Corinth would disappear from the map for more than a century.

CHAPTER 2

"Let the Die Be Cast"
The Crisis of the Roman Republic

The victories over the Carthaginians and the Greeks gave the Roman Republic a worldwide empire. However, within decades the Republic entered a crisis that would endure for much of the following century and ultimately lead to its destruction.

One of the major challenges facing Rome was its system of landownership. Hannibal's presence in Italy between 218 and 203 BCE—a time of continuous raiding and fighting— led not only to the destruction of four hundred cities (as Hannibal boasted) but also to the devastation of the rural landscape: both sides burned crops, slaughtered livestock, destroyed farms, and massacred local populations. These terrible conditions forced many small subsistence farmers from their land, especially in the South, where Hannibal's troops were based. Their places were taken by much larger and wealthier landowners who, gobbling up huge portions of public land, defied the rule of a maximum of 500 jugera (125 hectares; a jugerum was the amount of land an ox could plough in a single day) of arable land per person. In the 130s BCE, a land reform was attempted by the politician Tiberius Gracchus, a grandson of Scipio Africanus. He advocated enforcing the 500-jugera law and redistributing their usurped territories more widely and evenly among the poor and landless. His plans proved unpopular with the large landowners and many senators (two groups with a considerable overlap). His efforts at reform ended abruptly in 133 BCE, when he was clubbed to death with a chair leg in the Senate and his body tossed into the Tiber. It was Rome's first act of political violence for many centuries and a dark prelude of much that was soon to come.

The Republic faced an even more dangerous problem with, as in the old days, warfare between Rome and its neighbors. As we have seen, the Republic pursued a successful policy of military alliances, which meant the disparate tribes, cities, and political communities inhabiting the peninsula were united under its rule. This unity was sorely tested on occasions such as Hannibal's invasion, but the greatest challenge came with the Social War (that is, war of the *socii*) at the beginning of the first century BCE. The war ended with, for all intents and purposes, the unification of Italy on a cultural and linguistic as well as a political level.

The Social War featured a coalition of the *socii* rising against Rome. It was prompted in part by the demand of some of them for Roman citizenship—for the rights and privileges jealously denied to them by the Romans, who referred to their allies dismissively as *peregrini* (foreigners). Citizenship had become a significant issue since the days of Tiberius Gracchus because only Roman citizens, and not the *socii*, were eligible to receive land as part of the planned reforms. The rebellion began in 91 BCE with the Marsi, an Oscan-speaking people whose most important city, Marruvium, was 68 miles (110 km) east of Rome.

They were quickly joined by other tribes, such as the Piceni, the Vestini, the Marrucini, and the Samnites. The war is sometimes known as the Italic War because the allies, looking for a unifying identity against Rome, began using the term *Italia* to describe their lands. And here we find, besides the mythical King Italus, a different and more probable origin for the name Italy: either the ancient Oscan word for a calf (*víteliú*, coming from the Sanskrit *vatsá*) or the Greek word for an ox (ἰταλοί). "For in Italy," a Roman writer later observed by way of explanation, "there was a great abundance of cattle, and in that land pastures are numerous and grazing is a frequent employment."[1] More to the point, birds and animals, including bulls, oxen, and calves, served as totems for the Oscan-speaking peoples. Whatever the case, in 90 BCE, the rebels gave to an otherwise undistinguished town 100 miles (160 km) east of Rome, Corfinium, a resounding new name: Italia. They made it their seat of government and planned for it to serve as their capital once Rome was defeated. They struck a coin showing the Oscan bull goring the Roman wolf.

A coin issued in Corfinium showing a personification of "Italia" crowned in laurels, as well as the bull goring the Roman wolf

The Social War took a deadly toll on both sides. A historian named Velleius Paterculus, whose great-grandfather fought on the side of the Italian federation, estimated the total deaths, over the war's two years, at three hundred thousand. That must have been an exaggeration, but after a bloody stalemate the Romans agreed to the allies' demand for citizenship. Henceforth everyone on the peninsula south of the Po would hold Roman citizenship, united as a political community sharing the same rights and privileges as well as, increasingly, the same language: Latin would soon become widespread, with the various Oscan dialects dying out in the decades that followed. The only other language that would endure this Latin domination, especially in the cities of the former Magna Graecia and among the educated Romans, was Greek.

"Italia" had been defeated, but a new and different Italia was born from this bloodshed. Only a few decades after the Social War, the orator and statesman Cicero delivered a speech in which he declared that the glory of Rome and the renown of its people were due to their recognition—based on the example of Romulus and the Sabines—that "this State ought to be enlarged by the admission even of enemies as citizens."[2] Rome's traditional enemies, such as the Samnites, had themselves become Roman citizens. And yet unity on the peninsula, and indeed within Rome itself, was still fragile and fluctuating. The decades that followed the Social War were blighted by violent power struggles between military strongmen who finally pushed the Roman Republic over the brink of extinction.

These strongmen were enabled by reforms carried out in the Roman army during the last decade of the second century BCE by the general and statesman Gaius Marius. Rome's war machine had formerly been staffed by an army of citizens raised by levies (the word "legion"—the name for the bodies of infantry comprising some 4,500 men—comes from *legio*, "levying"). But since the soldiers needed to pay for their own food and weapons, receiving in return only a small stipend, the poor and propertyless were excluded from service. Rome's acquisition of overseas territories in Spain, Africa, and Greece required long campaigns and a permanent military presence— an impossible task for the conscripts in a citizen army who needed to return to their homes, farms, and businesses. Marius therefore introduced reforms by which military service was opened to the poor, who would receive not only war booty but also, at the end of their service, grants of land. These rewards (which made war and conquest inherently necessary) became the responsibility not of the state but of their general, to whom the legions swore an oath of loyalty. And so arose what were more professional but essentially private armies: bodies of thousands of fighting men who owed their allegiance not to the Roman state but to their military commander.

Gaius Marius was to experience the implications of his reforms firsthand. The first great clash, in the early 80s BCE, was between him and his one-time deputy, Lucius Cornelius Sulla. The casus belli was who got to lead the campaign against Mithridates VI of the Hellenistic kingdom of Pontus, a vast territory that encompassed most of modern Turkey and encircled the Black Sea. Sulla ultimately prevailed over Marius thanks to extraordinary ferocity in a civil war that left thousands dead. In 81 BCE he declared himself "dictator" (an ancient but little-used title) with sweeping powers that made him the sole ruler of the Roman world. It was a tremendously powerful position from which, perhaps surprisingly, he stepped down after two years, returning sovereignty to the Senate and people.

Yet internal peace and stability still eluded the Roman Republic as another power struggle developed. One of the parties was a former ally of Sulla named Gnaeus Pompeius, or Pompey. Few men have ever had a more adamant sense of their own grandeur. An admirer of Alexander the Great, Pompey had added Magnus, "the Great," to his name when he was only twenty-five—an indication of his huge aspirations and self-regard. Cruel military exploits in Sicily and Africa earned him another nickname: *adulescentulus carnifex* (teenage butcher). He added to his savage luster in 71 BCE by crucifying thousands of fugitives along Via Appia following the slave revolt led by the gladiator Spartacus. Pompey's greatest triumph, however, came in the East, where he captured Jerusalem, made Syria a Roman province, and founded thirty-nine cities, one of which, with typical lack of modesty, he christened Pompeiopolis.

Pompey's success in Asia and his popularity with the people of Rome alarmed many of the senators, who balked at his requests to have them ratify his settlements in the East and give his retiring veterans—as they had been promised—their plots of land. To achieve his ends, around 60 BCE (the exact date is debated) Pompey made an alliance with another ambitious commander and adroit political operator feared by the aristocrats in the Senate: Gaius Julius Caesar.

Born in 100 BCE into a distinguished but impoverished Roman family, Caesar was the nephew of Gaius Marius. He also believed himself to be descended from both Ancus Marcius, the fourth King of Rome, and, further back, no less a figure than the goddess Venus—which conferred on him, he claimed, the power of kings and the reverence due to gods. By the age of forty, he was a rising political star whose energetic self-promotion spooked the senators. A third party was added to this coalition when Caesar, deploying his able diplomatic skills, reconciled Pompey with Marcus Licinius Crassus, a former rival whom Pompey had deeply offended by claiming credit for defeating Spartacus. The secret alliance became known (to us, though not to the ancients) as the First Triumvirate, a Gang of Three who combined the political acumen of Caesar, the military prestige of Pompey, and the wealth of Crassus, by far the richest man in Rome.

The alliance eventually fell apart. Crassus was removed from the scene when in 55 BCE, dreaming of glorious military triumphs to match those of Pompey, he clattered eastward with seven legions, bent on attacking the Parthians, whose empire sprawled across present-day Iran and Iraq. Instead of finding the success he craved, he died in battle in Mesopotamia, after which the Parthians used his disembodied head onstage as a prop in a production of a play by Euripides. Caesar enjoyed greater success with his own military enterprise when he marched north of the Alps and spent much of the next decade fighting the Gallic Wars against the Celtic tribes. He brought vast territories, including modern-day northern France and Belgium, under Roman control, at the expense, according to ancient estimates, of perhaps a million dead. In repeating the success of Pompey in Asia, he developed kingly ambitions. Pompey soon grew jealous of Caesar's triumphs since for the previous few years he had been in Rome conducting more modest bread-and-circuses affairs, such as arranging shipments of grain and combats between wild beasts.

Following his conquests in Gaul, Caesar was ordered by the Senate to return to Rome after surrendering his command and disbanding his troops, as all generals were required to do before entering Roman territory. This disarmament was the time-honored way of stopping generals and their armies from marching into Rome and seizing power. Caesar crossed the Alps with his battle-hardened legions, and sometime in early January 49 BCE performed one of the most famous and momentous border-crossings in history. It began inauspiciously as, setting off at dusk with mules taken from a local bakery, he got lost when his torches were extinguished, and he found himself wandering aimlessly on dark paths until he managed to find a local guide. But as he reached the southern boundary of his command, marked by a river named (because of its ruddy waters) the Rubicon, he spoke the first of his famous phrases: "Let the die be cast." His 13th Legion, armed to the teeth, entered Roman territory. Such was the panic and confusion that Romans fled the city for the safety of the countryside, and people from the countryside fled their villages for the safety of Rome.

Pompey had assured the Senate that he would raise troops to battle Caesar, but when his legions failed to appear—most of his army was away in Spain—he, too, panicked and fled Rome, with most of the senators following hard on his heels. This latest head-to-head then witnessed Caesar pursuing Pompey, first across the Italian peninsula on Via Appia from Rome to Brundisium (Brindisi), then across the Ionian Sea to Greece—where Caesar trounced Pompey's troops at Pharsalia—and finally into Egypt. Here Pompey's magnificent career ended on a strand of beach at the behest of the fifteen-year-old pharaoh Ptolemy XIII, the brother of Cleopatra.

He later presented Caesar with the gift of his rival's severed head. Cleopatra, meanwhile, was smuggled into Caesar's presence in a rolled-up mattress. She later gave birth to a child pointedly named Caesarion ("Little Caesar" in Greek).

With Pompey and Crassus gone, Caesar's pretensions were unbounded. Back in Rome, he occupied a golden throne in the Senate and took to donning a purple toga (the costume worn by the Etruscan kings). He placed his head on coins and statues of himself in temples. In one famous and controversial episode, during a festival in the Forum, perched on a throne, he was offered a crown, which he made a hasty show of rejecting once the revelers showed a distinct lack of enthusiasm for this coronation. He did take to wearing a crown of laurel leaves, which allowed him to conceal his balding pate. Worst of all for his critics, early in 44 BCE he became *dictator perpetuo* (dictator for life)—a position that looked little different from that of a monarch. The very name of the post made it highly dubious that, like Sulla, he would ever relinquish his powers.

Caesar's overweening ambitions and the drastic shift to one-man rule quickly became too much for many Romans to bear. A conspiracy against him, involving sixty senators, was hatched by the men Caesar called "those pale, thin ones"[3]: Gaius Cassius Longinus and Marcus Junius Brutus, the latter supposedly a descendant of the Brutus who founded the Roman Republic. The attempt on his life came on one of the most famous dates in history, the Ides of March (March 15) in 44 BCE. On that day he went to the Senate, temporarily housed in Pompey's magnificent theater because the Senate building had burned down eight years earlier during a violent altercation between warring factions.

Jean-Léon Gérôme's 1867 The Death of Caesar, *showing Caesar sprawled at the foot of Pompey's statue*

Once inside, the assassins pounced, skewering him with twenty-three wounds. The only assailant against whom he made no show of defending himself was Brutus, who stabbed him in the groin. According to the historian Suetonius, he uttered not the Latin phrase (*Et tu, Brute?*) made famous by Shakespeare but, rather, "You too, my child?" which he spoke in Greek (καὶ σύ, τέκνον).⁴ (Rumor had it that Brutus was Caesar's illegitimate son.) Caesar then slumped against the blood-spattered pedestal of a statue of Pompey.

The motives of the conspirators and the justification for their actions have been debated for more than two millennia. Was his murder a foul crime or an idealistic and patriotic act performed by Brutus, "the noblest Roman of them all"? The ancient sources report a wide range of motives among the killers, not all of them especially high-minded. Many were inspired by grudges, believing, rightly or wrongly, that Caesar had impeded their careers. Brutus, too, may have been spurred into action for personal reasons: Caesar's treatment of Brutus's mother, Servilia, his longtime mistress. In any case, the varied and, in some cases, petty personal motives of the conspirators meant that with Caesar gone they possessed no unifying vision or principle, and no single-minded commitment to, or plan for, restoring the Roman Republic. It can be no surprise, then, that what followed was a dozen more years of chaos and violence.

CHAPTER 3

"Masters of All in Existence"
The Roman Empire

By the time of Caesar's assassination, the Roman Republic had survived for almost five hundred years. As we've seen, however, for most of the previous century it had been in crisis thanks to civil war, political violence, and government dysfunction. The years immediately following the death of Caesar did nothing to shore up the Republic's fissured and failing foundations, shaken by the ambitions of military strongmen.

Brutus and Cassius would be revered, both in their own day and later, as defenders of republican liberty. However, they found it prudent to leave Rome following popular expressions of support for the murdered dictator, who had provided generously for the poor. The pair fled to Greece where, defeated by the army of Caesar's longtime ally, Mark Antony, both committed suicide, Cassius apparently by the same dagger with which he had stabbed Caesar.

Another triumvirate was formed in November 43 BCE. It was composed of Mark Antony and another of Caesar's longtime supporters named Marcus Aemilius Lepidus. The third member was Caesar's handpicked heir, his great-nephew Gaius Octavius (Octavian), then twenty years old and bent on avenging Caesar's death. Although their title called them "triumvirs for the restoration of the state," this new Gang of Three provided no more stability than the first one. The political violence continued with the execution in December 43 BCE of the great orator and statesman Cicero, a staunch defender of the Republic. His disembodied head was exposed in the Forum and then abused—spat upon, the tongue pierced with hairpins—by Mark Antony's third wife, Fulvia (soon to be replaced by Octavian's sister, Octavia).

The triumvirate quickly fell prey to rivalries. Antony and Lepidus were deftly outmaneuvered by Octavian, with Lepidus elbowed aside and Antony, in September 31 BCE, defeated by Octavian's forces in the Ionian Sea off Actium in northern Greece. Antony fled to Alexandria, where he committed suicide, followed by his lover, Cleopatra, by then the mother of three of his children. Octavian took the precaution of killing Caesarion, Cleopatra's seventeen-year-old son with Caesar.

Octavian returned as the conqueror of Egypt and the sole ruler of Rome. Inheriting Caesar's fabulous wealth, he also took his name, going by Gaius Julius Caesar Octavianus after the dictator's death. In January 27 BCE, the Senate awarded him an invented title, "Augustus" (Revered One)—the name by which history remembers him. He went on to rule for the next forty years in relative tranquility. The secret of his success was his personal style of leadership. Needing to avoid alienating the Romans by becoming an autocrat like Julius Caesar, he presented himself to Romans as a restorer of the social and political order. The word he chose to designate his position was not "Imperator" (Emperor) but "Princeps" (in effect, First Citizen). Augustus made a show of returning power to the Senate, which retained many of its traditional roles in government and administration, including taking joint responsibility with Augustus for the running of the Empire. The ultimate basis of his rule—or so he claimed in a famous statement—was the fact that he "surpassed everyone in *auctoritas*" even though officially he held no more power than any other politician or magistrate. What exactly he meant by *auctoritas* is much debated, but it seems to have been a kind of moral authority based on his personal prestige.

Portrait of Augustus, cast in bronze and featuring his staring, lifelike eyes done in glass paste

Augustus's political achievements in bringing stability to the Empire were mirrored by cultural achievements that made Augustan Rome one of history's greatest ages for art and architecture. Shortly before his death in 14 CE, he compiled a list of his many accomplishments, known as the *Res Gestae Divi Augusti* (Achievements of the Divine Augustus). It pointed out such feats as restoring liberty to Rome and placing "the whole world" under the sovereignty of the Roman people. His contributions to the city's built environment were summed up by his boast (reported by Suetonius) that he had found Rome "built of brick and left it in marble."[1] Augustus did indeed adorn the city with wonderful new monuments. One of his greatest buildings was the magnificent Theatre of Marcellus, constructed on the right bank of the Tiber and named in honor of his beloved nephew and

The Theatre of Marcellus, opened by Augustus in 12 BCE

intended heir, Marcus Claudius Marcellus, who died in 23 BCE at the age of nineteen. We can still admire the graceful crescent of pockmarked limestone arches, albeit stripped of the marble and stucco decorations, and less than a third of the original building's imposing sweep.

Augustus encouraged other wealthy Romans to follow suit and adorn the city with splendid monuments. One of them was his wealthy friend and trusted adviser, Gaius Maecenas, who ultimately gave his name, thanks to his generous promotion of Latin poets such as Horace and Virgil, to munificent patrons of the arts everywhere. The most prolific enthusiast for beautifying Rome became Augustus's loyal supporter, Marcus Agrippa, whose naval command had been decisive in the battle against Antony and Cleopatra at Actium. Agrippa restored Rome's sewers (even taking a boat tour to carry out a personal inspection) and built two new aqueducts, which together provided the city with nearly forty million gallons of water per day—a vital resource for a population, during Augustus's reign, of more than a million people. Agrippa also raised a temple to all the gods known as the Pantheon (subsequently rebuilt in spectacular style, as we'll see, more than a century later). Another important builder during Augustus's reign was his wife, Livia Drusilla. She restored various temples and constructed both a market (the Macellum Liviae, or "Livia's Market") and the Portico of Livia, a spectacular covered walkway and garden on the Esquiline Hill.

Augustus launched major building projects throughout the peninsula, perceiving the need for infrastructure spending in the hinterlands so badly devastated during decades of warfare. Roads, ports, bridges, walls, gates, sewers—their construction was extensive and prolific throughout Italy's countryside and towns. Rome had long enjoyed an extensive road system, including Via Appia, the "queen of roads" constructed in 312 BCE and running south from Rome to Brundisium. However, by the time of Augustus, the roads, like so much else, were in dire need of repair. Augustus proudly took the title *curator viarum* (commissioner of roads) and funded both their repair and upkeep from his own coffers, encouraging his wealthy friends to follow suit. Not just Rome but the Italian hinterlands, too, were given a brick-to-marble makeover.

It's a credit to Augustus that the system he devised would survive for the next few centuries, in part because of reverence for his memory—for his *auctoritas*. And it survived despite the inevitable problems of succession and the many "bad emperors" who followed in his wake.

The problem of succession stemmed from the fact that despite his three marriages, Augustus produced no male children. His only child, Julia, was born to his second wife, Scribonia, in the same year (39 BCE) that Augustus divorced Scribonia to marry Livia Drusilla. Livia, too, got a divorce that year, from Tiberius Claudius Nero. He came from an ancient and noble family, the Claudii, who traced themselves back to the earliest days of Rome (they claimed to be of Sabine descent). Tiberius Claudius Nero may have been shunted aside, but his name and bloodline would live on, and the four emperors after Augustus are known as the Julio-Claudians because of this mixing of the Julii and the Claudii.

The imperial family was a blended one: Augustus and Livia with their three children from earlier spouses. Family relations intertwined further when Tiberius became the third husband of his stepsister Julia, Augustus's intelligent and high-spirited daughter (one of whose previous husbands had been Marcus Agrippa). The imperial family's lineage, with its tangled convolutions, was not a family tree so much as a hopelessly intertwining kudzu vine whose coils regularly produced blighted tendrils and poisonous blossoms. For the next few decades, the Roman Empire would become a family drama, its fate dependent on a dizzying series of gruesome personal relationships that tumbled, violently and chaotically, down the generations, featuring everything from matricide and mariticide (the act of killing one's spouse) to incest.

The marriage between Tiberius and Julia, stepbrother and stepsister, did not prove a success. The union was heirless (their son died in infancy) and, ultimately, loveless. Julia became notorious for promiscuity and adultery. Her conduct became distinctly awkward for Augustus, who banished her from Rome to a volcanic island in the Tyrrhenian Sea some 50 miles (80 km) from Naples; so harsh and cruel were

The Julio - Claudians

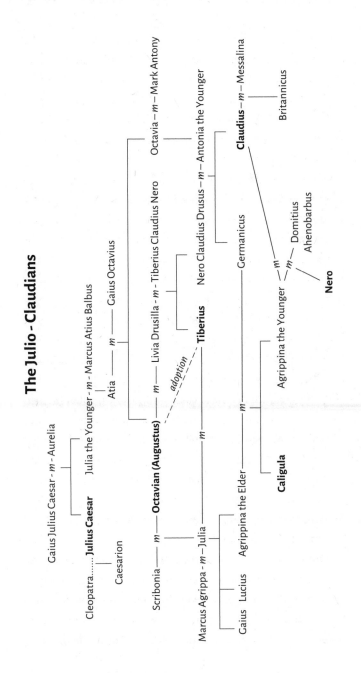

her privations that she was allowed neither wine nor male company. Following the deaths, possibly suspicious, of two of Julia's children with Agrippa, in 4 CE Augustus grudgingly adopted Tiberius as his son and heir. Tiberius became emperor a decade later when Augustus died at the age of seventy-seven (possibly helped on his way by Livia, eager for her son Tiberius to take over). Aware that a smooth transition was essential in order to avoid the chaos and violence of the civil wars of the previous century, the Senate quickly granted Tiberius all the powers formerly held by Augustus.

It cannot have been easy for Tiberius, fifty-five years old at the time, to succeed Augustus, a man who had held the reins of power for more than forty years, and who, following his death, was proclaimed a god. Tiberius's reign set a pattern to be followed with terrible regularity by so many of his successors: an admirable and encouraging start—respect for the laws and the Senate—followed by a rapid and disastrous decline into mass killings and sexual depravity. His reign of terror finally came to an end in 37 CE when he died from a wasting illness that raised suspicions of poison. The alleged culprit was one of the few members of his extended family whom he had spared death, a twenty-four-year-old great-nephew he took with him, virtually as a prisoner, to his sumptuous residence on Capri, where he had diverted himself from the cares of state by cavorting with a lewd entourage of sexual acrobats.

This great-nephew bore the impressive name Gaius Caesar Augustus Germanicus. He was better known, however, as Caligula ("Bootsie") because of the child-size hobnailed sandals (*caligae*) he had worn as a toddler when accompanying his father, Germanicus, on military campaigns. He proved a popular successor among the people of Rome. Germanicus, the nephew of Tiberius, had been a handsome, brilliant, and wildly popular general who in 19 CE died (like so many of Tiberius's kin) in suspicious circumstances. Caligula quickly began repaying the love of the people and the faith of the Senate, instituting a series of popular measures—lowering taxes on sales at auction, allowing the circulation of books banned by Tiberius—and putting on gladiatorial combats and chariot races. He completed large public works, such as rebuilding the port at Rhegium, refurbishing the Theatre of Pompey (badly damaged in a recent fire), and bringing an 84-foot-high (25 m) obelisk (the one now in St. Peter's Square) from Egypt. Construction also started on a new aqueduct and another amphitheater.

Although his reign seemed to bode well, some of Caligula's antics—dressing up as a woman or a gladiator or carrying around a toy thunderbolt—must have caused disquiet among attentive observers. Likewise, his plan (never actually carried out) of making his horse Incitatus ("Speedy") a consul, or his practice of sending to Athens for famous statues of Greek gods, then having their heads removed and replaced with his own. Other of Caligula's whims proved far more

Gaius Caesar Augustus Germanicus, aka Caligula: His dangerous lunacy ensured a brief reign.

lethal, and it soon became patently obvious that the new Princeps was severely and dangerously deranged. Suetonius claimed that he was driven mad by an aphrodisiac given to him by his wife, but it's difficult to imagine how any such concoction could have been responsible for his gratuitous and sadistic violence. Few were safe from his psychopathic whims, from a senator who was dismembered in the street and a playwright burned alive to a distinguished visiting guest and important ally, King Ptolemy of Mauretania, a descendant of the daughter of Mark Antony and Cleopatra: he was murdered when Caligula grew jealous of the crowd's ardent admiration for his magnificent purple cloak. Such homicidal lunacy ensured a short career, and in 41 CE he was killed by a member of the Praetorian Guard, the elite troops who protected the emperor and his family.

When reports reached the Senate of Caligula's death, the senators held an emergency debate, bickering about whether they should restore the Republic or elect one of their own as emperor. Soon, however, the Praetorian Guard and the people of Rome mobbing outside the Senate came to their own, different conclusion: they wanted Claudius, the fifty-year-old nephew of Tiberius and uncle of Caligula. No one in the imperial family had ever entertained the slightest thought of Claudius becoming emperor. Regarded as a bumbling imbecile, he was deliberately kept from the spotlight. Caligula had not viewed Claudius as any kind of threat, which explains how he survived his crazed nephew's reign of terror.

The trajectory of Claudius's reign matched all too tragically those of Tiberius and Caligula. He made a promising start, abolishing the taxes Caligula imposed to fund his extravagances, allowing exiles to return, respecting the authority of the Senate, and completing the construction of various of Caligula's projects, including the aqueduct known as the Aqua Claudia (whose remains can still be seen cutting through Rome's Parco degli Acquedotti). His armies conquered the Catuvellauni in southeast England and thereby added a new province, Britannia, to the Roman Empire.

Claudius's greatest achievement was to open public offices in Rome, including in the Senate, to people from the provinces. As someone who studied history, he could appreciate that Rome's greatness came about thanks to its assimilation of Sabines, Samnites, Etruscans, and other tribes and ethnic groups with whom the city had once been at war. He therefore began expanding the Senate to include members from across Italy and the provinces. Much resistance came from the old Roman families who dreaded the thought of the Senate and important public offices filling up with people from the provinces, such as the long-haired Celts from the North. However, Claudius argued passionately for senators who could represent the entire peninsula, including men from the Gallic tribes. He won the debate, and the doors of the Senate swung open to men Claudius proudly called "the stoutest of the provincials."[2]

Ancient historians such as Suetonius and Tacitus, writing decades later, place much of the blame for Claudius's downfall on the sexual antics and homicidal intrigues of the final two of his six wives. Both were, in the way of the Julio-Claudians, closely related to him. When he became emperor, he was married to his fifth wife, his cousin Messalina. Her two grandmothers were half-sisters, while her grandmother and Claudius's grandmother were full sisters—the daughters of Octavia and Mark Antony.

Such inbreeding did not bode well, and the marriage, as in the case of so many Julio-Claudian unions, was anything but blissful. Messalina was an enthusiastic adulteress, and in 48 CE, with Claudius away from Rome, she conducted a marriage ceremony with her handsome lover, an ambitious politician who had designs on usurping Claudius. Stunned by this turn of events, Claudius put the pair of them to death and then vowed not to remarry. After all, he already had a son and heir, Britannicus, born to Messalina in 41 CE and proudly named after his new province. However, soon afterward he changed his mind and married someone even more closely related to him than Messalina, and if anything, even more cut-throat and power-hungry: his niece Agrippina, the daughter of Germanicus and the younger sister of Caligula. In order for the marriage to take place, Claudius needed to revoke a law against uncles marrying their nieces.

The thirty-five-year-old Agrippina had been married twice already. She had poisoned her second husband, but from her first—a nephew of Augustus—she had a child, a boy named Nero, born in 37 CE. Following his marriage to Agrippina, Claudius adopted Nero and then married him to Octavia, his daughter from Messalina. It was no doubt to hasten Nero's succession, against the claims of Britannicus, that in October 54 CE Agrippina served Claudius a dish of mushrooms poisoned by an expert in such matters, a woman named Locusta. The poison quickly took effect, and Locusta was to do a brisk business in the imperial palaces in the years that followed.

Coming from an old Oscan word meaning "strong and valiant," the name Nero regularly appeared in the Claudii family tree. But Nero Claudius Caesar Augustus Germanicus—to give him his full name—did not share the heroic military background of so many of his strong and valiant forebears and namesakes. Blue-eyed with curly blond hair, Nero had a passion for art and music rather than warfare.

Military heroics must scarcely have seemed needed when Nero became emperor at the age of sixteen: the Roman Empire was enjoying a period of peace. And despite his youth and inexperience, Nero, like so many of his ill-fated predecessors, made a decent start to his reign. However, he soon revealed how, like his Uncle Caligula, he was woefully unfit for office, eccentric at best and, at worst, depraved. The first flickers of concern may have been raised by his obsession with his own artistic performances. He took to the stage to sing, play the harp, and act in plays, something widely considered beneath the dignity of an emperor. Although the poor quality of his voice made his audience cry with laughter, Nero took the precaution of stationing thousands of soldiers in the crowd to whip up enthusiasm with stage-managed hurrahs. He forbade anyone to leave the theater when he was performing—an edict so strictly enforced that women gave birth in their seats and men faked death so they could be carried away.

Agrippina probably murdered Claudius so that Nero would become emperor when he was still young enough for her to control. Mother and son ruled together, and so close were the pair, according to Suetonius, that whenever they rode together in a litter their mutual fondness was betrayed by telltale stains on Nero's clothing. This tender bond would soon be broken as Nero began taking offense at Agrippina's criticisms and her attempts to control and dominate. Following several bungled assassination attempts—tampering with a bedroom ceiling to make it collapse, and with the hull of a boat to make it sink—he finally disposed of her by a more forthright method: one of his goons ran a sword through her womb.

Agrippina was the latest example of an unruly Roman woman—the kind of wife or mother who, if we choose to believe the sources, exerted a malign influence on her husband or children, revealing the dangers that supposedly loomed if women ever wielded power. Rome offered very few public roles for women: they were rigorously excluded from political life, allowed neither to vote nor to hold political office. As one politician of the first century CE demanded: "What have women to do with public meetings? According to the tradition of our forefathers, nothing!"[3] It is revealing that the most prominent and important women in Rome were the six priestesses known as the vestal virgins. Their duties included keeping alight the sacred fire of Vesta (goddess of the hearth), baking little cakes (the *mola salsa*, or "salted flour"), and sweeping and cleaning the Temple of Vesta. Despite their sacred nature, these rituals were not unlike the cooking and cleaning obligations of the average Roman matron whose costume—a headband (the *vitta*) and an ankle-length, girdled dress called the stola—the Vestal Virgins shared.

Roman women were expected to discharge their obligations in the home as obedient daughters, loyal wives, and devoted mothers. These much-desired qualities are reflected in funerary inscriptions for wives, a study of which shows the most common adjectives to be *dulcissima* (sweetest), *pia* (dutiful), and *sanctissima* (most chaste).[4] Yet many Roman women were not the weak, passive, and frivolous characters their men wanted or believed them to be—and nor were they necessarily the homicidal harridans of legend. Roman history offers numerous examples of intelligent and well-educated women who exerted positive influences when, defying the standards of the age, they took their places in the public sphere. Prominent among them was Cornelia, daughter of Scipio Africanus and the mother of Tiberius and Gaius Gracchus. She supervised their education and advised them in politics. After her death, a bronze statue (the base of which survives) was raised in her honor in Rome—the first monument to a Roman woman, as opposed to a goddess, ever put on public display.

Another notable woman was Hortensia, who in 42 BCE delivered a speech in the Roman Forum, from whose public assemblies women were normally excluded. She and many other Roman women objected to a tax that Antony, Lepidus, and Octavian had imposed on 1,400 particularly wealthy women. "Why should we pay taxes," Hortensia demanded, "when we have no access to the offices or the honors or the military commands or the entire political process, which you have now brought to such a sorry state by your rivalries?" No taxation, in other words, without representation. The triumvirs, enraged that the women had become "boldly assertive," tried to have them ousted, but an assembled crowd began booing and the triumvirs relented, ultimately drawing up a list of only four hundred women obliged to pay taxes.[5]

Nero is probably most associated in the popular mind with the events that began in the early hours of July 10, 64 CE, when a fire broke out in Rome and, over the course of a week, destroyed much of the city. Historians such as Suetonius put the blame on Nero's desire to clear some choice parcels of land where he could build a pleasure palace. He supposedly enjoyed the spectacle of the conflagration from the tower of a palace on the Esquiline Hill, from which, dressed in his lyre-player's garb, he regaled the beleaguered, fleeing Romans with snatches of song from one of his own compositions, an epic on the fall of Troy.

Yet according to another historian, Tacitus, Nero was in fact away from Rome, at Antium (Anzio), when the fire broke out. He hurried back, directed the fire-fighting operations, and made provisions for those made homeless by opening up his gardens and providing supplies of grain. The question remains as to whether the fires were actually started on his orders; he certainly benefited personally, claiming for himself a large area, where he built his Golden House (*Domus Aurea*). This vast complex included parks, lakes, and—in a gesture typical of his delusions of grandeur—an awe-inspiring 100-foot-high (30 m) bronze statue of himself wearing a crown shaped like the sun. Created by an artist named Zenodorus, the Colossus (as it became known) stood at the entrance to the Golden House—testament to what Tacitus grudgingly called Nero's "passion for the incredible."[6]

Nero presided over the rapid rebuilding of Rome, introducing a new code of safety for buildings and making sacrifices to appease the gods. Still, suspicions continued to linger regarding his responsibility for the fire. To scotch the rumors and divert the blame, he needed a scapegoat, and he found one soon enough. "Nero substituted as culprits," wrote Tacitus, "and punished with the utmost refinements of cruelty, a class of men, loathed for their vices, whom the crowd styled Christians."[7]

Religious persecution was relatively uncommon in Italy. Roman religion was polytheistic and eclectic, with different gods worshipped in different places and for different purposes. The Romans treated foreign gods in much the same way they treated the foreigners themselves—by assimilating them. Alongside the official Roman cults, with their priests, temples, festivals, and gods, various other religions had been imported from abroad by soldiers and immigrants, especially from the East. One of the larger religious groups in Rome was the Jews. Having arrived in Italy by at least the second or third century BCE, the community by Nero's time could count a dozen synagogues and a population of fifty thousand. Julius Caesar and Augustus had given them freedom of worship and exemption from military service.

Within a decade or so of Christ's execution during the reign of Tiberius, a small Christian community had taken root in Rome. Tacitus claimed that the Roman people detested the pernicious superstition of the Christians, hence their appeal for Nero as scapegoats. But Tacitus was writing several decades later, and it's debatable how much the average Roman in the 60s CE actually knew about the beliefs and practices of this religious minority. After all, they numbered only in their hundreds in a city of more than a million people. Whatever the case, the leaders of the community were arrested, convicted, and executed. Tacitus reported that as a gruesome spectator sport they were covered with the skins of wild animals and torn to pieces by dogs. Nero crucified many of them in the gardens of his palace and then, when darkness fell, burned them alive "to serve as lamps by night." The strategy ultimately backfired. Tacitus wrote that the savagery of these reprisals touched the hearts of a bloodthirsty

Roman mob inured even to the most extreme scenes of gore and violence.[8]

One of the many victims may have been Paul of Tarsus (the future St. Paul), who had come to Rome (his privilege as a Roman citizen) to answer a charge of stirring up sedition in Judaea. He was beheaded (likewise his privilege as a Roman citizen) along Via Ostiense outside the walls of Rome. Another victim, according to tradition, was a fisherman from the Sea of Galilee named Shim'on, better known, thanks to his christening by Christ, as Peter the Apostle. What happened next was crucial for ecclesiastical and architectural history. According to tradition, Peter was buried next to the site of his martyrdom in a cemetery on the west bank of the Tiber. Close by the Circus of Nero, this cemetery was situated in a marshy valley beneath the gentle slope of one of Rome's many hills, the Mons Vaticanus, or Vatican Hill. The word Vaticanus comes from *vates* (a prophet or soothsayer) and *cano* (to sing)—an indication that in centuries past it had been a sacred place of divination or revelation. With the persecution of the Christians and the arrival of the bones of Peter the Apostle, the Vatican would once again become a vitally important holy site.

Nero's megalomania and paranoia hastened his end. After an assassination plot was uncovered in 65 CE, he took vicious retribution. Mutterings of discontent grew into a full chorus as he lost the support of several of his provincial governors and their legions. Rebellion broke out first in Gallia Lugdunensis (in what is now northern France) and then in Hispania Tarraconensis (the largest province in Spain). The governor of the latter, Servius Sulpicius Galba, was proclaimed by his legions as the new representative of the Senate and people of Rome—in effect, the new emperor. Realizing the cause was lost, Nero sent for Locusta, who obliged him with a fatal concoction, but his servants, as they looted the palace, made off with the fatal vial along with most of his other possessions. Two further suicide attempts miscarried before his end came at a villa a few miles outside Rome, to which he fled in disguise. "What an artist the world is losing!" he wept while watching as the firewood was gathered for his cremation.[9] As Galba's soldiers came for him, he thrust a dagger into his throat: a final, faltering performance.

CHAPTER 4

"From a Kingdom of Gold to One of Iron and Rust"
Decline and Fall of the Empire

The Julio-Claudian line of emperors was extinguished with Nero. The question of who would rule the Empire therefore became monumental and acute. Transitions of power had so far been relatively peaceful. To be sure, Tiberius, Caligula, Claudius, and Nero all met violent or suspicious ends. But in each case the succession had followed the line of least resistance through the extended Julio-Claudian dynasty, and the new emperor was accepted, at least at first, by the Senate and the people. But with the Julio-Claudian family tree having flung out its last stunted and misshapen branches, the succession, on this occasion, came to be settled by bloodshed rather than bloodlines. Governors from several of Rome's provinces jockeyed for position, their legions and the Praetorian Guard serving as kingmakers. What followed Nero's death has become known to history as the "Year of the Four Emperors"—testament to a rapid and murderous turnover.

The man who emerged from the carnage was a rugged sixty-year-old general named Vespasian. He would reign for the next decade, dying in June 79 CE of natural causes—a rare feat indeed for a Roman emperor. *Vae*, he quipped on his deathbed, *puto deus fio*. ("Dear me, I think I'm becoming a god.") He was indeed deified by Titus, his son and successor. They were the first two of the three emperors in what is known (after their family, the Flavii) as the Flavian Dynasty, which ruled from 69 to 96 CE.

The Flavians adorned Rome with what has become its most famous and iconic monument—a gigantic, oval-shaped sports stadium, the Flavian Amphitheatre. Begun by Vespasian in about 72 CE, it was completed and opened by Titus eight years later (with a rhinoceros as the guest of honor). The building's more familiar name, the Colosseum, comes not, as we might expect, from its massive size but because it was built near the Colossus of Nero. Stretching more than 600 feet (180 m) through what had previously been an artificial lake in Nero's private pleasure park, the amphitheater was a venue for spectacular and bloody entertainment, such as gladiatorial battles and animal hunts. A marvel of

The Flavian Amphitheatre, better known as the Colosseum, opened for bloody spectacles in 80 CE.

architecture and engineering, the Colosseum could seat fifty thousand people and featured eighty entrances (two reserved for the use of the emperor and his family) and a series of underground winches, cages, and ramps that dramatically propelled the lions and tigers into the "arena," a wooden platform covered with a layer of sand (*arena* in Latin) that absorbed the blood.

The Roman Empire continued its inexorable expansion under the Flavians, and indeed funds for the Colosseum came from the spoils of the sack of Jerusalem in 70 CE. Roman legions annexed the north of England, pacified Wales, advanced into Scotland, and even, under the brilliant general Agricola, contemplated an invasion of Ireland. The legions were carrying out the policy of "Romanization"—bringing the culture and institutions of Rome to the farthest hinterlands of the Empire. But the grim and gory flipside of Roman civilization is seen in the words that Tacitus (Agricola's son-in-law) put into the mouth of a British chieftain named Calgacus who fought the Romans in Scotland in 83 CE. Calgacus exhorts his countrymen to resist these rapacious "robbers of the world" who have invaded their island. "To plunder, butcher, steal," he declares, "these things they misname empire: they make a desolation and they call it peace."[1]

Two months after he succeeded his father as emperor, Titus was faced with one of history's most famous natural disasters: the eruption of Mount Vesuvius. The giant volcano had occasionally spewed forth fire and ash, but the eruption in 79 CE was on a different scale from anything seen before. The number of dead has been estimated at around sixteen thousand, which in some respects is remarkably low considering that Pompeii's population might have been as high as thirty thousand, with another five thousand in Herculaneum. However, people had time to flee—perhaps as much as a day or two—as the giant rumbled, smoked, and shook their homes as a prelude to its explosion.

Titus's brief reign was troubled not only by Vesuvius but also by a fire in 80 CE that once again destroyed large swaths of Rome, including Marcus Agrippa's Pantheon, built more than a century earlier. "I am ruined," Titus supposedly exclaimed as he watched the conflagration, no doubt aware of how the Great Fire of 64 had contributed to the fall of Nero. He died soon afterward, in September 81 CE, either due to an outbreak of plague—yet another disaster that struck Rome—or from poison administered by his thirty-year-old brother Domitian, who succeeded him as emperor. Like the Julio-Claudians, Domitian made a good start, launching a building program in Rome and pushing back the boundaries of the Empire by consolidating the conquest of Britain. But he soon—again, like the Julio-Claudians—turned into a power-mad autocrat and, as Suetonius claimed, an object of terror and hatred to all. He became so paranoid that he lined the walkways of his palace with reflective surfaces so he could spot assassins sneaking up behind him. They got him nonetheless, in September 96 CE, after fifteen years in power, killing him in his bedroom as he went for his midday nap.

If it looked like the bad days of the Julio-Claudians were returning, what followed instead was a kind of Golden Age for the Roman Empire: the period of the "Five Good Emperors"—five men in succession who ruled the Empire for the next eight decades, during the period of its greatest majesty and success. Unlike the Flavians and Julio-Claudians, these men were for the most part unrelated or, if related, only very distantly. They were selected and promoted on the basis of ability rather than blood (or indeed bloodshed). The system would break down only when the role of emperor once again began descending along a family line.

The first of the "good" emperors was Nerva, a veteran politician and a former adviser to Nero. He proved an able operator with an amiable disposition, endearing himself to the senators by issuing coins with such reassuring slogans as "Public Freedom," "Equity," and "Justice." He died early in 98 CE, after only eighteen months in power and with no children of his own. He handily solved the problem of succession by means of adoption: he chose a tall, handsome, forty-five-year-old Spanish-born soldier who was serving as governor of Upper Germany: Marcus Ulpius Traianus, better known as Trajan.

Trajan became Rome's greatest ruler since Augustus, and arguably its greatest ever. "The sufferings of the past are over," exulted Pliny the Younger, a high-ranking public official, in a speech in 100 CE. "Times are different."[2] Trajan ruled, he pointed out, as a fellow citizen rather than a tyrant, and he was modest and courteous, affable and humane, inspiring affection and joy rather than—like so many of his predecessors—hatred and terror. The Senate gave him the official title *Optimus Princeps* (Best Prince), and later emperors would be greeted by senators with the words *felicior Augusto, melior Traiano*. ("May you be luckier than Augustus and better than Trajan.") Under his rule, the Roman Empire achieved its greatest and most mind-boggling territorial expanse, stretching from the north of England to the shores of both the Caspian Sea and the Persian Gulf.

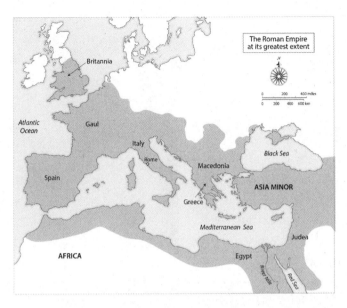

The Roman Empire
at its greatest extent

Britannia

Atlantic
Ocean

Gaul

Italy

Rome

Spain

Macedonia

Black Sea

ASIA MINOR

Greece

Mediterranean Sea

Judea

AFRICA

Egypt

River Nile

Red Sea

Like Nerva, Trajan had no children. On his deathbed, he
therefore adopted as his son and heir a distant relation—a
son of his father's cousin who hailed from the same town
in Spain, and who in 100 CE had married another of Trajan's relatives, his great-niece Vibia Sabina. Hadrian was
forty-one years old when he became emperor in 117. He
proved a ruler of a very different stripe from Trajan. Rather
than a warrior, he was a highly cultivated aesthete, a lover
of music, philosophy, literature, and architecture. A great
admirer of Greek culture, he became known as Graeculus
("Little Greek"). He became the first emperor to wear a
beard—an allusion to the Greeks of old whose images he
admired in portrait busts. He even took as his lover a Greek
youth, Antinous, mourning extravagantly when, during
a visit to Egypt, the boy drowned in mysterious circumstances in the Nile.

Hadrian beautified Rome by lavishing on the city more than thirty building projects. His greatest architectural legacy was his rebuilding of the Pantheon, the temple in the Campus Martius built at Marcus Agrippa's expense during the early years of Augustus's reign. Badly damaged in the fire of 80 CE, thirty years later, in 110, it was struck by lightning. Hadrian

Hadrian, with his Greek-style beard: His curly locks were tended by specially trained slaves.

began rebuilding the temple soon after he became emperor. In doing so, he made changes such that it became one of Rome's, and the world's, most audacious, unique, and breathtaking buildings: one with a beautiful cupola that soars skyward with no visible means of support, pierced at the top by an opening, 27 feet (9 m) in diameter, that lets in sunlight and rain. The building is a tour de force of shock-and-awe architecture and engineering.

Hadrian's final building was his tomb—a gigantic, cylindrical mausoleum (today's Castel Sant'Angelo) that, minus the garden and its enormous statue of Hadrian driving a chariot, still rears its immense bulk above the Tiber. Hadrian thought much about his death in his final years, and when he died in the summer of 138, at the age of sixty-two, he had made careful plans for a transfer of power. He adopted a fifty-two-year-old named Titus Aurelius Antoninus, the husband of his niece, and stipulated that Antoninus in turn should adopt as his heirs two fatherless boys, a seven-year-old named Lucius Verus (the son of Hadrian's planned successor who had died prematurely) and the great-grandnephew of Trajan, a seventeen-year-old prodigy named Marcus Aurelius.

Antoninus proved a worthy choice, warmly welcomed by the Senate, which soon christened him Antoninus Pius because of (among other admirable qualities) his loyalty and filial piety toward Hadrian. Under him, the Roman Empire enjoyed one of its greatest periods of peace and prosperity. Before he died in 161, after twenty-three years in power, his final watchword to his guards was *aequanimitas* (equanimity): yet another of his virtues.

Antoninus Pius had enjoyed a close relationship with his eldest adopted son, Marcus Aurelius, an enthusiastic scholar of Greek philosophy. He greatly favored Marcus over the younger of the pair, Lucius Verus. Marcus was studious and solemn, wearing a Greek mantle and honoring his teachers of Latin and Greek with statues, while Lucius was fun-loving and carefree, fond of gambling, gladiators, chariot races, and extravagant all-night banquets. Antoninus had sidelined the young man, naming Marcus as his sole heir, but when Marcus came to the throne, he made Lucius his co-emperor, marking the first time two emperors had ruled together. The arrangement proved a success. Marcus looked after affairs in Rome while the more vigorous Lucius, when war broke out against the Parthian Empire, took charge of military matters, setting off for the East in the summer of 162. By 165 CE, the Parthians had been defeated and Lucius and the victorious legions returned home in the summer of 166.

Besides booty from the East, the Roman legions unwittingly brought with them what history has come to know as the Antonine plague. Over the next three decades, its steady outbreaks killed perhaps a tenth of the Empire's population—as many as ten million people. The tremendous death rate took a toll whose magnitude and consequences (as well as the exact identity of the pathogen) historians still debate. One historian, writing in the 1930s, argued that the depopulation caused by the plague "contributed perhaps more than any other factor to the decline of the Empire."[3] Not all historians today make such bold pronouncements, and we shall see that plenty of other factors were involved in the decline and fall. But the plague wreaked undeniably devastating havoc. Farms were abandoned in the countryside, towns depopulated, and government positions left unfilled. One of the most drastic effects was on the Roman army. The physician Galen (whose description of its symptoms led to it sometimes being called the "Plague of Galen") claimed to have witnessed the death of most of the legions gathered at Aquileia in northern Italy. So substantial were the losses that, to find replacements, Marcus Aurelius was forced to conscript slaves, gladiators, rural policemen (a force known as the *diogmitae*), and even bandits. He also hired warriors from the German tribes to fight in the upcoming war— against the German tribes. For, even as the pestilence raged, the Roman Empire faced a terrible threat on its northern frontier.

The northern border of the Roman Empire had long been a fraught one. Two rivers, the Rhine and the Danube, provided a natural separation between Rome and the warlike tribes who in the first century BCE had gradually migrated

Marcus Aurelius, a "good emperor" who faced threats from plague and war

south from Scandinavia and the Baltic coast, displacing many of the Celts. The Romans called them the Germani, which, according to one theory, comes from the Celtic word *gairmeanna* (cries, exclamations), presumably a reference to their blood-curdling war cries. The Romans had neither the forces nor the inclination to take possession of the vast, heavily forested, swamp-infested lands beyond the Rhine and Danube. Instead, they were happy to keep themselves separated from what they called the barbarians, establishing a series of palisades, ditches, garrisons, and watchtowers that stretched from the mouth of the Rhine to the banks of the Danube.

Late in 166, an alliance of Germanic tribes, taking advantage of the pandemic ravaging the Roman legions, crossed the frontier in a series of concerted attacks. Marcus Aurelius spent the last decade and a half of his life fighting the Germans (in what is now known as the Marcomannic Wars) and reinforcing the increasingly porous northern frontier.

He died in the spring of 180 while still campaigning north of the Danube near what is now Vienna. His death (probably from the plague) marked the end of the era of the Five Good Emperors—and, according to the historian Dio Cassius, the moment when the Roman Empire descended from "a kingdom of gold to one of iron and rust."[4]

The rust began with Marcus Aurelius's successor, his son Lucius Aurelius Commodus. Not yet nineteen years old, Commodus was already offering ample displays of the cruelty, vengefulness, and incompetence that would mark his reign. Marcus supposedly died fearing his son would become another Caligula, Nero, or Domitian—and so he proved to be. Ridley Scott's 2000 film *Gladiator* depicts all too accurately Commodus's obsession with gladiatorial combat. The contrast with his father was so extreme that rumor hinted he was the result of his mother's adulterous liaison with a gladiator. After several assassination attempts failed, in December 192, following a dozen years in power, Commodus went the same way as his fellow bad emperors. His lover Marcia served him a cup of poisoned wine after spotting her name on a hit list carelessly left lying about. When the potion failed to take full effect, she summoned Narcissus, the brawny wrestler who served as Commodus's personal trainer. Accepting a handsome reward, Narcissus throttled his pupil in his bedchamber.

The death of Commodus led to a frantic scramble around the Empire as various generals, supported by their legions, vied for the imperial purple. The "Year of the Five Emperors" followed, from which the forty-eight-year-old Lucius Septimius Severus emerged victorious, having defeated his rivals in battle and then killed them. Although he became the first in what historians called the "Severan Dynasty," Septimius promoted himself as one of the Antonines, for in 195, in a gesture bizarre even by the standards of Roman emperors, he declared himself the adopted son of Marcus Aurelius (who had died fifteen years earlier). He even renamed his eldest son: Lucius Septimius Bassianus became Marcus Aurelius Antoninus. The fictitious adoption and sudden name change were intended to legitimize Septimius's reign—to present him as a natural and obvious successor to the Antonines rather than a military adventurer who crushed the opposition on the battlefield and then slaughtered the dozens of senators who had favored his rivals.

Septimius died in England in February 211 while on a military campaign with his two sons, aged twenty-three and twenty-two, whom he named as his heirs and successors, hoping they would rule together. The elder of the pair had other ideas, and within the year he had slain his brother—yet another Roman fratricide. This older brother, the so-called Marcus Aurelius Antoninus, was better known by the nickname he earned because of the hooded, ankle-length Celtic-style cloak, known as a *caracallus*, that he always wore. Caracalla therefore became the second emperor, after Caligula, to be named for a fashion accessory. He also became the latest in Rome's depressing roster of bad emperors.

Caracalla possessed all the gruesome whimsies and mad fantasies of fellow bad emperors, such as massacring bears and lions in the Colosseum, along with his scarcely less prolific culls of perceived enemies in the Senate. His own particular obsession was with Alexander the Great: he proclaimed to a startled Senate that he was Alexander's reincarnation. This crazed enthusiasm proved one of the reasons for the end of his short, bloody reign. Believing it to be his destiny to push eastward like Alexander, he mounted a campaign against the Parthian Empire. While fighting in Mesopotamia in 217, he took a detour to pay his respects at a temple in Carrhae in what is now southern Turkey. Dismounting en route to answer a call of nature, he was stabbed to death by one of his Praetorians,

A marble bust of Caracalla that features his typically menacing gaze

probably on orders from their head, Marcus Opellius Macrinus, who succeeded him as emperor.

Caracalla left behind numerous portrait busts that depicted him, no doubt all too accurately, as a sinister, scowling brute. But he also left behind one of the greatest legacies any emperor could claim: the Constitutio Antoniniana, known as the Edict of Caracalla. Issued in 212, this decree gave all free inhabitants across the Roman Empire the same rights and privileges as Italians. Caracalla's edict took to the limit the generous enfranchisement policies of Romulus and Claudius. It seems counterintuitive that a sanguinary tyrant such as Caracalla should have been behind such a liberal policy. Historians have long been suspicious that he issued the decree for financial reasons, since millions more people, at a stroke, suddenly became liable for Roman taxes. Even so, neither the savage character of Caracalla nor any base economic motive should detract from the grandeur of his gesture: one that made millions of people across Europe and beyond, in theory at least, equal citizens before the law.

In the third century CE, the Roman Empire faced what historians call the Crisis of the Third Century: a political, military, and economic plight that threatened the integrity and even the existence of the Empire. Its causes were multiple: everything from bad governance and financial woes to barbarian invasions, further outbreaks of plague, and a powerful new enemy rising in the East.

The Crisis of the Third Century took place during the decades between 235 and the accession of Diocletian in 284. One of its most prominent characteristics was political instability caused by a dizzyingly fast turnover of emperors. Between 235 and 284, some thirty emperors (depending on which are counted as true emperors rather than pretenders) held power, many only for a few months before their various deaths by assassination, suicide, battle, or plague. There was even, in 238, the homicidal rotation of the "Year of the Six Emperors." The lack of continuity and stability was made worse by renewed attacks from the Germanic tribes. In 250, the Goths, who had migrated down the Vistula River from Scandinavia, invaded the Roman province of Moesia (modern Serbia and Bulgaria). At the same time, another tribe, the Carpi, invaded Dacia. Even Rome itself came under threat in 271 when the Juthungi—yet another Germanic tribe—crossed into northern Italy, sacked the city of Placentia (Piacenza), and began slogging implacably south. They were repelled and destroyed thanks to decisive action by the emperor Aurelian, a brilliant general and one of the few capable rulers during the decades-long crisis. But in 275, Aurelian met the same fate as so many of his predecessors when he was murdered by his Praetorian Guard.

In 284, a humbly born, forty-something Dalmatian cavalry commander named Gaius Valerius Diocles finally brought a measure of order and stability to the crumbling Empire. This new emperor, who would soon be known more grandly as Diocletianus, or Diocletian, managed to shore up and preserve the Empire through a series of administrative reforms and economic strategies (including the world's first experiment with wage and price control). One of the most effective solutions was to devise a system of power-sharing. Realizing the Empire was far too large to be governed by a single person, he named a co-emperor: a fellow humbly born Illyrian named Maximian, a skilled soldier. Their responsibilities were divided into geographical spheres. Maximian, based at Mediolanum (Milan), governed the West and kept an eye on the Germans; Diocletian, based at Nicomedia (İzmit in modern Turkey), governed the East and kept watch on the Sassanids. Powers were further divided, and an attempt made to solve the problem of succession, when in 293 each of these two "augustuses" chose a "caesar" to assist and, in the fullness of time, succeed him. These junior emperors were Constantius (based in Trier, on the northern frontier) and Galerius (based in Sirmium, in modern Serbia). So was born the Tetrarchy, or rule of four—what came to be known as the *quattuor principes mundi* (four princes of the world).

The formation of this Gang of Four revealed the deflection of power away from Rome and, indeed, from Italy. None of the four emperors had been born in Italy (Galerius started life herding sheep in Dacia) and none was based in Rome, which had been supplanted by Mediolanum as the capital in the West. Diocletian visited Rome on only a single occasion, in 303, almost twenty years into his reign, an indication of how the "Caput Mundi" (capital of the world)—as Rome had been called since at least the first century BCE—and its ancient institutions were becoming increasingly marginalized. Diocletian's numerous administrative reforms were aimed mainly at a decentralization of power and the separation of civil from military rule—that is, removing political clout from the legions that, over the past half-century of military anarchy, had so ruthlessly created and destroyed emperors. The Tetrarchy did not, in the end, provide for orderly transitions of power. Diocletian and his fellow augustus, Maximian, retired in 305, to be succeeded, as planned, by their caesars. But the system broke down a few years later with a bitter rivalry for supremacy in the West between Maximian's son Maxentius and Constantius's son Constantine, both of whom claimed to be augustus. In the spring of 312, Constantine, who had been campaigning against the Franks, crossed the Alps with an army of forty thousand men en route to the battle that was arguably the most important of the millennium, that of Milvian Bridge.

On the eve of the battle, Constantine received his famous and fateful omen. Two writers, Lactantius and Eusebius, both Christians, and both close to Constantine, purported to explain what happened. According to Lactantius, Constantine experienced a dream in which he was commanded to exploit a particular sign, the Chi-Rho, a sacred emblem that used the Greek letters X and P, the first two letters of ΧΡΙΣΤΟΣ (Christ). Eusebius, writing three decades later, claimed that Constantine's vision was not simply a private dream but instead a celestial apparition that he and his entire army witnessed. Instead of sacrificing to the traditional Roman gods—which he noted had all too frequently failed previous emperors—he decided to pray to the god of the Christians. He was in the midst of an earnest prayer when he received his vision of a cross of light in the heavens accompanied by the Greek words ἐν τούτῳ νίκα (Latinized as *in hoc signo vinces*—"in this sign shall you conquer"). Constantine duly placed the cross not on the shields but, with the help of workers, in gold and precious stones on his battle standard. The next morning, he faced the forces of Maxentius as they poured across the Tiber. The date was October 28, 312.

Maxentius hoped to resist Constantine's assault thanks to his numerically superior force of one hundred thousand troops as well as a reassuring prophecy that an enemy of the Romans would perish in battle. Made bold by this pronouncement, he marched his men through the Porta Flaminia on Rome's north side, only to lose not only the battle but also, as his drowned corpse was fished from the Tiber and decapitated, his head. On the following day, Constantine entered Rome as the undisputed emperor of the West, and as a victor who believed his success was down to the divine intervention of the god of the Christians. He endeavored to repay his debt. In 313, he met at Mediolanum with the augustus of the East, Licinius, and together they issued the Edict of Toleration, granting Christians—who had recently been persecuted under Diocletian—full rights of worship. He returned property confiscated during Diocletian's persecutions, exempted the Church and its clergy from taxation, and offered plots of land on which Christians could build their churches. He wisely left the monument-rich ceremonial center of Rome intact, but two new Christian basilicas rose on the outskirts of Rome: St. Peter's on the western outskirts and St. John Lateran to the southeast.

Constantine departed from Rome in January 313, only a few months after his victory. He made a brief return in 315 and then another, equally short, in 326. During his long reign, he spent fewer than six months in total in Rome. Under his rule, the Empire's center of gravity shifted eastward, and on November 8, 324, he founded a "New Rome"—named Constantinople—on the west side of the Bosporus Strait, on the site of the ancient Greek-speaking city of Byzantion (known in Latin as Byzantium). The new capital's impregnability as well as its quick access to the frontiers of both the Danube (where lurked hostile Germanic tribes) and Mesopotamia (the Sassanids) made it of far greater strategic importance than Rome. This "New Rome" would grow and prosper as the old Rome steadily diminished in both size and importance.

By the time of Constantine's death in 337, Christianity had made deep inroads into the population. By 400, a decade after Emperor Theodosius banned most forms of pagan worship, Christians probably accounted for a large majority of the population. But the Christianization of the Roman Empire coincided with further crises and political decline. In the 370s, a nomadic people from the steppes of central Asia, the Huns, swept westward, displacing Gothic tribes from their lands along the Dnieper and triggering a mass migration that, over the next few decades, would witness the collapse of the imperial frontiers and, finally, that of the Empire in the West.

In the winter of 406–407, Germanic tribes such as the Vandals and the Suevi crossed the Rhine in vast numbers, fleeing the irresistible westward expansion of the Huns (whose arrival in regular waves seemed to coincide with adverse climatic events in the East). The Huns themselves crossed the Rhine in 451, under Attila, but were defeated at Châlons by a combined army of Romans and Visigoths (one of the largest of the Germanic groups). Attila then swept into Italy, plundering a dozen cities, including (to give their modern names) Aquileia, Padua, Pavia, Bergamo, Vicenza, Verona, and Milan. Many of the inhabitants took refuge in the brackish lagoons on the scattering of islands along the Adriatic coast. Here, safe in their watery mazes, they would pound pylons into the mud and raise buildings alongside the channels of water. Attila, who once boasted that grass never grew again on the ground where his horse had trod, in fact left a remarkable legacy in his wake: the city of Venice.

As Attila moved south, the embassy that arrived to negotiate with him was led not by the emperor, Valentinian, but by a sixty-something aristocrat, Pope Leo I, later known as Leo the Great.

The title of pope as we know it today did not exist until later centuries. Leo was the bishop of Rome and as such was entitled, like other bishops, to call himself papa (from the Greek *pappas*, "father"). Not until the turn of the second millennium was the title exclusively reserved for bishops of Rome—at which point former bishops of Rome (from St. Peter onward) retrospectively became "popes." The pope today is still the bishop of Rome.

Dressed in his ecclesiastical finery, Leo met Attila at Ambuleium, near Ravenna, the capital of the Western Empire since 402: its surrounding swamps and waterways made it much more impregnable than either Rome or Milan. His eloquence and priestly robes impressed the king of the Huns, as did the enormous sum of money he offered Attila to vacate Italy. It was therefore the pope rather than the emperor who now took charge of the affairs of Italy and especially Rome: a prestigious and charismatic leader who embodied authority—political as well as religious—and commanded respect. The popes and their bishops were assuming many of the roles once performed by the emperors and other Roman officials, while the Church had become the largest landowner, after the state, in Western Europe.

The power and importance of the pope and the Church increased in the decades and then the centuries that followed. The Empire survived in the East and would continue to do so until the conquest of Constantinople by the Ottoman Turks in 1453—the year that marks the true end of the Roman Empire. But in the West, the Empire ended on a September day in 476, in Ravenna, with the toppling of its last emperor. By a fitting but ironic symmetry, he was named Romulus. A child emperor, he was known by the title Augustulus, or "Little Augustus." On September 4, 476, a German mercenary named Odovacar captured Ravenna and deposed Romulus Augustus, on whom, because of his youthful beauty, Odovacar took pity. The last Roman emperor, he was sent to live out his days in a sumptuous villa in southern Italy.

Odovacar was proclaimed king by his troops, although, crucially, not emperor, a role for which he seems to have had little appetite. He modestly signed documents as *Odovacer Rex*—Odovacar the King (though he did add an imperial flourish to his name, calling himself Flavius Odovacar). A coin minted the following year in Ravenna depicts him without imperial finery, titles, or insignia. Instead, he sports a pudding-bowl haircut and a moustache—the latter a sight so rare among the Romans that there was no word for it in Latin.

Rome's "decline and fall" was far more complex than any single cause or event. However, one of the most popular explanations was, and still is, the rise of Christianity. A number of ancient Romans, pagan holdouts, believed that abandoning the old gods and traditions had much to do with Rome's decline, prompting St. Augustine to write *The City of God* to counter the argument. In fact, Christianity is only one of the (according to one recent count by a German historian) 210 reasons given over the centuries for the fall of the Empire.[5] Included among them are physical afflictions, including gout, lead poisoning, and malaria; environmental problems, such as deforestation, drought, and soil erosion; cultural issues, such as poor education, racial discrimination, and female emancipation; the supposed moral failings of hedonism, homosexuality, and individualism; and traits including militarism and the lust for glory—but also the contrasting qualities of passivism, lethargy, celibacy, and impotence. The latter was the result, apparently, of spending too much time in the hot waters of Roman baths, a habit of "luxury and inertia" that, according to one stern Victorian writer, was "among the principal causes of the decline and fall of Rome."[6]

Whatever the causes, one great civilization on the Italian peninsula had ended. Even so, the legacy of Rome would endure, not merely in Italy but across the world: in politics, law, language, art, and culture. Some aspects of this inheritance are as hotly contested as the debates about the causes of the decline and fall. Certainly, some of Rome's legacies are unsettling, not least the many bloody conquests that Calgacus deplored as desolations. Moreover, although the Romans did not invent slavery, much of their civilization relied and rested upon it. By the time of Augustus, the Italian peninsula was home to approximately two million slaves, a third of the total population (a ratio similar to the later slave societies of the New World). Conditions for the slaves were bad enough that households and landowners needed to hire slave-catchers (*fugitivarii*) to bring back the desperate runaways. The revolt of Spartacus was only one of several large slave rebellions that were quashed with great brutality.

Unlike New World slave societies, however, the Romans were colorblind, enslaving people of every origin and race. Most slaves were prisoners of war, but debtors, criminals, unfortunates captured by pirates, and even children found abandoned in the street—all could find themselves enslaved regardless of their skin color and ethnic or geographic origin. The Romans appear to have held few, if any, negative views about different racial types, in part because they were themselves, in many cases, racially and ethnically mixed. As one demographic study claimed, only "a very small percentage" of people walking the streets of Rome "could prove unmixed Italian descent."[7] Septimius Severus, for example, came from Leptis Magna, a city 75 miles (120 km) east along the coast from Tripoli in modern Libya. Swarthy and dark-haired, he was the son of a Roman mother and a father of Carthaginian (and perhaps also Berber) blood—a fact that caused neither comment nor controversy. The Romans certainly did not entertain anything like the "white" racial consciousness or identity recently imposed on them by far-right groups, including those at the 2017 "Unite the Right" rally in Charlottesville, Virginia, who marched behind images of Hadrian and Marcus Aurelius inscribed with slogans such as "Protect Your Heritage." In fact, the satirist Juvenal mocked the Germans for their "blue eyes and yellow hair."[8] The misguided distortions of history by white supremacists have been one of Rome's more unfortunate and offensive legacies. The claims about Rome made by such hate groups continue to be vigorously and expertly contested.[9]

Other of Rome's bequests have been more positive. The idea of separating government into three branches was widely copied by modern-day states determined to provide a system of checks and balances against abuses of power. The Roman legal texts known as the Twelve Tables (after the dozen bronze plates on which they were inscribed during the fifth century BCE) became one of the most important legal documents in history. They dealt with contracts, debts, family relations, legal guardianship, inheritance, and property rights, and they stressed the concept of the equality of all before the law, no matter the social status (apart, of course, from slaves). They were expanded during the Middle Ages and ultimately became the basis for much European law.

Rome's other great legacies include not only Latin—one of the great products of the human mind—but also the languages into which Latin evolved as it spread around the Empire in Western Europe: Romance languages such as

Italian, French, Spanish, Catalan, Portuguese, and Romanian. Roman architecture likewise traveled across the centuries and over a vast geographical area. Just as Roman politics and law permeated the government and legal system of the United States, so, too, the vocabulary of Roman building—with its clear geometries and elegant symmetries—infused early American building styles. Thomas Jefferson's design for the State Capitol in Virginia, for example, was based on the Maison Carrée in Nîmes, a Roman temple from the time of Augustus.

One of Rome's greatest gifts to posterity was its infrastructure of roads—50,000 miles (80,000 km) of them scything across great tracts of the Empire. Although originally for military transport and provisioning, these roads, paved and straight, with bridges, embankments, and milestones, also sped up communication and cultural exchange, spreading ideas and, in many cases, prosperity to conquered territories. And this prosperity has continued. A team from the University of Gothenburg recently superimposed a satellite image of Europe over a map of Roman roads, using light intensity at night as an indicator of economic activity. They found a strong correlation exists between the old Roman roads and modern concentrations of economic affluence—yet another example of something the Romans have done for us.[10]

CHAPTER 5

Goths, Longbeards, Franks, Saracens, and Normans
Italy under the "Barbarians"

The centuries following the collapse of the Empire in the West would bring further wars, plagues, and other disasters. The violence and disruption of the Germanic and Hunnic invasions led to the loss of the literacy, prosperity, and cultural values on which so much Roman civilization was based—not to mention that of material comforts such as roof tiles and well-wrought cooking pots.[1] Italy was invaded by successive conquerors who, frequently at war with one another, carved the peninsula into competing spheres of influence. This state of affairs would keep Italy internally divided, separated by politics and even language for well over a thousand years, with large territories often ruled by absentee leaders based north of the Alps or in Constantinople. These invasions by "barbarians," as well as the resulting loss of both unity and political autonomy, is often blamed for plunging Italy into the Dark Ages, from which, according to traditional chronologies, it would fail to emerge until the Renaissance. The full story is more subtle and complex, with periods of undeniable desolation followed by attempts, often impressive, to restore Rome's cultural and political grandeur.

The Empire in Italy ended with neither a bang nor a whimper. Life on the peninsula in the first years after 476 CE continued much as before, albeit probably more peacefully, on the whole, than for many decades or even centuries. Odovacar maintained good relations with the pope as well as with the emperor of the East, who ruled the eastern provinces of the Empire from Constantinople. (Historians later began referring to the Emperors of the East as "Byzantine" emperors, a reference to Constantinople's origins in Byzantium, although the incumbents regarded themselves as Roman emperors whose lineage went back in a direct line through Constantine and Diocletian to Augustus.) Trouble arose when, in 489, another mustachioed Gothic chieftain, Theoderic, crossed the Alps. Theoderic had been the leader of a Germanic tribe called the Amali (or Amalungs) who joined various other groups of barbarians to become one of the Germanic "supergroups," the Ostrogoths—the "eastern" Goths (as opposed to the "western" Visigoths). For several decades, the Ostrogoths had been crisscrossing the Balkans in a restless and sometimes violent search for lands in which to settle. In 489, with the blessing of the Byzantine emperor, who wanted them gone, they began a final journey, a kind of migrant caravan that took them—soldiers, women, children—into Italy: possibly as many as two hundred thousand people, along with a baggage train, pack animals, cattle, and sheep.

For three years Theoderic and his soldiers besieged Ravenna, a prolonged assault that certified the city's impregnability. Finally, in 493, weary of battle, both sides agreed to a power-sharing agreement that finished with a celebratory banquet, at the end of which Theoderic, after warmly toasting Odovacar, murdered him. Yet if the Ostrogothic

Kingdom of Italy began with this act of treachery and violence, the next three decades would be, thanks to Theoderic, a period of peace and prosperity—and a brief return to the grandeur that was Rome.

Theoderic, like Odovacar, never aspired to be emperor. Although he received permission from the Byzantine emperor to wear a purple robe, his position for the next thirty-three years was that of a king who served as the emperor's nominal vassal. However, he eventually came to govern vast territories that included not only Italy but also Sicily, Dalmatia, and (thanks to strategic marriages and military intervention) large areas of Spain and southern Gaul. As in the old days, much of Western Europe was therefore governed by a power anchored on the Italian peninsula. Theoderic came to be hailed as "forever Augustus" and the "propagator of the Roman name."[2] The Roman Empire, it seemed, had been restored to something of its former glory—thanks, ironically, to a barbarian chieftain.

The Ostrogothic Kingdom did not long survive Theoderic, who, after he died in 526, was succeeded by his daughter, Amalasuntha. She ruled for less than a decade before, following a palace intrigue, she was strangled in her bath. The emperor in Constantinople, Justinian, took advantage of the crisis in succession to claw back Italian territory from the Ostrogoths. Justinian's chief aim was to restore the unity and historical boundaries of the Roman world that had been shattered in the previous century. He began a series of military campaigns in the West, capturing the lands ruled by the Vandals in Africa and the Ostrogoths in Italy as well as part of Spain (then under Visigothic rule). He largely achieved his aims, and by the time of his death in 565, most of the lands washed by the Mediterranean were once more dominated by the emperor, albeit now from Constantinople rather than Rome.

Two years after he came to power, in 529, Justinian sent an edict to Athens banning the teaching of philosophy (and thereby obliging seven suddenly out-of-work Platonists to traipse off to Persia in search of their fortunes). This closure of the Academy in Athens—founded by Plato in 387 BCE—has often been seen by historians as a watershed: the end of the classical world and the onset of the Dark Ages. In fact, much of the literature and philosophy of the classical world was preserved thanks to the efforts of the Christians. Around the year 500, a young man from Norcia in Umbria, the future St. Benedict, retired to live the rigorous life of a hermit in a remote cave near Subiaco, 40 miles (65 km) east of Rome. (The word "monk," *monaco* in Italian, comes from the Greek *monos*, "alone": a reference to how during the third century the Christian hermits such as St. Anthony of Egypt retreated into the Egyptian desert for lives of austere solitude.) Soon locally famous for his asceticism and sanctity, Benedict attracted numerous followers and in 529—the same year as Justinian's decree—founded the great monastery of Montecassino, midway between Naples and Rome. Here he composed his famous "Rule" for a communal living that combined prayer with work (*ora et labora*). The latter involved, besides toiling in the gardens or fields, copying manuscripts by hand in the scriptorium.

The Benedictine Rule became a pillar of monastic life, widely adopted across Western Europe and responsible for, among other things, encouraging literacy and establishing libraries: each monastery was to supply a collection of manuscripts for the monks to read. The furnishing of these libraries with books meant ancient knowledge was preserved and handed on to posterity, thanks to the transfer of Greek and Roman works from papyrus (the perishable writing support of the pagans) onto parchment (the more durable choice of the Christians). Indeed, virtually all the classical works that have survived into our time have done so only because in the dim and distant past they were laboriously copied out by monks clutching goosequills as they hunched over leaves of parchment.

Despite the efforts of Justinian, the Western Empire had hardly been rejuvenated. The long war, as well as the continual ravages of the plague, took a dreadful toll on Italy. A later historian, Paul the Deacon, painted a bleak picture of deserted farms, abandoned villages, shriveled vineyards, and unburied corpses. His account was probably no great exaggeration, since in the second half of the 500s the population of Italy was little more than half of what it had been during the reign of Augustus.[3] Even so, the Empire may have recovered and sustained itself but for the appearance of a formidable new enemy: the Lombards.

The Lombards originated several centuries earlier in Scandinavia as the Winnili, a name that seems to have meant something along the lines of "demon dogs." They gradually migrated southward through Europe, taking over Pannonia (modern Hungary) in 489. They got their new name, Langobardi, or "Longbeards," either from their abundant facial hair or else from Langbaror, one of the names of Odin, the Norse god whom they worshipped. In 568, under their king, Alboin, these long-haired demon dogs descended into Italy, accompanied by Heruli, Goths, and Saxons, as well as their women, children, slaves, and livestock—a force of perhaps as many as two hundred thousand people.[4]

The Lombards would dominate large parts of the Italian peninsula for more than two centuries, from 568 to 774. This occupation would prove economically, socially, and culturally catastrophic, and in many ways 568 is a more convincing date for the end of the Roman Empire in the West than the victory of Odovacar in 476. As the great nineteenth-century historian Ferdinand Gregorovius wrote, "The Goths had protected Latin civilization, the Lombards destroyed it."[5]

The Lombards burst into Italy virtually unopposed by the imperial forces and an exhausted local population suffering from famine on top of the plague. Although they quickly captured cities and territories in northern Italy (a large part of it known ever since as Lombardy), their conquest was a prolonged and intermittent affair. Their occupation led to the fragmentation of Italy into different pockets of influence—a political reality that was to have far-reaching consequences. They followed the same settlement pattern they practiced in northern Europe, based on the independent excursions of clans or family groups called *fare* (related to the German *fahren*, to go or travel). More than thirty of these *fare* fanned out across the Italian peninsula, each several thousand strong and claiming for itself (usually through violence) territory thereafter ruled by the head of the clan. These clan leaders soon adopted an old Roman title, *dux*, or duke, and, ensconced in their castles and military outposts, demanded of the beleaguered local populations the tribute of one-third of the produce of their land.

Ruling their various chunks of territory as petty tyrants, the Lombard dukes turned Italy into a patchwork of fiefdoms nominally ruled by their king, based in Pavia. Some of the Lombard dukes, aggressively independent, grew so powerful and entrenched (especially in Spoleto and Benevento) that future Lombard kings were hard-pressed to control them. The fragmentation of the peninsula was made more extreme by the fact that the Lombards proved unable to conquer the whole of Italy: large areas of the south, including Puglia and Calabria—the heel and toe of the Italian boot—as well as Naples, Sicily, and a strip of land linking Rome to Ravenna, remained under the control of Constantinople. The emperor's man in Italy, based in Ravenna, was the exarch (from the Greek *exarchos*, "leader").

The third power contending for control on the peninsula during these decades was the Church, which assumed political importance in Rome and the surrounding territory, known as the Duchy of Rome. The duchy was technically an imperial possession governed by the pope on behalf of the Byzantine emperor. However, by the turn of the seventh century, the papacy was asserting itself as an independent power thanks to the efforts of many popes, exemplified in the figure of Pope Gregory I (St. Gregory the Great). Gregory had been a monk when, in 578, the reigning pope, Pelagius II, sent him as a legate to Constantinople to plead for assistance from the Byzantine emperor against the Lombards. These dealings proved a revelation to Gregory. When no significant help was forthcoming from the East, he realized that only decisive and independent actions on the part of the Church could safeguard Rome.

Gregory accordingly took swift and vigorous measures when he was elected pope in 590. He provided for refugees from the Lombard rampages, offering them alms and supplying the corn dole (in the old days, the task of the emperor) from the estates of the Church. When the Lombards besieged Rome and Naples, it was Gregory who negotiated peace directly with them, much to the annoyance of the exarch in Ravenna and the emperor in Constantinople. But henceforth the popes rather than the emperors would manage civic and institutional affairs in the Duchy of Rome. Indeed, for many on the peninsula, both inside Rome and beyond, the popes became the preferred and seemingly more natural leaders than either the "barbarian" Lombard dukes or the Byzantine emperors, the latter of whom were remote figures based in faraway Constantinople.

Italy in the decades following the Lombard invasions was, at best, feeble and moribund, and at worst, terrifying and dangerous. The seventh century in Italy was, almost uniquely, a time of extremely limited literary and cultural expression—the darkest period of the Dark Ages. The Lombards appear to have been, during their first decades of rule, completely illiterate: not a single text written in the Lombardic language, not even one full sentence, has survived. They eventually abandoned their own language (extinct by the ninth century) and instead used the vernacular Latin of the locals, to which, however, they contributed a bit of their own vocabulary. Italian words with Lombard roots include *agguato* (an ambush), *arraffare* (to grab), *bara* (coffin), *baruffa* (a brawl), *faida* (a feud), *ghermire* (to seize), *guerra* (war), *rubare* (to rob), *tregua* (a truce), and *sgherro* (a thug or goon)—all evoking a world of war, violence, and smash-and-grab looting. These long-haired warriors also provided Italian with the word for dandruff (*forfora*). Lombard names, too, summon a picture of a warrior culture in which parents named their children after fierce beasts and frightening weapons: Aistulf (Raging Wolf), Agilulf (Scary Wolf), Garipald (Valiant with a Spear), and Liutprand (Sword of the People). Some Lombardic names, Italianized, survived well beyond the time of the Kingdom of the Lombards: personal names such as Alberto, Bernardo, Guido, and Raimondo, as well as surnames including Arnolfini, Grimaldi, and even Garibaldi.

Despite generally cordial relations between the Lombards and the papacy during the 600s CE, by the eighth century the popes came to resent and fear Lombard expansion. To thwart these aims, at various times they turned north of the

Alps for military help from the Franks (whose kingdom stretched across virtually all of modern France and parts of Germany). Such was the case in 751, when a Lombard king named Aistulf finally captured the last vestiges of Byzantine-controlled lands in northern Italy. Fearing for the safety of his domains, Pope Stephen II appealed to the king of the Franks, Pepin the Short, whose army descended into Italy and forced the Lombards to relinquish some of their recently captured imperial domains. These lands Pepin offered not to the Byzantine emperor but, crucially, to the pope. Endowed in perpetuity to the Catholic Church, these territories became the Papal States: a total of twenty-two cities plus extensive lands stretching across the peninsula, from Rome to the Adriatic coast. Henceforth, the popes would rule as secular as well as religious leaders. The pope's sovereignty over these lands—challenged countless times by various warriors and princes in the centuries that followed—would last until the middle of the nineteenth century.

A generation later, Aistulf's successor, Desiderius, likewise hoping to expand Lombard power, once more threatened the papacy. And once more the pope responded by summoning military assistance from the Franks. Since Pepin had died in 768, there was a new king of the Franks: Pepin's strapping twenty-six-year-old son, Charles, the future Charlemagne. In October 773, Charlemagne's troops overran northern Italy and besieged Pavia, the Lombard capital, capturing it the following June. Desiderius, fated to be the last monarch of Lombard blood, was marched off to exile in a monastery while Charlemagne became king of the Lombards as well as king of the Franks. Most of northern Italy (apart from Venice and the Papal States) was absorbed into the Frankish Empire.

The ancient lands of the Roman emperors made a deep impression on Charlemagne. His courtiers, already comparing him to King David, Solomon, and Moses, began hailing him as *novus Constantinus* (the new Constantine). Their flattery fell on eager ears. With domains that stretched from the North Sea to the Danube, throughout Germania, and, thanks to this latest conquest, down to Rome, Charlemagne regarded himself as the restorer of the Roman Empire in the West. But he also considered himself the defender of the Christian faith—a sacred mission imposed on him, he believed, because the Byzantine emperors were drastically weak, beset by invasions and internal struggles, and unable or unwilling to offer protection to the papacy and the Church. "In you alone," proclaimed Charlemagne's chief adviser, Alcuin of York, "rests the salvation of the Church of Christ."[6]

In December 800, during a stay in Rome, Charlemagne took himself off to the Basilica of St. Peter's for a solemn Mass. During the ceremony, Pope Leo III approached him, prostrated himself, and then, rising to his feet, placed an imperial crown on Charlemagne's head. The congregation intoned three times: "Long live Charles, the most pious Augustus, crowned by God, the great, peace-giving Emperor." Extinct for almost 325 years, the title of Roman Emperor was renewed in the West—albeit now with a distinctly Christian emphasis: Charlemagne was proclaimed "Holy" Roman Emperor.

For centuries thereafter, many people in Italy, the popes in particular, had good cause to rue that fateful day. The coronation of an emperor by a pope raised difficult questions regarding the authority of each with respect to the other. Did the pope have jurisdiction in the world of politics and therefore, by extension, over the emperor? Did the emperor have authority in religious matters and therefore, by extension, over the pope? These unresolved pope-versus-emperor questions would become the source of much bitter conflict in the centuries that followed.

The dispute plumbed its murky depths with the "Investiture Controversy" that began in 1075 when Pope Gregory VII announced that only the pope possessed the authority to appoint clergy. The Holy Roman Emperor, Henry IV, took exception, declaring Gregory's election invalid and demanding his abdication. Gregory promptly excommunicated Henry, forcing the hapless emperor—whose position at home was endangered by disgruntled German aristocrats looking for any excuse to depose him—to perform his infamous and humiliating "Walk to Canossa," the castle overlooking badlands 90 miles (150 km) southeast of Milan where the pope was staying as the guest of his staunch supporter, Matilda of Tuscany. Here, in the dead of winter, at the end of January 1077, Henry was forced to wait for three days outside the castle walls, shivering barefoot in the snow and wearing the hairshirt of a humble penitent. At last, the gates groaned open, Gregory admitted him, and, with Henry on bended knee, offered him absolution.

The tedious dispute at least threw into relief the figure of Matilda, known as *la Gran Contessa*, one of the great characters of medieval Italy. Born in Lucca to a Tuscan aristocrat in about 1046, as a young woman she had spurned female arts such as embroidery in favor of masculine pursuits: she donned suits of armor, galloped about on horseback, and wielded swords and battleaxes. She left an unhappy marriage to Godfrey the Hunchback, Duke of Lower Lorraine, to return to her Italian homeland and (if the gossip can be believed) the arms of Pope Gregory. After Godfrey was killed while answering a nocturnal call of nature, many fingers of blame pointed Matilda's way. A decade later, then in her forties, she married a seventeen-year-old named Welf, the Duke of Bavaria and Carinthia. It proved another unhappy union, not helped when she shaved her head and donned a hairshirt on their wedding night. But the marriage truly collapsed when Welf sided with Henry IV, the man against whom Matilda fought for the better part of a quarter of a century. A later chronicler marveled how Matilda, "armed like a warrior," appeared at the head of her armies, proving "that courage and valor in mankind is not indeed a matter of sex, but of heart and spirit."[7] She was held in such esteem by later popes that, in the seventeenth century, her remains were interred in the Basilica of St. Peter in Rome, beneath a marble effigy carved by the great sculptor Gianlorenzo Bernini. A century earlier, another sculptor, Michelangelo, had proudly claimed to be Matilda's descendant.

The ninth century brought into Italy a new onslaught of "barbarian" invaders. These latest arrivals came not through the Alpine passes, as so many had done before, but rather on boats. The Muslim war fleets had swept out of the Arabian Peninsula soon after Muhammad's death in 632. The Arab conquests in the Mediterranean included Egypt in the first half of the 600s, North Africa (including Carthage) in the second half, and the entirety of Iberia by 713. Their conquest of Sicily was a decades-long affair that began in 827 and was finally completed, apart from some fortresses that remained in Byzantine hands, with the capture of Taormina in 902.

Muslim raiders frequently attacked along the Italian mainland, the peninsula known in Arabic as *al-Ard al-Kabira* ("The Great Land"). (The memory of these "Saracens" coming ashore survives in the name for the shutter of corrugated sheet metal used for protecting shops at night or during riots: *saracinesca*.) In the summer of 846, a fleet sailed up the Tiber, attacked Rome, and sacked the Basilica of St. Peter. A year later, Muslims captured (from the Lombard duke of Benevento) the Adriatic port of Bari on the Italian heel, establishing an Islamic emirate. The first emir of "Barah," as the city became known, was one Kahlfun al-Barbari ("the Berber"). One of his successors, Sawdan al-Mawri ("the Moor"), appears, due to his name, to have come from sub-Saharan Africa, which meant that during Sawdan's fourteen years in power (857–871) southern Italy featured a Muslim enclave ruled by a black African. Sawdan seems to have been an efficient and well-organized ruler, expanding his influence over more than eighty castles. He adorned Barah with mosques and palaces, opened schools, and formed generally good relations with his Christian neighbors—apart, of course, from those in the towns that his men, in search of loot, pillaged and burned, or in the monasteries from which he extorted gold. Three monks passing through the emirate in 870 received courteous treatment and were duly impressed by "the prince of that state," as they called Sawdan, although they did not fail to notice how one of the ships in the harbor held a cargo of nine thousand Christian slaves bound for points east.[8]

The emirate of Barah was conquered in 871 by the army of Louis II, the Frankish ruler of Italy. Sawdan spent four years in a Benevento dungeon before vanishing from history.

Today nothing remains in Bari of its decades-long Saracen interlude, for in the 1100s the city was completely destroyed by the Normans—the next great invasion force in Italy.

The Normans first arrived in Italy as mercenaries to help the Lombards in their struggles against the Byzantines. As we've seen, in the middle of the eighth century, the Lombards under King Aistulf had ended Byzantine control in peninsular Italy. However, the Byzantines returned in force to the South, capturing all of Calabria in the 880s and then Benevento in 891. Once the "Catepanate of Italy" (from the Greek *katepáno*, "topmost," from which we get "captain") was established in the tenth century, the Italian boot was submerged to its ankle in Byzantine authority. However, the natives—that is, the Lombards, established in the South for almost five hundred years—became restless. An increasing tax burden imposed by Constantinople as well as the demand for greater political autonomy led a disaffected Lombard nobleman named Melus of Bari to stage a revolt in 1009. Although defeated by an imperial army, Melus regrouped his forces in the years that followed. He conscripted into Lombard service a group of Norman mercenaries encountered, according to legend, at the shrine of St. Michael the Archangel on Monte Gargano, a rocky, forested spur jutting out from the coast of Puglia. This band of some 250 adventurers had fetched up at the holy site not to pray so much as to offer protection, for a price, to pilgrims for whom the shrine was a stopover before they caught ships to the Holy Land from the nearby port of Bari.

Melus's new recruits would change the course of Italian history. The Normans were the descendants of the Vikings, who in past centuries had menaced much of Europe before, in 911, Charles the Simple, the great-great-grandson of Charlemagne, bought them off with the lands in northern France that became the Duchy of Normandy. Since then, the Normans had earned a reputation as feared mercenaries. The band at Monte Gargano were led by one Rainulf Drengot, who had been expelled from Normandy after he threw "from a very high place" a man who boasted of seducing his niece.[9] What followed in the South over the next few decades were further rebellions and battles against the Byzantines. At first the Normans fought alongside the Lombards before exploiting the region's instability for their own ends (initially plunder, later territory) and establishing shifting alliances with various Italian powers, from Lombard princes to the pope and even—since they switched sides with carefree consciences whenever it suited their needs— the Byzantine emperor. In 1030, Rainulf became count of the hamlet of Aversa, building a fortress with moats and high hedges that constituted the first Norman settlement on the Italian peninsula. Strategically placed between Capua and Naples, Aversa quickly became a magnet for landless Norman knights and fortune-seeking younger sons.

One of these adventurers, arriving in about 1046 with a small band of horsemen, was Robert d'Hauteville, known as Guiscard (from the Norman *wischard*, "cunning"). A ruddy-faced, flaxen-haired giant, Guiscard supported himself at first through banditry and kidnapping, terrorizing the roads and hills of Calabria and, in the words of one chronicler, committing "much bloodshed and many murders."[10] He soon captured Calabria from the Byzantines, and over the next few decades, the Normans under Guiscard and his numerous brothers and half-brothers subdued all of southern Italy and brought to an end not only Byzantine but also Lombard control. Then, in 1091, Guiscard's younger brother Roger d'Hauteville captured Sicily, ending centuries of Muslim domination. Even so, the Islamic influence would linger in, for example, many hundreds of words in the Sicilian dialect, including (as we'll see) the word *mafia*. It also survived in the cuisine: cassata (a sponge cake), cannoli (cream-filled pastries), even frozen desserts such as gelato, granità, and sorbetto—all Arab inventions or imports.

The Normans eventually turned Sicily into Europe's newest kingdom. Roger's son and successor, Roger II, united Sicily to the mainland Norman possessions in Calabria and Puglia, and in 1130, on Christmas Day, he was crowned King of Sicily. Under Roger II, who spoke Arabic thanks to his Muslim tutors, the Normans participated in a brilliant and sophisticated culture on an island populated by large numbers of Arabs and Greeks. His kingdom was characterized by a fusion of Western, Byzantine, and Arabic arts and traditions epitomized by buildings such as the cathedral of Monreale and the Cappella Palatina in the Royal Palace in Palermo. Both feature Byzantine-style mosaics—some 7,000 square feet (650 sq km) in the case of the former, which also has interlocking pointed arches similar to those in the Great Mosque in Córdoba, built in the tenth century. The Cappella Palatina shows even more emphatic Islamic influences and motifs, from the honeycomb (or *muqarnas*) vaulting in the nave, reminiscent of mosques and mausoleums in the Arab world, to the Arab inscriptions painted on the ceiling. An Arabic inscription likewise features on the embroidered silk mantle made for Roger II in the early 1130s (now in the

Imperial Treasury in Vienna). The Kufic lettering praises the royal workshop in Palermo for its "industry and perfection," and Roger himself for his "magnanimity and majesty." It also celebrates the "felicitous days and nights without cease or change" in the Kingdom of Sicily. Much would in fact change in Sicily in the centuries that followed, but for a brief period the Normans, descendants of the axe-wielding Norse marauders, had become, beneath the bright Mediterranean sun, the most tolerant and civilized people in Europe.

CHAPTER 6

"All the Cities of Italy"
The Middle Ages

In about 1165, a Jewish traveler from Spain, Benjamin of Tudela, en route to the Holy Land, arrived in the port city of Pisa. He was suitably impressed with what he saw. "Pisa is a very great city, with about 10,000 turreted houses for battle at times of strife," he observed. "All its inhabitants are mighty men. They possess neither king nor prince to govern them, but only the judges appointed by themselves."[1]

As a populous, prosperous, and self-governing urban center, Pisa marked an astonishing change from the Italian cities of many previous centuries. What's more, Pisa was far from unique: by 1200, at least two hundred and perhaps as many as three hundred cities and towns in central and northern Italy were ruled not by kings or princes but by collective governments of officials elected by the city-dwellers themselves.[2] These self-governing cities would have far-reaching consequences, not the least of which was the creation of the kind of vibrant urban society in which, some two centuries later, the culture of the Italian Renaissance could be born.

Italy had been a land of cities at least since Etruscan times. Most Italian cities survived the collapse of the Empire in the West more or less intact, and Italy remained the most urbanized region of Western Europe. However, between the fifth and the tenth centuries, urban life had drastically declined. Rome dropped from a population of a million people in the second century to an estimated fifty thousand in the sixth century[3]—with further losses in the centuries that followed. The buildings were humbler and more ramshackle, made from wood rather than stone. Roman baths fell into disuse and disrepair because of problems maintaining an adequate water supply—an acute problem in Rome after the Ostrogoths, in 537, severed the aqueducts that fed the bathing complexes. Not without reason did a nineteenth-century historian characterize the Middle Ages as "one thousand years without a bath."[4]

The countryside beyond the city walls had also changed since the days of Augustus or Trajan. The threat from barbarian invaders meant people living in exposed hamlets and villages on the coasts and plains uprooted themselves to occupy more secure and defensible locations, clustering in and around fortified centers, such as hilltop towns and castles. Historians call this process *incastellamento* (roughly translatable as "encastling").[5] This heading-for-the-fortified-hills appears to have begun spontaneously in the sixth and seventh centuries: the time, unsurprisingly, of the violent Lombard takeover. Later, the local nobles invited these migrants to live beside, or even within, their fortresses, thereby intensifying their control over the population.

As a consequence of the barbarian invasions and the breakdown of any strong centralized authority, a relationship of mutual loyalty and support developed between the castle-dwelling nobles and their clutches of dependents. These vassals (from *vassus*, "servant") performed military duties and other personal services (known as *feodalitas*) for the lord, such as upkeep of castles and laboring in the fields. In return, the vassal received protection and sometimes a plot of land known as a *feudum* (a word whose Germanic root, *fehu*, refers to cattle). This arrangement of oaths, ties of dependence, and complicated land-tenure schemes later came to be known, of course, as feudalism—a byword for the economically and socially backward Middle Ages.

By the turn of the millennium, these feudal ties began to fray. The lords became increasingly powerful, levying tolls, dispensing justice, and exercising unchecked powers that led to abuses and, occasionally, protests and revolts. At the same time, the countryside became more peaceable and prosperous as the barbarian raids ended. New agricultural tools, especially the heavy plough—which tilled the soil far more effectively than the ancient plough—made for more productive agriculture. So, too, did the three-field system of crop rotation, which increased yield by some 30 to 50 percent.[6] Italian marshes were reclaimed thanks to drains and dykes. Irrigation canals were dug, hillsides terraced, forests cleared—all of which meant the growing population could be fed. The cities began recovering their numbers as many peasants, newly unconstrained by the ties of vassalage, made their way into urban centers, where a distinctive and dynamic economic and political life was beginning.

These cities had begun flourishing due to the lack of a strong centralized control. The Holy Roman Emperors showed little interest in the Italian peninsula, leaving the actual administration to the bishops. These were imperial appointees, usually German, who were given palaces, extensive lands, far-reaching secular powers, and titles of nobility, which meant they differed little from other feudal potentates apart from the fact that they also wielded ecclesiastical power. They became unpopular thanks to the imposition of fiscal measures, such as customs duties and road tolls. In 1031, in Cremona, the inhabitants rebelled against a bishop named Hubald, chasing him from the city and destroying his palace. Similar uprisings against the imperial overlords followed in Milan and Parma in 1037.

Known in Roman times as "the Golden City," Parma was by this time affluent from the wool trade. Many cities around Italy likewise had buoyant economies by the turn of the millennium. Genoa, Pisa, Venice, Bari, and Amalfi, to give conspicuous examples from along the coasts, had become thriving maritime and commercial centers. Amalfi gained its independence from the Lombards in the ninth century, and then, in the tenth and eleventh, established itself as a maritime power. The seafaring skills of the Amalfitani owed much to their perfection of the mariner's compass, already known to the Arabs and improved, as legend had it, by Flavio Gioia (a statue of whom stands along the seafront in Amalfi). Banks, warehouses, and trading depots owned or run by Amalfi merchants could be found scattered around the Mediterranean, including in Tripoli, Alexandria, Antioch, and Constantinople. Ships set sail from Amalfi with loads of timber, salt, and grain; they returned with spices, perfumes, silk, and carpets. They sold many of their wares in Rome, where the papal court was a reliable consumer of luxury goods.

Across the peninsula, Venice dominated the Adriatic. Founded for defensive purposes in the watery mazes of the lagoons during the barbarian invasions, it gained its autonomy from the Byzantine empire in the middle of the eighth century. A hundred years later, the Venetians were trading with Sicily and Egypt. In 1082, in exchange for military assistance, the Byzantine emperor granted them lucrative trading privileges in the East, including an exemption from all customs duties and the right to own shops, wharves. and warehouses in Constantinople. Like the Amalfitani, the Venetians exported products such as salt and timber while bringing back silks, precious skins, exotic feathers, and spices, especially pepper, the demand for which was so great that Venetian ships would soon import more than a million pounds each year from Alexandria.[7]

Venice's political independence and burgeoning commercial life coincided with the development of new structures by which the citizens came to be governed by men "appointed by themselves." As early as the eighth century, the Venetians had established a republican form of government. Their head of state was the doge (from the Latin *dux*), an official, elected for life, enjoying great prestige and elaborate ceremonies but carefully circumscribed powers: he was to be addressed not as "prince" or "lord" but only as "Messer lo Doge" (Mr. Doge). He was advised and assisted by a bewildering variety of councils, the members of which provided an intricate system of checks and balances. Elected for short terms, most of these officials were wealthy merchants—traders with business interests around the Mediterranean.

For several centuries Venice's republican form of government remained unique in Italy. However, by the late 1000s and early 1100s, power in other towns and cities in northern Italy began passing from the bishops and feudal lords to organized groups of citizens within the cities themselves. The end result was the development of the Italian city-states or "communes": scores of independent political entities in which elected officials (known as consuls, after the officials in Ancient Rome) served short terms in office, made collective decisions about war, legislation, and taxes, and remained free from all but nominal control by superior powers such as the local bishop or faraway Holy Roman Emperor. It was this state of affairs that so impressed Benjamin of Tudela in Pisa, and that could be found throughout the cities all over northern Italy.

Various Holy Roman Emperors attempted, with limited success, to bring these independent-minded Italian city-states to heel. The most vigorous response was mounted in the second half of the twelfth century by Frederick Hohenstaufen, crowned King of Germany in 1152. Three years later, Frederick, known in Italy as "Barbarossa" because of his long red beard, was crowned Holy Roman Emperor by Pope Adrian IV (an Englishman, Nicholas Breakspear). Determined to assert imperial control, in 1158 he invaded northern Italy and besieged Milan. Not prepared to lose their hard-won autonomy to a foreigner from beyond the Alps, many of the city-states banded together, forming an anti-imperial alliance known as the Lombard League, a confederation that included Milan, Venice, Bologna, Brescia, Mantua, Padua, Vicenza, and Treviso. In May 1176, the army of the Lombard League trounced Barbarossa's troops at the Battle of Legnano—a stunning victory that ensured the alliance's iconic status, many centuries later, as a precursor of the Italian struggles for independence against foreign control. The battle would become the subject of an opera by Giuseppe Verdi, and in 1847 Legnano (a city 20 miles/30 km northwest of Milan) was patriotically name-checked in

Goffredo Mameli's "Fratelli d'Italia," later to become the Italian national anthem.

Following his defeat at Legnano, Barbarossa struck a deal with the communes by which they retained their autonomy at the price of paying a tax and swearing an oath to the Holy Roman Emperor. A short peace ensued, although the communes needed to revive the Lombard League in the 1230s when Barbarossa's grandson Frederick II—a cosmopolitan polymath known as the *stupor mundi*, or "wonder of the world"—took his own stab at reasserting imperial control. In 1248, the army of the Lombard League took advantage of Frederick's absence from his camp outside Parma (he had gone hunting with falcons) to rout his forces. Frederick died two years later, and not for another 250 years would an emperor arise powerful and ambitious enough to trouble the peninsula.

The communes gradually began to fall apart over the next few decades as another, unhappier story began unfolding. The tension between landed and mercantile interests, and competition within these groups themselves, resulted in factions and feuds within the communes. In Bergamo, northeast of Milan, the townspeople were forced to take vows promising to stop brawling in the streets, stabbing each other to death, and hurling missiles from high places onto each other's heads.[8] Beginning in 1177, Florence witnessed twenty-seven months of violent riots and pitched battles in the streets after the powerful Uberti clan refused to recognize the election results. Much of the city burned down. In the early 1300s, Dante would lament how people "thrown together within the same wall and ditch / Cannot live without biting one another." He offered as a sorry example two

The skyline of San Gimignano, where fourteen of what used to be seventy-two tower-houses survive

warring factions in Verona, the Montecchi and the Cappelletti, later immortalized (as the Montagues and Capulets) in Shakespeare's *Romeo and Juliet*.[9]

Such intramural feuds led families to band together in what were known as *consorterie*. The members of these kinship-based groups swore oaths of loyalty to each other, raised militias armed with weapons such as catapults and crossbows, and shared fortified houses, often with tall towers—powerful fortifications intended to protect the clan not from foreigners but from their own fellow citizens in the neighboring streets. Here they could gather in times of tumult and violence, safe behind thick walls, raining rocks and arrows onto their rivals in the streets below. The cityscapes of Florence, Genoa, Lucca, Milan, Parma, Pavia, Siena, and Verona were dominated by forests of these family towers (examples of which can still be seen today in the Tuscan town of San Gimignano). By the 1180s, Florence had around a hundred of them. Bearing names such as "Iron Mouth" and "Cat's Kiss," they rose to heights of 200 to 230 feet (60–70 m). The tower of one *consorteria* in Bologna (the Asinelli Tower, still standing) soars to nearly 320 feet (97 m) above the city, more than twenty stories—slightly higher than the Statue of Liberty. Such architectural exclamation points were about intimidation and prestige as much as defense, accommodation, or refuge.

In order to bring some order to their feuding communes, many cities introduced a special official, a chief magistrate known as the *podestà* (from the Latin *potestas*, "power"). He was always a foreigner, that is, someone from another city and therefore (theoretically) impartial, able to resolve the factional conflicts besetting the city where he served his term of office—usually lasting only a year to prevent the danger of his becoming entrenched. However, in many cases, figures more robust than the *podestà* took the communes in hand and, in the end, extinguished them. Various local strongmen, in the name of law and order, took control of individual cities, effecting a transition from municipality to principality (or, indeed, tyranny). For example, Ferrara had become a commune by the early 1100s, but a century later, after battles between the Torelli and Este clans, the latter seized power. Ruled by the Este for centuries thereafter, Ferrara eventually became a dukedom. Likewise, Milan: it was a commune by 1097, but then, after the mid-1200s, fell for the next two centuries under the sway of the Visconti, a family descended from the city's feudal lords who, after 1395, ruled as dukes. Such takeovers were typical, as during the thirteenth and fourteenth centuries the communal, republican governments of northern and central Italy fell one by one into the hands of strongmen bent on establishing dynasties. Dante bitterly complained that "all the cities of Italy are full / Of tyrants."[10] Communes that managed to resist this political swing, such as Florence and Siena, were remarkable exceptions.

Frederick Barbarossa's coronation in Rome in 1155 had been immediately preceded by a solemn task imposed on him by Pope Adrian IV: capturing and killing an austere, devout, and eloquent priest named Arnaldus, known to history as Arnold of Brescia.

Pope Adrian had been hoping to quell a growing new movement for which Arnold was the charismatic figurehead. Born in Brescia around the turn of the twelfth century, Arnold came to resent the financial wealth and temporal power of the Church. Some of the same ecclesiastical sins that would offend Martin Luther and the reformers during the sixteenth century—dissolute and corrupt bishops, ignorant priests, the aggressive fleecing of the poor—existed fully fledged by the 1100s. Arnold's remedy was for the Church to divest itself of both material possessions and political territories and ambitions, and to return to the poverty and holiness of Christ and the Apostles. The ecclesiastical authorities, horrified, promptly excommunicated him as a heretic. Tasked by the pope with the job of getting rid of him, Barbarossa was happy to oblige: he captured and hanged Arnold on the eve of his coronation.

Yet Arnold's teachings and ideals lived on. Decades later, in 1184, the Council of Verona excommunicated various groups deemed heretics—men and women united in their opposition to clerical wealth and corruption—for whom the

Church used the umbrella term "Arnaldisti." In the summer of 1209, some twenty thousand members of one of these groups, the Cathars, were slaughtered in Béziers in southern France after Pope Innocent III declared a crusade against them. Yet less than a year later, remarkably, another poverty movement gained the favor of Pope Innocent and acceptance into the good graces of the Church.

The story is enthralling, however tinged with myth and wishful thinking. A few years before the Council of Verona, a son had been born to one of the wealthiest men in Umbria, a cloth merchant named Pietro di Bernardone. Pietro traveled each year to the cloth fairs in France, where he met his French wife. She gave birth to a son while he was away on one of these business trips, christening him Giovanni. However, Pietro was fond enough of France that when he returned, he renamed his son Francesco, or "Frenchy." If Pietro was an example of the commercial revolution by which, in the 1100s and 1200s, Italian merchants were becoming rich and successful through trade, his son Francesco—St. Francis of Assisi—marked the repudiation of worldly affluence in favor of a search for spiritual values. By 1210, his message had attracted enough followers to the beautiful little hill town of Assisi that he and twelve companions (the number was not coincidental) made the 100-mile (160 km) trip south to Rome. The gambit was dangerous given that Francis and his followers rejected the wealth, power, and worldliness of the Church. Determined not to be branded a heretic like the ill-fated Cathars, Francis hoped to have his new religious order, the Friars Minor, or "Lesser Brothers," accepted by the pope. He was fortunate to find in Pope Innocent a brilliant and shrewd tactician.

The encounter between Francis and Pope Innocent is the stuff of legends (many composed by biographers in the decades after Francis's death). The pope supposedly mistook the bearded, bedraggled Francis for a swineherd, then granted him the Rule after a dream about a humble man of small stature holding up Rome's cathedral, St. John Lateran. Many episodes in the life of St. Francis were illustrated in the famous fresco cycle painted in the 1290s in the Upper Church of San Francesco in Assisi—part of a massive complex constructed, ironically and highly controversially, at huge expense. These landmark frescoes used to be attributed to the great Florentine artist Giotto di Bondone, although few art historians today believe him to have been responsible: more likely it was a team of painters from Rome. Whoever painted them, these frescoes are monumentally important, no less significant because we cannot attach Giotto's name to them, nor is Giotto less important as an artist for not having painted them.

One of these scenes depicts an episode that happened in the tiny hill town of Greccio, some 60 miles (100 km) south of Assisi, in December 1223. Francis asked a local man to construct a manger scene for him, the better to explain to the villagers the miracle of Christ's birth. The man took to his task with gusto, supplying a manger in the woods complete with an ox, a donkey, and a pile of hay in the midst of which, according to one witness, a sleeping child suddenly appeared, to be cuddled by a joyously weeping Francis. The point of this performance was to help the congregation engage emotionally with the Christian story by having it presented to them visually—quite literally staged for them—in all its wonder, pathos, and simple humanity.

A fresco in Assisi showing the Nativity scene enacted at Greccio, with St. Francis cuddling the Christ Child

This aspiration of Francis was ultimately of greater consequence for history and culture than his devotion to poverty. Neither the Church nor Western society as a whole ever embraced poverty, and even the Franciscans themselves, after Francis's death, were bitterly split on the issue. But his intimate and emotive engagement with the Scriptures, and with the figure of Christ, both buttressed the Church's teachings and played an important part in kickstarting the revolution in the visual arts so emphatically demonstrated by the frescoists who worked in Assisi's Upper Church. Several decades after Francis's death, an English Franciscan philosopher named Roger Bacon argued passionately for the Scriptures to be "placed before our eyes in corporeal figurations"—that is, for the Christian story to be depicted realistically through geometrical techniques such as perspective. By means of such artworks, "the evil of the world would be destroyed," Bacon confidently asserted, "by a deluge of grace."[11] This sort of desire for convincing realism in sacred art (as opposed to the more rigid and abstracted forms of Byzantine art) found its fulfillment in the art of Giotto and his followers as they developed (for example, in Giotto's frescoes in the Scrovegni Chapel in Padua) a series of special effects by means of which they brought both a third dimension and a human element into painting. They created a more convincing illusion of architectural space in which their figures—thanks to individuality, compelling gestures, and naturalistically rendered bodily forms—could act out their dramatic roles. As the nineteenth-century critic John Ruskin wrote, when Giotto depicted the Madonna with St. Joseph and the Christ Child, he humanized and domesticated them as "Mamma, Papa, and the Baby."[12]

The Franciscan demands for empathy and verisimilitude appear to have led to a new source of inspiration for art. The Italian sculpture and painting of the second half of the 1200s and first half of the 1300s—a period often known as the Proto-Renaissance—were partly inspired by a productive engagement with the antique. The art of these decades is full of classical allusions or "quotations" from pagan art. Sculptors such as Giovanni Pisano and painters including Giotto and, in Siena, Ambrogio Lorenzetti incorporated into their work many poses and figures studied from the scattered artistic vestiges of the Roman world seen in artifacts such as sarcophagi. Giotto, for example, adapted many figures and poses that he saw in Etruscan reliefs and ancient Roman urns. This innovative use and creative manipulation of ancient models from the pagan past became part of a technique that would make Italy the cultural leader of Europe for the next two centuries at least.

The engagement with the ancient world was interrupted in the middle of the 1300s. Art historians have long noted that Tuscan painting of the second half of the 1300s differed in style from that of the first half. The qualities that Ruskin later admired in Giotto—warm intimacy, down-to-earth humanity, truth to nature—were conspicuously absent from much art in the second half of the century. Instead, artists steered away from individuality and the human element in favor of the divine and the universal. Flatness and rigidity replaced movement, expression, and voluminous contours. This change is perhaps best appreciated in Andrea Orcagna's work in the Strozzi Chapel in the Basilica di Santa Maria Novella in Florence. Here Orcagna's magnificent altarpiece, with its gold background and intimidating figure of Christ, crowned and haloed, fixing viewers with the blank stare of a Byzantine icon, provides a sharp contrast with *The Crucifix* by Giotto painted a half-century earlier. The latter hangs only a few yards from the Strozzi Chapel but occupies— with its anatomically accurate depiction of the very dead, and very human, Christ—what seems to be a completely different world.

Orcagna's world was indeed different from that of the late 1200s when Giotto painted his *Crucifix*. The most significant change had been a worldwide pandemic, the Black Death, that arrived in Italy at the end of 1347, on Genoese ships returning from Crimea. The disease quickly spread across Europe, killing perhaps a third of the population over the next few years, and possibly half that of cities such as Florence and Siena. The deadly pandemic has been held responsible, in a classic study by the art historian Millard Meiss, for the more severe and archaic art of Orcagna and his generation—a

Giotto's Crucifix *in Santa Maria Novella: Special attention is paid to the deceased Christ's humanity.*

"Black Death style" that reflected a renewed religiosity in the chastened population.[13] Meiss's fascinating thesis has been challenged by those who point out that many supposed examples of the Black Death style actually preceded 1348, which suggests other and earlier causes for the profound artistic and religious changes of the 1300s. And indeed, there was certainly disaster aplenty—economic, social, political, and spiritual.

One of the worst disasters was repeated crop failures and famines. The period that climatologists (examining ice-core samples and tree rings) call the Medieval Climatic Optimum and the Medieval Warm Period ran from roughly 900 until 1300, at which point the weather in Europe began to change: glaciers advanced, lakes froze, storms raged, rivers and fields flooded. Bad weather between 1309 and 1311 caused a failure of cereal crops in central Italy. Conditions worsened in the coming years as violent storms followed long periods of drought. In the spring of 1315, heavy rains began falling across Europe, causing crop failures from Scotland to Russia and down through Italy (where the drowned fields were blamed on a comet that appeared in 1314). A serious famine struck Italy again in 1328, causing bread riots in Florence and Rome. In 1346–47, during another famine, some four thousand people died of starvation in Florence alone.

The prosperity of the previous decades disappeared with the spectacular failure of Europe's largest merchant banks, the Bardi and Peruzzi, multinational concerns based in Florence that a historian has dubbed "super-companies."[14] Both companies went bankrupt (the former in 1343, the latter in 1346) when King Edward III of England, to whom they had loaned 1.5 million florins to finance his war against France, defaulted on his payments. Begun in 1337, this war, later known all too aptly as the Hundred Years' War, caused yet more economic hardship as it disrupted European trade. Recessions led to civil unrest, the most spectacular example of which, the Tumult of the Ciompi, took place in Florence in 1378. The Ciompi were poor, unskilled textile workers who led a mass insurrection against Florence's government, burning palaces and hanging *popolani grassi* (fat cats). They stormed the town hall and briefly seized political power.

The Church could provide no leadership because the papacy had been in crisis throughout the 1300s. The city of Rome was controlled politically and militarily by feudal barons, such as the Colonna and Orsini, from whose ranks many popes had been elected. Often violently at odds with each other, they challenged the power of popes coming from rival clans or, especially, from outside Rome. Pope Clement V, a Frenchman elected in 1305, possessed little desire to confront these powerful gang lords who had entrenched themselves in their strongholds in the ruins of the Colosseum and the Theatre of Marcellus. Refusing to move to Rome, he relocated the papal court to Avignon, counting on the protection of the French monarch, Philip IV (the Fair). The city on the Rhône would host the papacy for the next sixty-eight years, during what became known as its Babylonian Captivity. Even after the papacy finally returned to Rome in 1377, successive rival claimants popping up in Avignon led to the Western Schism, a period of four decades when popes ruled (or claimed to rule) in both Rome and Avignon at the same time.

The "calamitous" fourteenth century (as one historian has dubbed it) ended with no signs of respite.[15] Plague struck Italy again in the summer of 1399. People grew desperate. Throughout northern Italy, seemingly spontaneously, thousands of people—thirty thousand in Genoa alone—began taking to the streets and squares. They paraded behind crucifixes, sang hymns and (in time-honored penitential fashion) scourged their flesh with whips. Many wore hooded white robes with holes cut for their eyes—the garb from which they got their name, Bianchi (Whites). It was an act born of the destruction wrought by decades of war, plague, and poverty. They began descending on Rome in such numbers that, by the autumn, the city hosted 120,000 of them. Pope Boniface IX declared a Jubilee for the year 1400, which brought even more pilgrims to the city—and also, in greater force, the plague, which tragically overwhelmed and brought a ruthless end to the Bianchi movement.

The new century therefore dawned with much of Italy devastated and wretched, seemingly abandoned by God. And yet the 1400s in Italy were to become what the French philosopher Voltaire later called one of the great ages of the world, equal to the cultures of Periclean Athens and Augustan Rome.

CHAPTER 7

Italy's Age of Gold
The Renaissance

In 1492, a Florentine priest and scholar named Marsilio Ficino wrote to a friend recounting the remarkable accomplishments of the previous decades. The fifteenth century had been, he said, a "golden age" for the liberal arts, with such disciplines as grammar, poetry, oratory, painting, sculpture, and architecture restored to light—"and all of this in Florence."[1]

This praise serves as one of the earliest descriptions of what we have come to call the Italian Renaissance. The concept of the Renaissance—which means rebirth—suggests a rescue from neglect and a miraculous return to life. Ficino may have somewhat exaggerated the importance of Florence, but he was absolutely right about this enthusiastic revival of learning: a revival in which he, as the translator from Greek into Latin of the complete works of Plato, played a major part.

Historians no longer look for "Big Bang" explanations of how and why, in the 1400s, Florence in particular became the site of such vibrant and innovative cultural explorations. But the undeniable fact that the city produced such a tremendous and unprecedented range of art with so many astonishing stylistic innovations—in painting, sculpture, and architecture—has nevertheless tempted scholars into trying to guess the riddle of the Sphinx.

Attempts have been made to explain the phenomenon in terms of economics. Florence in the early 1400s was one of the wealthiest cities in Europe, its bankers and merchants having pioneered a series of innovative business techniques, such as bills of exchange, double-entry bookkeeping, and partnership contracts. However, the city's population had decreased dramatically due to famines and the Black Death, falling from at least one hundred thousand in the time of Dante and Giotto to fewer than forty thousand by the 1420s. Moreover, the wool industry, one of the primary sources of the city's wealth, was in steep decline by the 1400s. If the commercial revolution of the Middle Ages had witnessed an economic boom with expanding trade, the 150 years that followed the arrival of the Black Death were characterized by—according to a famous study by Robert S. Lopez—a reversal of fortune. One curious feature of the Italian Renaissance is that it appears to have taken place against a century-long background of demographic decline, stagnating industry, contracting trade, and falling profits. The Renaissance was a combination of what Lopez called "economic depression and artistic splendor." He speculated that the paradox of expenditure on luxuries such as art and architecture coming at a time of financial hardship could be explained by the fact that the difficult and uncertain economic times and limited investment opportunities led merchants to shy away from risky business ventures and to plunge their wealth instead into luxury goods and prestige items.[2]

This "hardship" thesis has been challenged ever since it was first aired in 1953, not least, perhaps, because we are used to imagining the arts and culture as offshoots of affluence. Other historians have pointed out that many people, in Florence as elsewhere in Italy, actually grew richer in the decades following the Black Death since the existing wealth was shared among fewer people. Unemployment fell along with the prices of food and rent, while workers' wages rose in the city as well as the countryside, where new agricultural products such as olives and mulberry trees (for the lucrative new silk industry) were introduced. However, wealth in a city like Florence was not widely or evenly spread: one study has found that fully half its wealth was concentrated in the hands of fewer than 350 men—less than 1 percent of the population.[3] Even so, other studies point to an increasing affluence and high standard of living in Florence, where the greater wealth among the middle classes led to the flourishing of trades producing relatively cheap products in the "luxury-arts sector"—paintings, statues, and decorative arts such as terra cotta.[4]

To be sure, many great works of Florentine art in the 1400s were commissioned and funded by corporations or wealthy individuals, such as the banker Cosimo de' Medici, one of Europe's richest men. He underwrote the construction of the Dominican convent of San Marco and then its decoration with frescoes and an altarpiece by Fra Angelico. Over the course of several decades, his family—including his grandson, Lorenzo the Magnificent—would spend hundreds of thousands of florins on art and architecture. But the middle classes were involved as well, as indicated by Masaccio's *Holy Trinity* in Santa Maria Novella. This fresco is an accomplished demonstration of single-point perspective, illusionistic architecture, true-to-life naturalism, and even (thanks to the recumbent skeleton) anatomical skill—an icon of the innovative "new art" of Florence. Yet the patron was not a prince, wealthy plutocrat, or powerful corporation but, rather, one Domenico Lenzi, a linen dealer.

Domenico appears with his wife in the fresco: an embodiment of the shrewd, rational, and religiously devout merchants who brought a cautious prosperity to Florence along with a series of artistic masterpieces.

The surviving evidence indicates that many other merchants commissioned paintings, especially portraits of themselves. People of lower social status likewise kept artists busy: a carpenter asked Andrea del Sarto for a Madonna, a tailor gave Jacopo Pontormo

Masaccio's Holy Trinity: *an example of the Renaissance interest in architecture, perspective, and anatomy*

his first commission, and an agricultural laborer near Perugia left money in his will for a painting of Christ to adorn his grave. It's worth reflecting that Leonardo da Vinci's first commission, albeit when he was still an adolescent, came from a peasant in Vinci who wanted an image painted on a wooden shield. This passion for images at all levels of society, as well as an ability to pay for them, helps explain why over the centuries the Italians produced such art in such abundance.

Besides economic explanations for the origins of the Renaissance in Florence, political ones have also been put forward. One of the most famous and appealing explanations points to the influence of the Republic of Florence's wars against Milan in the 1390s and early 1400s.[5] The ruler of Milan, Giangaleazzo Visconti, after capturing Verona and Padua in the 1380s, had begun casting a covetous eye over Tuscany. The war that broke out in 1390 was contested on many fronts—military, diplomatic, and, not least, literary. As they fought to maintain their independence, the Florentines came to regard themselves as bastions of liberty and republicanism who preserved from the despotism of Milan their values of free speech, self-government, political participation, and equality under the law. They took their inspiration from the Roman Republic, with Florentine scholars and politicians such as Coluccio Salutati representing the Florentines as Rome's true heirs, and as upholders of traditions and values that were civic and communal, involving an active and patriotic commitment to the state by its citizens. (In fact, Florence was every bit as ruthlessly imperialistic as Milan, greedily gobbling up territories all across Tuscany: Volterra in 1361, Arezzo in 1384, Pisa in 1406, Cortona in 1411, and Livorno in 1421.)

Giangaleazzo captured Bologna in the summer of 1402 and, seemingly unstoppable, was poised to attack Florence when, in early September, he died suddenly in his camp from either the plague (still raging) or malaria. The Florentines' faith in their heritage and destiny seemed to have been amply rewarded (though war with Milan would drag on for decades). The question for historians became whether this political background influenced and motivated Florence's artistic revolution—whether the extraordinary innovations in the visual arts, so redolent of Ancient Rome, had anything to do with this kind of political propaganda churned out by Salutati and his fellow intellectuals.

An argument in the affirmative was made in the 1960s by Frederick Hartt, who noted that the greatest progress in Florentine art came in the first two decades of the 1400s, not in painting but in sculpture, thanks primarily to Donatello.[6] Painting at this time was largely devotional, destined for the altars of churches or private chapels, and concerned with directing the spectator's thoughts to the hereafter. Much Florentine sculpture, on the other hand, addressed the here and now. Often destined for display not in ecclesiastical settings but, rather, in the public sphere of the city's streets and piazzas, this "civic art" was intended to inspire not religious reverence but patriotic pride—to instill in Florentines the values necessary to defend the liberty of the republic against tyrannical aggressors. As such, the statues needed to present themselves as believable human figures rather than the stiff, staring, and otherworldly mannequins of much religious art.

Most conspicuous among these statues in Florence were those in the niches on the exterior of the oratory of Orsanmichele. Rather than by priests and prelates, these works, in both marble and bronze, were commissioned by silk dealers, sword makers, stonemasons, and bankers. Donatello's work at Orsanmichele reveals not only advances such as single-point perspective but also, in his *St. George*, carved for the guild of armorers in 1415–17, a compelling psychological portrait showing the saint, with his pensive expression and taut stance, gathering his reserves for a battle in defense of Florentine liberty. A down-to-earth military hero, he harks back to the glories of the Romans. This kind of patriotic figure, shown marshaling his strength and prepared to vigorously defend the institutions of the republic against threatening behemoths, would reappear many decades later (minus the armor and toga) in Michelangelo's *David*.

Whether or not Donatello imbibed any of this political philosophy is an open question. However, there can be no doubt that Donatello's art took much inspiration, like Giotto's a century earlier, from ancient Roman statues and sarcophagi.

Donatello's steely, determined St. George, *today on display in Florence's Bargello Museum*

According to legend, as an adolescent he visited Rome with Filippo Brunelleschi, who sold a farm near Florence to fund their journey. Thunderstruck at the beauty and majesty of the ancient buildings, the pair excavated and studied the ruins, with Donatello becoming determined, according to an early biographer, to "recover the beauty of the ancients, which had been lost for so many years."[7] Although the story of the trip to Rome may be no more than a myth, the powerful and well-proportioned figures in Donatello's works certainly "quote" ancient Roman prototypes. Yet his works are varied and strikingly original. His bronze *David*, cast for Cosimo de' Medici, suggests not public-spirited martial vigor but, in the slim, androgynous, and nude adolescent lost in an erotic reverie over his beheaded foe, unabashed homoeroticism. Replete with meanings that are private and individual, it marks a new moment in the history of art.

Brunelleschi, too, sought to recover ancient beauty in architecture through a reworking of classical models. His loggia for the Ospedale degli Innocenti—Florence's home for foundlings and orphans—launched an aesthetic revolution by means of a vocabulary of semicircular arches over round columns topped by Corinthian capitals, and by its adherence to a modular plan by which the dimensions of every part (columns, arches, windows) bore a proportional relation to every other part. Architects who followed Brunelleschi would substitute these antique forms and decorative motifs in place of those (pointed arches, capitals decorated with gargoyles, and dragons) borrowed from France or Germany.

Brunelleschi's buildings proved so beautiful and novel that, according to his biographer, people gathered round the building sites to gawk. He became even more renowned by his contemporaries for performing the greatest engineering feat of the age. In 1420, he inherited the decades-old plan to top the Florentine cathedral of Santa Maria del Fiore, begun in 1294, with the world's largest dome: one that would not only exceed by some 18 inches (46 cm) the span of the Pantheon but also rise, thanks to its pointed profile, to the much greater height of 276 feet (84 m). The fabled trip to Rome, where he would have been exposed to the massive vaults of ancient Roman structures—the Pantheon as well as the Baths of Caracalla and the Basilica of Maxentius and Constantine—no doubt fired his enthusiasm for surpassing

The cathedral of Santa Maria del Fiore in Florence, topped by Brunelleschi's magnificent dome

the ancients. The unprecedented magnitude of the cupola, completed in 1436, called for such invention and ingenuity on Brunelleschi's part that his demonstration of the art of the possible in brick and stone transformed not only the built environment but also the view of human worth and ability.

In 1452, the Florentine scholar Giannozzo Manetti wrote *On the Dignity and Excellence of Man*, a treatise arguing that the divinity of the human mind was best revealed by works of art such as the frescoes of Giotto, the sculptures of Lorenzo Ghiberti, and the cupola of Brunelleschi—examples of the "dignity and excellence" of which humanity was capable. Florentines such as Leonardo da Vinci and Michelangelo, and Italian artists and architects in general, would offer many more such examples in the decades, and then the centuries, that followed.

Even as Marsilio Ficino wrote his praise of the "golden

age" of Florence in September 1492, events were underway that would severely jeopardize Italy's long and spectacular economic and cultural reign. The following month, on October 12, Christopher Columbus, in search of a passage to Cathay, India, and the Spice Islands, made landfall along a strip of white sand in the Bahamas. The arrival of Europeans on the American continent meant the world's economy would steadily shift from the Mediterranean to the Atlantic, favoring those countries—first Spain and Portugal, then the Netherlands, England, and France— with seaports on the ocean.

Italy missing the transatlantic boat, so to speak, was not without certain bitter ironies. Not only was Columbus born in Genoa, but so, too, perhaps (his exact origins are a mystery) was another Italian navigator, Giovanni Caboto, aka John Cabot, who, sponsored by King Henry VII of England, reached Newfoundland in 1497. The name America comes, moreover, from a Florentine, Amerigo Vespucci, who in the course of two voyages done on behalf of the Spanish and Portuguese, in 1499 and 1501, respectively, became the first European to explore virtually the entire Atlantic coast of South America, and the first to realize that this landmass was not in fact Asia (as Columbus believed) but a continent hitherto unknown to Europeans.

A more immediate and dramatic threat to Italy's place in the world came in 1494. For the previous four decades, Italy had enjoyed a rare and unaccustomed period of peace. Unlike France, England, Portugal, or Spain, Italy was still divided into numerous dukedoms, marquisates, and republics. A document from 1455 listing the political entities on the Italian peninsula recorded more than 120 of them. These divisions suited the papacy, which since the time of the Byzantines and the Lombards had pursued the goal of preventing the unification of Italy under a single power. A major and obvious disadvantage of this disunity had been the bitter territorial conflicts in the first half of the 1400s. However, in 1454, the five major powers (Venice, Milan, Naples, Florence, and the pope) put their signatures to a treaty (the Peace of Lodi) and then, a year later, to a pact of nonaggression and mutual defense (the Italic League). Their newfound enthusiasm for peace and cooperation was inspired at least in part by the conquest of Constantinople by the Ottoman Turks in 1453—the year that marks the end of the Roman Empire in the East.

Despite the occasional skirmish, an uneasy peace generally held. Then, in January 1494, the seventy-year-old king of Naples, Ferdinand I, dropped dead. Although he was succeeded by his son, Alfonso II, another contender for the throne, King Charles VIII, unexpectedly emerged in faraway France. Later that year, intent on pressing his tenuous claim to Naples, Charles invaded the peninsula with an army of thirty thousand men. He appeared almost effortlessly to achieve his aims as he swept through the Apennine valleys, and Alfonso abdicated and fled to a Sicilian monastery. Charles entered Naples as a liberator in February 1495, wearing a richly bejeweled crown and holding a golden orb in one hand and a scepter in the other. He was hailed by the members of his court as the new Augustus, the new Charlemagne, and "Most August Emperor."

Charles's triumph was short-lived. For several months

Italy in 1494

CHAMBERY
DUCHY OF SAVOY
TURIN
ASTI
SALLUZO
M. OF MONTFERRAT
GENOA
REP. OF GENOA
FRANCE
Nice
Monaco

MILAN
Bergamo
REP. OF MILAN
Brescia
Parma
MANTUA
MODENA
D. OF MODENA
LUCCA
FLORENCE
REP. OF FLORENCE
SIENA
REP. OF SIENA

Belluno
REP. OF VENICE
Verona
Padua
VENICE
FERRARA
Bologna
Ranenna
Forli
Istria

Ancona
Perugia
Foligno
Terni
Aquila
Pescara

OTTOMAN EMPIRE
Dalmatia
Adriatic Sea
Lissa
Ragusa
REP. OF RAGUSA

CORSICA

PAPAL STATES
ROME
Tremiti

Gaeta
NAPLES
Foggia
Andria
Bari
Monopoli
BENEVENTO
Salerno
Potenza
Brindisi
Lecce
KINGDOM OF NAPLES

Asinara
Sassari
SARDINIA
Cagliari

Tyrrhenian Sea

Cosenza
Crotone

Lipari
Messina
Palermo
Reggio
Marsala
KINGDOM OF SICILY
Catania
Ragusa
Siracusa

Ionian Sea

Mediterranean Sea

Pantelleria

IFRIQIYA

MALTA

Lampedusa

N

0   50   100 miles
0 50 100 150 km

he dallied among the delights of Naples, where his soldiers spread a terrifying new disease known to the locals as the *mal francese* (French disease) and to the French as the *maladie napolitaine* (Neapolitan disease)—that is, syphilis, possibly (but by no means certainly) brought back from the New World by Christopher Columbus's sailors. Returning north, he suffered defeat at the Battle of Fornovo, near Parma, at the hands of a combined force of Venetians, Milanese, and Mantuans. At first either neutral or active supporters of the French, all three had undergone swift changes of heart. Charles aborted his Italian enterprise and beat his retreat across the Alps. He was planning a second expedition in April 1498 when he died after banging his head on a door lintel as he hurried to a tennis match. It was a surprising end for a man so short that an Italian diplomat had mocked him as a dwarf.

Italy's calamities did not end with Charles's death. A later popular expression would ruefully claim that Italy was shaped like a boot because everyone walked all over it. The last days of the Roman Empire had witnessed the descent into Italy of Huns, Vandals, Ostrogoths, and Visigoths, while, in the centuries that followed, the peninsula fell prey to successive waves of Lombards, Byzantines, Franks, and Normans. New barbarian invasions were now unleashed as the peninsula became the battleground for the expansionist ambitions of the French and Spanish monarchies. For the next seven decades, these two superpowers fought a series of brutal battles known to history as the Italian Wars.

A second French invasion had quickly followed on the death of Charles VIII. Charles's successor, Louis XII, laid claim not only to the Kingdom of Naples but also, through his grandmother, to the Duchy of Milan. He invaded and captured Milan in 1499 (causing Leonardo da Vinci, who had just finished *The Last Supper*, to flee to Venice and then Florence). A year later, he signed a treaty with Spain by which the Kingdom of Naples was to be split between them. Although King Federigo of Naples (Alfonso's younger brother) frantically recruited twenty thousand Ottoman mercenaries, the French and Spanish troops easily overran the kingdom before (because the finer territorial details of the agreement had not yet been worked out) they ultimately and inevitably began turning their guns on each other. The Spaniards defeated the French in 1503, and, by 1504, they were in possession of the entirety of the South as well as Sicily and Sardinia.

The French, meanwhile, dominated the north of Italy from their base in Milan (destined to change hands multiple times in the decades that followed) from which they threatened Venice and occasionally Rome. Pope Julius II, the "Warrior Pope" elected in 1503, tried unsuccessfully to oust them with the battle slogan *Fuori i barbari* ("Out with the barbarians"). His cry was taken up a few years later by the Florentine Niccolò Machiavelli, who, in *The Prince*, composed in 1513, lamented that Italy was "without a leader, without order, beaten, despoiled, ripped apart, overrun, and having suffered every sort of ruin." He appealed for a strong leader, a valiant and decisive prince, to "seize Italy and free her from the barbarians."[8]

No such figure would appear for more than three centuries, and for the next few decades the desolation and destruction would continue virtually unabated. Incessant clashes were punctuated by occasional atrocities, the most shocking of which was the Sack of Rome in 1527 by unruly German and Spanish mercenaries in the pay of Charles V. Reigning as both the King of Spain and the Holy Roman Emperor, Charles was the most dominant figure to appear in Europe since Charlemagne. Hoping to check his power, Pope Clement VII, a Medici, joined forces in 1526 with Charles's traditional foe, King François I of France, as well as with Florence and Venice. The alliance proved drastically ineffective, and at dawn on May 6, 1527, under the cover of heavy fog, the imperial troops breached the walls and poured into Rome. Eyewitnesses described gruesome tortures, butchered bodies, cardinals dragged through the streets, and the looting of papal tombs. "Hell made a better sight," reflected one horrified witness.[9] After soldiers broke into the Vatican, a German soldier used his pike to scratch into one of Raphael's frescoes in the Stanza della Segnatura—painted for Pope Julius less than two decades earlier—the name that had already begun to haunt Europe: "Martinus Lutherus."

The long conflict between France and Spain finally ended in 1559 with the Peace of Cateau-Cambrésis. Political life on the peninsula, as well as on Sicily and Sardinia, was then dominated by Spain. The Spanish crown exercised direct sovereignty over both the Duchy of Milan and the Kingdom of Naples, as well as over Sicily and Sardinia. The duchies of Parma, Piacenza, Mantua, and Urbino were its vassal states, along with the Republic of Genoa. The only states remaining beyond Spanish control were the Duchy of Savoy, the Republic of Venice, Rome and the Papal States, and the Grand Duchy (as it became in 1569) of Tuscany—for the Republic of Florence had finally been extinguished by the Medici in 1530. All were hemmed in by Spanish territories and vulnerable by both land and sea, especially since the Spaniards held five garrison towns on the Tuscan coast (the so-called Stato dei Presidi) from which they could launch attacks.

Added to the loss of political autonomy was the repressive force of the Counter-Reformation, of which the Spaniards were rigorous and enthusiastic supporters. So, too, was Pope Paul IV, whose (mercifully) short reign between 1555 and 1559 witnessed the introduction of the *Index Librorum Prohibitorum* ("Index of Prohibited Books"), which banned works of more than five hundred authors, including Dante, Machiavelli, Giovanni Boccaccio, and, indeed, God, since it forbade vernacular translations of the Bible. Paul IV also issued the edict *Cum nimis absurdum* ("Since it is absurd") deploring the fact that, throughout much of Italy, Jews were living side by side with Christians. The exception was Venice, where, since 1516, the Jewish population had been forced into a "ghetto." The name comes from the verb *gettare* (to pour or cast), a reference to the cannon foundry that originally stood on the small Venetian island onto which the Jewish community was locked each night, with guards posted and a boat patrolling the canal outside. Eager to replicate this kind of segregation, Pope Paul compelled all Jews in Rome and throughout the Papal States to live in enclosed areas with only a single entrance and exit. After the Roman Ghetto was established in 1555, other cities around Italy followed suit: Florence in 1570, Siena in 1571, Verona in 1602, Padua in 1603, Mantua in 1612, and Ferrara in 1624. The historian Robert Bonfil has argued that these ghettos did not necessarily lead to a deterioration in the Jewish condition. On the contrary: Christian attitudes actually became more tolerant as the old anti-Semitic accusations and legends so prevalent in medieval times—of Jews ritually murdering children or defiling Communion wafers—began to disappear. Yet, as Bonfil points out, what this new attitude meant was that Christians could tolerate and accept Jews only if they were locked up each night inside gated walls.[10]

The combination of Spanish political control and Counter-Reformation zeal might have been expected to stifle the creativity and invention so brilliantly and prolifically exploited in the independent Italian city-states of earlier centuries. Certainly, conditions in the Kingdom of Naples, ruled by viceroys on behalf of the Spanish monarchs, were dismal from an economic and political point of view. The kingdom fell into degradation due to neglected roads, declining trade and commerce, and a feudal system of landownership. Bandits roamed the roads and pirates attacked the coasts. Each year the viceroy read a letter from the king of Spain announcing by how much taxes needed to be raised—an amount inversely proportional to the woeful abilities of the people to pay them.

And yet culture and learning did not die out in Naples. Quite the contrary. In the middle of the 1500s, a group calling itself the Accademia Segreta (Secret Academy) began conducting thousands of trials on "secrets"—that is, traditional medicinal recipes—to determine their effectiveness in treating everything from nosebleeds to leprosy, rabies, and the plague. These trials, carried out under strict observation in a purpose-built laboratory known as the *Filosophia*, deserve to be considered as the beginning—however crude and tentative—of experimental science.[11] Naples was equally accomplished in the arts. By the 1600s, the city could boast four conservatories of music, dozens of talented crafts-men who kept the Spanish monarchs amply supplied with luxury objects, and groups such as the Accademia degli Oziosi (Academy of Layabouts) whose members, the city's leading intellectual and literary lights, gathered for stimulating literary conversation. The city's vibrant artistic community included at various times Caravaggio, Anni-bale Carracci, Jusepe de Ribera, and Artemisia Gentileschi. The latter spent more than two decades working in Naples after 1630, running a large workshop and achieving such a level of celebrity that members of the Layabouts ardently addressed her in poems. Instead of confining herself to portraits and still lifes—the domain of most seventeenth-century women artists—Gentileschi ambitiously recreated historical and biblical scenes. Large in scale and dramatic in nature, with striking visual effects, her canvases often featured images of powerful and heroic women such as Judith and Esther.

The same cultural vitality could be found throughout much of the rest of Italy, which, from a cultural point of view, had never been stronger. Italians retained their dominance in the arts throughout the 1500s and 1600s. Michelangelo con-tinued to work for the better part of another four decades after the Sack of Rome, producing such masterpieces as the Laurentian Library in Florence, his statue of Moses on the tomb of Julius II, and—most spectacular of all—his cupola for the Basilica of St. Peter (completed after his death). In the 1540s and '50s, Rome could still provide inspiration for Andrea Palladio, who made five visits to the city and, accord-ing to a friend, "measured and made drawings of many of those sublime and beautiful buildings"—exactly like

Brunelleschi a century and a half earlier.[12] He went on to adorn the countryside around Vicenza with his elegant, classically inspired palaces and villas, prestigious monuments to the dolce vita enjoyed by aristocrats and landowners in northern Italy.

The greatest painter of the Venetian school, Titian, remained active until the 1570s, his coruscating colors and expressive brushwork

Sofonisba Anguissola, born to a wealthy family in Cremona in 1532, was the most successful of five sisters who became painters.

ensuring a brisk demand from aristocratic patrons in courts and palaces throughout Italy and Spain. Meanwhile, Caravaggio's dramatic storytelling and intensely personal, brilliantly realized figures—comparable in their emotive power to those of his contemporary William Shakespeare—bespeak a self-confidently thrusting and swaggeringly experimental culture and society. Female artists other than Artemisia Gentileschi began working at this time, too: Plautilla Nelli in Florence, Marietta Robusti (the daughter of Tintoretto) in Venice, and the Bolognese sculptor Properzia de' Rossi, who according to legend taught herself to sculpt by carving peach pits. Sofonisba Anguissola, from Cremona, became one of the greatest portrait painters of the second half of the 1500s. The Flemish painter Anthony Van Dyck sought her out in Sicily in 1623, reporting that she was ninety-six years old and, though nearly blind, still lively in spirit.

Italians dominated other cultural spheres as well. Italian cuisine served as the touchstone for the European courts, with Italian cooks the most creative in Europe. The first cookbook ever printed (in 1470) had been Bartolomeo Platina's *De Honesta Voluptate et Valetudine* ("On Honest Indulgence and Good Health"), compiled from the recipes of the man that Platina—the keeper of the Vatican Library—called "the prince of cooks," Martino da Como. A chef originally from Lombardy, Martino invented new dishes to grace the tables of cardinals and popes in the 1460s and '70s. Platina's cookbook was much translated and reprinted, and over the next century many other cookbooks appeared, such as Cristoforo da Messisbugo's *Banchetti, Composizioni di Vivande e Apparecchio Generale* ("Banquets, Food Preparation and Basic Utensils"). It served as a testament to the gastronomical delights (including caviar) served at the Este court in Ferrara where Messisbugo organized many a splendid feast in the first half of the 1500s. Various Italian recipes were imported into France by Catherine de' Medici, the great-granddaughter of Lorenzo the Magnificent and, between 1547 and 1559, queen of France. A kind of early lifestyle influencer, she introduced the French to, legend claims, such novelties as artichokes, forks, glazed earthenware, and a crimson-colored Florentine liqueur. Concocted from sugar, cinnamon, cloves, aniseed, orange peel, and various spices, this liqueur, alchermes, took its bright color from its magic ingredient, cochineal—the crushed bug that also lent its deep, vibrant color to artists such as Caravaggio.

Italy during the 1500s and 1600s was also at the forefront of European music and drama. *Commedia dell'arte* performances were staged from the middle of the sixteenth century as offshoots of courtly entertainments (with their jesters and buffoons) and Carnival amusements (with their dances, songs, and acrobats). Women appeared in *Commedia dell'arte* roles as early as 1564, when one "Lucrezia of Siena" trod the boards in Rome.[13] Their appearance on the stage—at a time when Shakespeare was forced to use boy actors in female costume—was one of the great innovations of Italian drama. Churchmen sometimes objected to their presence, as when a Jesuit railed against "extraordinarily beautiful" women, "frequently prostitutes on the game," who, he claimed, excited the libidos of audience members.[14] Such denunciations no doubt did little to keep the public away. The most famous and accomplished actress was Isabella Andreini, born in Padua in 1562. Enough of a celebrity to appear in two portraits and on a commemorative medallion, she not only acted but also wrote her own plays, such as *Mirtilla*, a drama first staged in 1588. Her extraordinary life was otherwise sadly typical of women of the time: she married at fourteen, bore seven children, and died in 1604 while giving birth to her eighth.

The Jesuit's description of the actresses as prostitutes was not necessarily wide of the mark. In the latter half of the 1500s, a number of them were almost certainly courtesans, specifically *cortigiane oneste*, or "honest courtesans": well-educated women known for their musical, literary, and artistic skills who granted sexual favors, for a price, to affluent and aristocratic customers. In Venice, the authorities kept a book, *Catalogo de Tutte le Principali e Più Onorate Cortigiane di Venetia*, which recorded their names, addresses, and fees. Among the most famous was Veronica Franco, widely celebrated for both her beauty and her cultural accomplishments.

A volume of her poetry, published in 1575, was dedicated to the Duke of Mantua, one of her many admirers, others of whom included princes, cardinals, writers, and artists. Equally accomplished was Tullia d'Aragona, illegitimate daughter of a cardinal. Born in Rome around 1500, she published sonnets, an epic poem (the first written by a woman ever published), and, in 1547, a philosophical treatise on the nature of romantic and sexual love.

Vittoria Colonna (1492–1547), friend of Michelangelo and leading cultural light

Other women who published during this period included poets such as Gaspara Stampa, Laura Battiferri, and Laura Terracina. The latter's collection of poems was reprinted five times in the first dozen years after its publication in 1548. There was also the remarkable Veronica Gambara who, besides writing poetry, assembled a glittering court at Correggio, which she ruled for more than three decades before her death in 1550. The most celebrated female poet of the century—and, indeed, one of its leading cultural figures—was Vittoria Colonna. Primarily known today through her close friendship with Michelangelo, she was the author of more than 150 sonnets. Such was her popularity in Ferrara that when an emissary arrived from Verona, trying to lure her away, the outraged people of Ferrara chased him from the city.

Among their other accomplishments, the Italians gifted the world with an entirely new musical genre. In the last decades of the 1500s, a group of writers and musicians who gathered at the home in Florence of Giovanni de' Bardi decided to revive Greek drama. Convinced that actors in Greek tragedies had sung the verses in a recitative style, this "Camerata de' Bardi" (as they called themselves) began composing music along with lyrics for a single melodic voice (as opposed to the polyphony then in vogue). Opera was thereby born: a combination of music, singing, drama, and elaborate stage sets. The first production, *Dafne*, performed during the Carnival in Florence in 1598, was followed two years later by *Euridice*, commissioned for the wedding of Maria de' Medici (daughter of Grand Duke Cosimo I) and King Henry IV of France. Both were composed by Jacopo Peri (music) and Ottavio Rinuccini (lyrics).

This new form of theater was taken up by Vincenzo Gonzaga, Duke of Mantua, whose court composer, Claudio Monteverdi, composed *L'Orfeo* for the Carnival of 1607. One excited court official promised that it would be "most unusual, as all the actors are to sing their parts."[15] The first opera house, the Teatro San Cassiano, opened in Venice in 1637. An Englishman in the audience in 1645 was not in the least disappointed. He declared the singers and "most excellent musicians," along with the "scenes painted and contrived with no less art of perspective," to be "one of the most magnificent and expensive diversions the wit of men can invent." Almost four hundred years later, the same can still be said of Italian opera.[16]

One of the musicians in Florence's Camerata de' Bardi had been a lutenist and music theorist named Vincenzo Galilei.

A pioneer of a process that he called *esperienza* (which we may translate loosely as "experiment"), Vincenzo claimed to be "motivated by the truth, based on the experience of things and many demonstrations."[17]

By taking observations from organ pipes and lute strings, he disproved long-held theories about how certain mathematical ratios determined pleasing, harmonious sounds. His combination of mathematical reasoning and practical skill played a crucial role in overturning classical musical theory.

Vincenzo's son Galileo would likewise use mathematical reasoning and direct observation of natural phenomena to overturn classical theories, in his case much more momentously. The most important figure in the Scientific Revolution, he would come to be known as the "father of modern science." Born in Pisa in 1564—incidentally, three days before Michelangelo's death—he became a professor of mathematics there in 1589. During his tenure, he dropped balls of different weights from (legend has it) the Leaning Tower to disprove Aristotle's theory that the speed of fall of a heavy object was directly proportional to its weight. In 1609, after learning about the "Dutch perspective glasses" invented a year or so earlier by a spectacle-maker in Middelburg, he fashioned an improved version with greater powers of magnification. At the end of the year, he began exploring the sky with what he called his "eye-reed" (*cannocchiale*). In 1610, he announced many of his discoveries in *Sidereus Nuncius* ("The Starry Messenger"), the book by which, as its most recent translator states, "we enter the modern world."[18] His studies with his telescope revealed how the moon was not a perfect, translucent sphere; how the surface of the sun was covered with blots; how Venus, like the moon, waxed and waned through a full series of phases; and how Jupiter was orbited by four moons. He named the moons the "Medicean Stars" in honor of his former pupil, Grand Duke Cosimo II, and his three brothers—a tribute that brought him a handsome stipend as Cosimo's court philosopher and mathematician. His astronomical observations led him to challenge the Earth-centered conception of the universe and thereby to shake the intellectual edifice of Europe.

Galileo's discoveries won him influential supporters and immense celebrity. He suffered a setback in 1615, however, when he was denounced to the Roman Inquisition by two Dominicans in Florence. Investigated and privately admonished, he was instructed neither to advocate nor defend heliocentric theory. However, the times suddenly appeared auspicious when, in 1623, his friend and supporter Maffeo Barberini became Pope Urban VIII. Galileo received permission to publish his defense of heliocentrism, *Dialogo Sopra i Due Massimi Sistemi del Mondo* ("Dialogue on the Two Chief World Systems"), which appeared in print in Florence in 1632. Yet he lost the support of the pope, among other reasons, because Urban believed that one of the characters in the dialogue, Simplicius, was used to caricature his own belief that it was impossible to decide which model of the universe was right. Moreover, Galileo could offer no definitive or final scientific proof of heliocentrism. For example, he ignored Tycho Brahe's system, which exactly matched his own observations but kept the Earth at the center of the Universe.

In any case, there were too many academic appointments and reputations at stake among the Aristotelians, and too many Jesuits who felt aggrieved after Galileo skewered them in satires, for his work to win official acceptance. In the summer of 1633, Galileo was hauled before a tribunal at the convent of Santa Maria sopra Minerva in Rome and informed that the inquisitorial process suspected him of heresy. He was forced to kneel before his judges and, under the threat of torture and with a prison sentence looming, abjure his "errors" and promise never to write or say anything of the sort ever again. He was nonetheless treated with respect and leniency, occupying a grand suite of rooms in the Palace of the Holy Office rather than one of the cells in the basement. He was spared prison and eventually allowed to return to Florence, where he lived under house arrest at his villa in Arcetri. He spent his remaining days (he died, blind, in 1642) pruning his vines and entertaining distinguished visitors such as Thomas Hobbes and the young John Milton. During these years, he also composed one of his most important books, *Discorsi e Dimostrazioni Matematiche Intorno a Due Nuove Scienze* ("Discourses and Mathematical Demonstrations Relating to Two New Sciences"), a work on the physics of motion that was to leave an important and lasting legacy in the history of science.

CHAPTER 8

"Go, thought, on golden wings"
Italy in the *Illuminismo*

A new century dawned, bringing changes to Italy. On the afternoon of November 1, 1700, All Saints Day, the King of Spain, Charles II, died childless in his palace in Madrid. King Charles, the great-great-grandson of the mighty Emperor Charles V, had cut a wretched, pitiful figure. Known as Carlos El Hechizado, or Charles the Bewitched, he was a product of the Habsburg dynasty's heedless inbreeding (his mother was also, in an amazing genealogical twist, his first cousin). Sickly and weak, he was the most pronounced and unfortunate bearer of the "Habsburg jaw"—a mandibular prognathism that caused his jaw to protrude such that, as an English envoy observed, "his two rows of teeth cannot meet."[1] His death, long expected, raised the question of what was to become of the vast possessions of the Spanish Empire, with those in Italy up for grabs.

The War of the Spanish Succession followed, at the end of which, in 1714, Spanish sovereignty in Italy was replaced by that of the Austrian Habsburgs, who gained control of Lombardy, Mantua, and the Kingdom of Naples. Meanwhile, under the terms of the peace treaty, the Duke of Savoy, Vittorio Amadeo II, became not only king of Savoy (which was upgraded from a duchy) but also king of Sicily—although a few years later he was forced to exchange his Sicilian crown, which went to Austria, for the less important one of Sardinia (though he kept Turin as his capital). Another crown changed hands in 1734 when Naples was recaptured by Spain, marking the beginning of the Bourbon dynasty in Naples. The kingdom was ruled by Charles of Bourbon, the son of King Philip V of Spain. Unlike so many previous monarchs, Charles actually lived in the kingdom (until, that is, he became king of Spain and moved to Madrid in 1759). In 1752, he began construction of the Reggia di Caserta, still the world's largest royal palace, sprawling over an area the size of seven soccer fields. Its awe-inspiring grandeur (1,200 rooms, 34 staircases, and a 23-mile-long/37 km aqueduct to fill the pools, fountains, and gilt-copper bathtub of the queen) in combination with the sadistic nature of its construction (the forced labor of convicts dragged from Neapolitan prisons and Turkish pirates captured by the Bourbon fleets) evoked, more than anything else built in the previous 1,500 years, the monumental edifices of the Roman emperors.

The second half of the eighteenth century brought an unaccustomed peace to Italy, perhaps the longest period the peninsula had ever known. With peace came both population growth and increased commercial and industrial productivity. Thanks to the cultivation of mulberry trees, Italy became Europe's largest producer of raw silk, and the silk mills in Bologna and Turin featured, with their spinning and twisting machines, some of the most advanced machines in preindustrial Europe. The wool industry recovered as cities including Schio (near Vicenza) and Prato (near Florence) began manufacturing lower-quality cloths, such as Prato's *mezzelane*, a mixture of linen and wool that could compete with the cheaper alternatives in England and Belgium. Trade was strengthened thanks to the establishment of free ports in coastal cities such as Trieste, Ancona, Civitavecchia, and Messina.

The latter half of the eighteenth century brought to Italy the same desire for political reform that swept across much of the rest of Europe. This was the era of the Enlightenment (or, in Italian, the *Illuminismo*): a period dedicated to the application of reason and the empirical method, the questioning of political and religious authority, and a faith in the progress and perfectibility of humanity and its institutions. By the middle of the century, the works of philosophers and writers such as John Locke, Voltaire, Montesquieu, and Jean-Jacques Rousseau had crossed the Alps and begun circulating among the cultural elites. In the early 1760s, a group of young men in Milan began convening at the home of a nobleman, Pietro Verri, and his younger brother Alessandro. After one exchange of opinion ended in fisticuffs, they named their group the Accademia dei Pugni (Academy of Punches). They also gathered at a coffeehouse operated by (according to their own mythology) a Greek refugee named Demetrius, who had arrived in Milan with a supply of "the most exquisite coffee in the world"—a beverage that had been lubricating and inspiring political conversations from London to Vienna.[2]

Coffee had been served in Italy at least since the first years of the 1600s, when Pope Clement VIII supposedly baptized coffee beans (imported from the lands of the "infidel" Muslims) to make them safe for Christian consumption. Coffeehouses began proliferating in Italy in the late 1600s, with the most famous, the Caffè Florian, opening in Venice in 1720. By the end of the eighteenth century, at least twenty other coffeehouses operated in Piazza San Marco. In the 1780s, an English traveler marveled that coffeehouses "remarkably abound in the Venetian dominions; at all towns, and even villages, where we passed, they are to be found."[3] As in England and elsewhere, many of these coffeehouses, stocked with newspapers and frequented by diverse social groups, became places of gossip, discussion, and the exchange of ideas. The members of the Accademia dei Pugni used Demetrius's coffeehouse in Milan as a place for their debates, and in June 1764, to preserve and disseminate their lively conversations, they launched a journal of ideas. Aptly named *Il Caffè* (which in Italian means both the coffee and the coffeehouse), it gave the *Illuminismo* a strong injection of caffeine.

The first issue of *Il Caffè* claimed its articles would cover "all things aimed at public utility" with the plan of "doing what good we can for our homeland, to spread useful knowledge among our citizens." For the next two years, articles appeared on physics, medicine, politics, and agriculture (including plans to introduce coffee crops into Italy), along with more whimsical and humorous items. Although much of the work was done by Pietro Verri, the most important member of the Accademia dei Pugni proved to be Cesare Beccaria, another young Milanese nobleman. Beccaria had studied at a Jesuit college in Parma, where his brilliance in mathematics earned him the nickname "Newtoncino." But in 1761, aged twenty-three, he read Montesquieu and became passionate about philosophical and social issues. Encouraged by Verri, he wrote a short treatise, *Dei Delitti e delle Pene* ("On Crimes and Punishments"), which a press in Livorno published in 1764. The work opened with an appeal "to the reader" that has become one of the fundamental texts of the Enlightenment. Addressing the followers of reason, Beccaria cast aside many centuries of legal tradition to argue passionately against torture and the death penalty, to beg for tolerance and equality, and to urge political leaders to work toward the maximum happiness of the greatest number of people.

Cesare Beccaria (1738–1794), a leading figure of the Illuminismo

Beccaria's success—and notoriety—were immediate. The work ran through six editions in the first eighteen months. It was translated into French in 1765 and English in 1766. The Catholic Church condemned the work and a Vallombrosan monk, in an indignant rebuttal, declared Beccaria a socialist. But its effects were far-reaching, especially in Tuscany, where in November 1786 the death penalty was stricken from the legal code (though, as we shall see, it was hastily reinstated a few years later).

The Enlightenment reached other parts of Italy as well. In the Kingdom of Naples, the reform movement was headed by a priest, Antonio Genovesi, a philosopher and economist born near Salerno in 1713, in the small town of Castiglione, now known in tribute as Castiglione del Genovesi. He taught philosophy at the University of Naples and hung out with a group of liberal-thinking intellectuals, the leader of whom was an expatriate Florentine polymath named Bartolomeo

Intieri. A latter-day Renaissance artist-engineer in the stamp of Leonardo da Vinci, Intieri had recently retired to a villa at Massaquano, in the hills near Sorrento, after spending his career trying to improve agricultural conditions through the invention and application of superior machinery to transport, grind, and store wheat. He found in Genovesi an enthusiastic disciple, and the pair fell into heady discussions (as Genovesi later fondly recalled) about "the progress of human reason, the arts, commerce, the economy, mechanics, and physics."[4] In 1754, Intieri funded a chair of "mechanics and commerce" at the University of Naples, to which he appointed his protégé. It was the first chair of political economy in Europe, and, crucially, marked the point in history in which the problems of the economy and society were deemed worthy of university study and instruction.

The political consequence of all of this enlightened thought, the French Revolution, quickly brought to an end Italy's unprecedented decades of peace and relative stability. At first many Italians greeted the news from across the Alps with enthusiasm. However, the Reign of Terror unleashed in 1793–94 fostered disillusionment among many Italian reformers and, at the same time, a determination by various Italian rulers to keep a tighter grip on power by cracking down on dissidents. Forty-eight suspected supporters of the French Revolution were arrested (and three executed) in Turin in 1794. A few years later, following a plot to kill the new king of Sardinia, Carlo Emanuele IV, some hundred suspects were put to death. Meanwhile, after the short hiatus, capital punishment was reinstated in Tuscany.

Italy in 1796

N

| 0 | 50 | 100 miles |
| 0 | 50 | 100 | 150 km |

REP. OF VENICE

• Belluno

TRENTO ⊙

Bergamo •
Brescia • Verona •
Padua •

KINGDOM OF SARDINIA

MILAN ⊙

VENICE

Istria

TURIN ⊙ • ASTI

MANTUA ⊙
Parma • MODENA ⊙ FERRARA
Pontremoli • Bologna •
Ranenna •
Forli •

OTTOMAN EMPIRE

GENOA ⊙

REP. OF GENOA

LUCCA ⊙ FLORENCE ⊙

Dalmatia

FRANCE • Monaco
Nice •

GR. DUCHY OF TUSCANY SIENA ⊙

• Ancona

Lissa

Adriatic Sea

REP. OF RAGUSA

Ragusa ⊙

Terni •
Talamone

• Perugia
• Foligno
Terni •
Aquila •

Tremiti

PAPAL STATES

⊙ ROME

CORSICA

• Pescara

Foggia •
Gaeta •
Andria •
Bari •

BENEVENTO
NAPLES ⊙
Salerno •
• Potenza

Monopoli
Brindisi
Lecce

Asinara

• Sassari

KINGDOM OF NAPLES

SARDINIA

Tyrrhenian Sea

Cosenza •
• Crotone

Cagliari •

Lipari
• Messina

Mediterranean Sea

Palermo

Marsala •

KINGDOM OF SICILY

• Reggio

Ionian Sea

Catania •
• Siracusa

Ragusa •

Pantelleria

KINGDOM OF TUNIS

Lampedusa ⊙

MALTA

Italy inevitably became involved in the decade-long French Revolutionary Wars that broke out in 1792 and pitted France against a coalition comprising powers such as the British, Austrians, Prussians, and Russians. In 1792, the French invaded and annexed Savoy, in part to thwart an Austrian invasion from the southeast and in part because they regarded Savoy as lying within their natural boundaries. Trouble truly arrived for Italy in the spring of 1796 when France's Army of Italy crossed the Alps with, at its head, the twenty-six-year-old Napoleon Bonaparte. He was determined to destroy the Austrians by defeating them on Italian soil—which he proceeded to do in short order, trouncing them in a series of battles in northern Italy that culminated at Rivoli, 15 miles (24 km) northwest of Verona, in January 1797.

Napoleon left Italy at the end of 1797 (he was about to invade Egypt) but by then he had taken a wrecking ball to the peninsula's borders and political institutions. The Republic of Genoa was dissolved, becoming the Ligurian Republic, a client state of France, while the Duchy of Milan became the Transpadane Republic before it was merged with the Cispadane Republic (consisting of territories in northern Italy such as the Duchy of Modena and Reggio) to become the Cisalpine Republic (with its capital in Milan), likewise a French vassal. Also included in the Cisalpine Republic were the Papal States. The French invaded the Romagna in February 1797 and quickly captured papal domains, despite a wave of "miracles" such as a portrait of the Madonna in Ancona that—thanks to a clever illusion produced by its glass case—wept crystalline tears. By such means had Pope Pius VI and his clergy tried to incite the rural masses to rise against these new barbarians.

As Napoleon's troops descended on Rome, Pope Pius was forced to negotiate terms, becoming the first pontiff in history to surrender his dominions—the lands given to the popes by Pepin the Short more than a thousand years earlier. The Treaty of Tolentino handed the Papal States to the French, who also took, in an unabashed looting spree, hundreds of artistic treasures from the Vatican together with five hundred manuscripts from its library. The Roman Republic was proclaimed in the ancient Forum and Pius forced into exile, first in Siena and then in a monastery outside Florence. After the French occupied the Grand Duchy of Tuscany—which in due time, with a wave of the Napoleonic wand, became the Kingdom of Etruria—the eighty-two-year-old pope was sent off to France, where he died in 1799 following a rigorous Alpine crossing.

Another venerable Italian political entity was destroyed by the irresistible pressure of Napoleon's army. The Venetians in their labyrinth of lagoons had withstood the advances and sieges of numerous enemies, from Charlemagne's son Pepin (whose ships they burned and whose soldiers—to prove the rich resources of their grain stores and the futility of a siege—they pelted with loaves of bread) to King Louis XII of France, who randomly fired six hundred cannons in the general direction of Venice so posterity might report that he had bombarded the impregnable city. But after the Austrians captured the Venetian possessions on the mainland and Napoleon reached the edge of the lagoons, the thousand-year-old Republic of Venice came to an end. The Treaty of Campo Formio, signed by France and Austria in October 1797, awarded Venice to the latter, though only after Napoleon and his soldiers had thoroughly pillaged the city, carting

Jacques-Louis David's heroic vision of Napoleon crossing the Alps to invade Italy

off treasures such as Paolo Veronese's 32-foot-wide (10 m) *Wedding Feast at Cana*. (Never repatriated, the spectacular canvas now hangs in the Louvre in a most unfortunate spot—opposite Leonardo's *Mona Lisa*.)

After the coalition forces drove the French beyond the Alps, Napoleon descended on Italy for a second time in 1800. The trip was immortalized in a series of paintings by Jacques-Louis David showing the bicorned Corsican valiantly astride a rearing white charger (in fact, Napoleon crossed the Alps

on a donkey). In the next few years, all of the newly constituted republics were swept away and the peninsula divvied
up between Napoleon and members of his family. He himself became king of Italy in May 1805 after an elaborate
ceremony in Milan in which he crowned himself. In the
South, having expelled the Bourbons, he created a vassal
state, the Kingdom of Naples, ruled over by his older brother
Joseph and then, after Joseph was promoted to king of Spain
in 1808, by his brother-in-law Joachim Murat (who reigned
as King Joachim-Napoleon). Nor did Napoleon neglect his
younger sister Elisa: he carved out for her a special domain,
the Principality of Lucca and Piombino, before, in April
1809, she entered Florence (already annexed to France) as the
Grand Duchess of Tuscany. She took up residence in Palazzo
Pitti, where her remodeling efforts resulted in a lavish new
bathroom with marble floors, a boiler for hot water, and a
bathtub fashioned by the sculptor Lorenzo Bartolini. The
remainder of the Italian peninsula—a vast swath stretching
from Piedmont down south of Rome—was subsumed into
the French Empire.

Napoleonic Italy brought about dramatic changes.
Borders were opened to trade, the administration was
rationalized and modernized, taxes reorganized, and the
Napoleonic legal code imposed in place of the confusion of
arcane and archaic jurisdictions. In the South, feudalism was
finally abolished and the privileges of the nobles suppressed.
Streetlights appeared in Naples and in the elegant Piazza del
Popolo in Rome. New and better roads were constructed
through the Alps. Throughout both the Kingdom of Italy
and the Kingdom of Naples, a middle class began emerging
thanks to the forced sale of lands and properties confiscated

from the Church and nobles—1,300 religious houses in the Kingdom of Naples alone.

Many Italian reformers applauded these initiatives, but Napoleon's vision of an Italy ruled by the Bonapartes as a satellite of France ended with his downfall and abdication in 1814. Normal service resumed as the Austrians, moving into Lombardy and occupying Milan, once

Marie-Louise, Duchess of Parma, the second wife of Napoleon: Her enlightened rule helped turn Parma into one of Italy's most elegant cities.

again became the dominant force, exerting direct or indirect dominion over the new political fragmentations. The old monarchs resumed their thrones in Turin and Naples, the Grand Duke returned to Florence, and various duchies such as that of Modena and Reggio were doled out to relatives of the Habsburgs. The ancient republics of Genoa and Venice were, however, never restored: the former went to the Kingdom of Sardinia (whose capital, we have seen, was Turin), the latter to Austria. Crucially, Napoleon's efforts at standardization came to an end as Italy once again returned to being a patchwork peninsula divided by different currencies, different systems of weights and measures, and with customs barriers between neighboring states.

Not all the progressive initiatives were immediately swept away by the reactionary forces. One of Napoleon's enduring legacies in Italy was his second wife, Marie-Louise, daughter of the Austrian Emperor Francis I. Napoleon wed her in 1810, when she was eighteen, in hopes of gaining an heir (produced the following year) and making the Bonaparte dynasty acceptable to the venerable European monarchies. Marie-Louise reigned as Empress of the French and Queen of Italy until Napoleon's fall in 1814, after which, according to her rights as the daughter of the Austrian emperor, she became Duchess of Parma. She took her demotion from the magnificent courts of Vienna and Versailles with good grace: "I have in my hands the way to make four hundred thousand souls happy," she enthused, "and to protect the arts and sciences."[5] Highly cultured and multilingual (she spoke German, French, English, Spanish, Italian, Latin, and Greek, as well as Czech and smatterings of Hungarian and Turkish), she devoted herself to the improvement and adornment of her new domains. Projects in Parma included a library, an orchestra, an art museum, a museum of antiquities, and a monumental theater (at which she kept the prices low so poor people might attend). She also gave Parma new roads, bridges, and hospices, as well as, in 1820, a new civil code. But her liberal instincts and generous gestures were ultimately frustrated by the more reactionary policies of her father. Before she died in 1847, she wrote a resigned note: "Don't make much noise about my death because, after all, I'm merely a woman who lived in an era greater than herself."[6]

This restoration of the old regimes, with their revocations of constitutions granted during the revolutionary period and their vigorous suppression of press freedoms and the right of assembly, led to the rise of secret societies dedicated to liberal ideals. One of the most influential was the Carboneria, which first appeared in the South during the reign of Joachim-Napoleon, possibly as an offshoot of Freemasonry from which the members borrowed oaths, rituals, and the concept of lodges (which they called *vendite*). The group eventually spread into Sicily and then the North. Its members, known as Carbonari

A band of Carbonari in their vendita *debate their next move.*

("charcoal-burners"), were committed to establishing constitutional governments, expelling the foreign powers, and even unifying the peninsula politically. They were said to be "enemies of every throne."[7] As such, they were persecuted by both Joachim-Napoleon and his successor, King Ferdinand, as well as by the pope, Pius VII, who excommunicated them.

In July 1820, the Carboneria was at the forefront of an insurrection in Naples, forcing King Ferdinand, many of whose troops began deserting to the rebel cause, to issue an edict promising a constitutional government with a citizens' assembly. The gambit emboldened, 500 miles (800 km) to the north, a Savoyard aristocrat and politician named Filippo Annibale Santorre, the Count of Santarosa. Author of *Delle Speranze degli Italiani* ("On the Hopes of the Italians") and a member of another secret society, the Federazione Italiana,

Santarosa hoped to force a liberal constitution on the authoritarian king of Sardinia, Vittorio Emanuele I. However, a constitutional government in Turin became a moot point as Austrian forces supported the royalists and then, in March 1821, marching southward, crushed the Neapolitan rebels, and brought to an end the Carboneria's brief experiment with constitutional government.

The last gasp of the Carboneria came in 1830 with an insurrection in Modena led by Ciro Menotti, a young entrepreneur who had made a small fortune from such diverse business interests as silkworm breeding, a distillery, and the manufacture of wood chips and straw hats. Once again, the Kingdom of Sardinia featured in the plan. Menotti and his fellow Carbonari hatched an ill-considered scheme whereby the duke of Modena and Reggio, Francesco IV, as the son-in-law of Vittore Emanuele I, would become king of Sardinia and ultimately—so the conspirators tickled the ear of the duke—king of a unified Italy. As a Habsburg who had already implemented repressive measures, including the execution of several Carbonari, Francesco should have seemed a gruesomely implausible ally in any liberal uprising. Indeed, he played the Carbonari false, apparently listening favorably to their blandishments before, in 1831, he had Menotti arrested, tried, and hanged.

In the months before his death, Menotti composed a rousing manifesto for his supporters. It was entitled "Ideas for Organizing Intelligences Between all the Cities of Italy for its Independence, Union and Freedom." The Carboneria was a spent force, but the struggle for Italian independence, union, and freedom was just beginning.

CHAPTER 9

"Here We Make Italy"
The Risorgimento

One of the people celebrating—prematurely, as it turned out—the Count of Santarosa's efforts in Turin was a thirty-six-year-old poet and dramatist from Milan named Alessandro Manzoni. During the vanishingly short stretch of time when it looked like the liberal uprising would succeed, Manzoni wrote "March 1821," a poem rejoicing at the expulsion of the Austrians and the unification of the Italians. Never again, he wrote, would barriers rise "between Italy and Italy," a people "united in arms, in language, in faith, / In memories, in blood, and in the heart."

In fact, Italy was very far from united in any respect, divided as it was into eight different states—many traditionally at war with one another—and multiple dialects. The dismissive barb of the Austrian chancellor, Prince Metternich, was all too true: the word Italy was a "geographical expression" that possessed no "political value."[1] However, Manzoni's poem became a kind of prophecy, and he would labor for its fulfilment decades hence.

Some of the first and most urgent efforts at unification were linguistic. Manzoni claimed in "March 1821" that Italy was united in language. Yet he himself knew only too well that was not the case. If Italy had not been unified politically since the fall of the Roman Empire in the West, neither was it unified linguistically.

It was, as a journalist pointed out in 1830, "a land of many races and of many tongues."[2] Leaving aside questions of grammar and syntax, we can look at the differences in basic vocabulary, which

Alessandro Manzoni (1785–1873): the dream of an Italy united in both politics and language

for father and mother ranged from *padre* and *madre* in Florence, to *patri* and *matri* in Sicily, and *pare* and *mare* in Venice. In parts of the South, among the speakers of Griko, a Greek-based dialect (the legacy of either Magna Graecia or the Byzantine occupation during the Middle Ages), mother and father were *ciura* and *mana*. In Florence, a fog was *una nebbia*, in Sicily *una negghia*, and in Venice *uno caivo* (or *caigo*)—supposedly a corruption of a phrase called out by Venetian boatmen (*Ca me ligo*, or "Here I tie") when the fog became too heavy to paddle and steer. A fog, for Griko speakers, was a *kamùla*.

The situation was little different from when Dante, some five hundred years earlier, had deplored what he called the "cacophony of the many varieties of Italian speech"—more than (by his reckoning) a thousand different types. Dante attempted to overcome this cacophony by crafting an elegant and expressive vernacular for his literary masterpiece, *The Divine Comedy*. He called his distinctive new language the *vulgare illustre*, or "illustrious vernacular": a courtly, spruced-up version of the language spoken by the educated classes, such as himself, in Florence. This illustrious vernacular was then adopted and further polished by the two other great writers of the fourteenth century, Petrarch and Giovanni Boccaccio.

This elegant, Florentine-inspired language became the model for Italian literature, and indeed for the letters, diaries, and accounts of many educated people up and down the peninsula. It was not, however, widely used in spoken language, or even by any means by all writers (dialect poetry and drama continued to flourish). Yet to a number of intellectuals in the early 1800s, it was clear that Italy could not come together politically until it possessed a common spoken language to act as a vehicle of unity.

Foremost among the linguistic unifiers was Manzoni, the grandson of Cesare Beccaria. In 1821, the year of his wishful thinking about Italians "united . . . in language," he lamented to a French friend that an Italian poet or dramatist from outside of Tuscany was forced to write in a language he had never actually spoken, and in a language spoken, moreover, by only a small number of Italians. There was, in other words, a fracture between literary and spoken Italian, one so great that the former, he wrote to a friend in 1806, "can almost be called a dead language."[3] The Tuscan language that descended from Dante and Petrarch might well have worked for grandiloquent poetry and drama, but what about a novel purporting to represent the speech and emotions of real people—the vast majority of whom were illiterate?

Manzoni grappled with this problem in his historical novel *I Promessi Sposi* ("The Betrothed"), begun in 1821 and first published to great acclaim in three volumes between

1825 and 1827. No sooner did the final volume appear than, dissatisfied with the work, whose language he believed was too reliant on the Milanese dialect, he set off from Milan to Florence to give the work what he later called a *risciacquatura in Arno*, or "rinsing in the Arno"—a linguistic revision that washed away the Lombardisms in favor of modern Florentine speech. The second, definitive edition of *I Promessi Sposi*, its language recast in a Florentine dialect both popular and literary, appeared in 1840. It offered testimony of Manzoni's belief that the common language of Italy must be the dialect spoken by educated Florentines, a point he made seven years later in *Sulla Lingua Italiana* (1847). His position was not that contemporary Florentine was any more beautiful, expressive, or authentic than other dialects; rather that its closeness to the literary language used by Italy's finest authors, from Dante forward, meant it had the best chance of being accepted by the rest of Italy as the common language. By the time Manzoni made this argument in 1847, the Risorgimento (Resurgence) was in full swing and the age-old language question had become ever more urgent.

One of the Carbonari frustrated by the failure of the 1821 uprisings was a slim, handsome, black-clad twenty-five-year-old doctor's son from Genoa named Giuseppe Mazzini. A law graduate and budding journalist, Mazzini was arrested along with other Carbonari in 1830. After several months of detention in the fortress in Savona, he was sent into exile and, in the summer of 1831, in Marseille, founded a new group called Giovine Italia (Young Italy), dedicated to the unification of an independent Italy as a democratic republic. His proposed means of achieving his goals were, first of all, the education and mobilization of the masses—especially young people—and, second, armed insurrection against the foreign oppressors. Another important part of the plan was God, who Mazzini believed would guide the people as they struggled for their free-dom—hence his famous slogan *Dio e popolo* ("God and the people"). By 1833, Giovine Italia could count some sixty thousand members.

Giuseppe Mazzini (1805–1872): Dio e Popolo!

Mazzini's insurrections did not go well, as Young Italy proved more effective with pens than guns, and God appeared, at best, indifferent to their efforts. In 1833, plans for an uprising in Genoa led by Young Italy were betrayed to the authorities before a single shot was fired. The new king of Sardinia, Carlos Alberto, retaliated with sweeping arrests and a dozen executions. A few months later, Mazzini, undaunted, led a group of a thousand insurrectionists in an invasion of Savoy, but his speeches and proclamations en route failed to rouse the spirits of the Savoyard masses, who spoke a different dialect. The episode proved a fiasco despite the presence of a new recruit to Young Italy whom Mazzini had recently met in Marseille: a burly twenty-six-year-old sailor from Nice named Giuseppe Garibaldi. Condemned to death in absentia, Garibaldi slipped away to Rio de Janeiro. Mazzini fled to Switzerland and then, after his expulsion in 1837, to London, where he lived in the "Little Italy" district of Clerkenwell, mesmerized by the inferno-like London fogs.

Other forces were mustering. In 1842, Giuseppe Verdi's opera *Nabucco* was performed for the first time at La Scala in Milan. In the rousing chorus of the Hebrew slaves, *Va, pensiero, sull'ali dorate* ("Go, thought, on golden wings"), with lines like *O mia patria, sì bella e perduta* ("O my country, so beautiful and lost"), Italian patriots had no difficulties seeing in the fate of the Jews oppressed by Nebuchadnezzar their own plight under the Austrians. Verdi's passion for the Risorgimento was later exaggerated by mythmakers in search of heroes for their niches and pedestals. However, the composer from Parma certainly knew and admired both Mazzini (the pair met in London) and Alessandro Manzoni. Verdi composed an unabashedly patriotic opera, *The Battle of Legnano*, chronicling the Lombard League's victory over Frederick Barbarossa in 1176 and featuring another stirring chorus: *Italia risorge vestita di gloria!* ("Italy rises again robed in glory!") And at the request of Mazzini, he also wrote a popular anthem, *Suona la Tromba* ("The Trumpet Sounds"), with words by Goffredi Mameli (composer of *Fratelli d'Italia*, which became the Italian national anthem).

Verdi sent "The Trumpet Sounds" to Mazzini in October 1848 with the words: "May this hymn soon be sung in the Lombard plains to the music of the cannons."[4] By that time, cannons were indeed roaring across the plains. The year 1848 was the *primavera dei popoli*, or "springtime of the people," in which beleaguered rulers, from Pope Pius IX and King Ferdinand II of the Two Sicilies (that is, Sicily and Naples) to the Grand Duke of Tuscany and King Carlos Alberto of Sardinia—authoritarians who a few years earlier were anything but inclined to address the grievances of their subjects—found themselves forced under the pressure of riots and insurrections to shore up their shaky regimes by hastily forming constitutional governments. The Austrian overlords in Italy also came under attack. In March 1848, in what became known as the *Cinque Giornate di Milano* (Five Days of Milan), the Milanese drove the Austrian governor and garrison from the city. They were assisted by a battalion of volunteers recruited in Naples and shipped north on a steamboat by a beautiful forty-year-old Milanese princess, Cristina Trivulzio di Belgiojoso, soon to be dubbed "the first lady of Italy."[5] The Venetians, likewise, rebelled against the Austrians in 1848, declaring independence as the "Republic of San Marco." Carlos Alberto then issued a proclamation that he would take up arms to defend the peoples of Lombardy and the Veneto against the Austrians—and so began the First Italian War of Independence.

Mazzini hurried back from exile to take part in the uprisings, wielding a rifle given to him by an English admirer, Emilie Ashurst. He was greeted in Milan by enthusiastic crowds. However, the Austrians soon inflicted heavy defeats on Carlo Alberto's troops and, in the summer, recaptured Milan. Without the stamina or heart for playing the role of a gun-toting guerrilla, Mazzini left Lombardy and went to Rome, from which Pius IX fled in November 1848. A constituent assembly, elected in Rome in February 1849, declared the end of the papacy's temporal power and the establishment of the Roman Republic. Ruled by a triumvirate that included Mazzini (hastily granted Roman citizenship), it promulgated a constitution that banned capital punishment and press censorship, and extended suffrage to all men over the age of twenty-one.

Such an experiment in liberal democracy and progressive social movements could hardly have been allowed to succeed, and Pius IX's pleas for help did not, therefore, fall on deaf ears. Various European despots scrambled to help extinguish this alarming example of people power. Spanish troops mustered for a march on Rome, and at the end of April, a French expeditionary force (dispatched by Napoleon's nephew, the new president of France, Louis-Napoleon Bonaparte) appeared along the coast, armed with formidable siege artillery. By early July, Rome was bombarded by French guns, one souvenir of which is an errant cannonball still embedded in the steps in the gallery of Palazzo Colonna. After the Roman Republic was crushed, the pope appointed a commission of cardinals that quickly and emphatically revoked all of the liberal measures. Mazzini slipped away to Switzerland and then to London for yet another spell of exile.

His war against the Austrians having failed, King Carlo Alberto of Sardinia abdicated his throne in March 1849. He went into a forlorn and aimless exile, traveling through France and Spain and eventually to Portugal, where, at the end of July, at a villa in Oporto, he died at the age of fifty. The new king was his eldest son, twenty-nine-year-old Victor Emmanuel II.

The other rulers and monarchs around Italy had been swift to rescind the constitutions so hastily granted during the "springtime of the people." However, Victor Emmanuel kept in place the one promulgated by his father in March 1848. The Albertine Statute, as it was known, provided for a constitutional monarchy by which the king shared legislative powers with a Senate and a Chamber of Deputies. The latter body was elected but the former directly appointed by the king, who was the supreme head of state in charge of foreign policy and the armed forces.

The Albertine Statute was a far cry from the liberal constitution of the defunct Roman Republic, and Victor Emmanuel was sometimes openly suspicious of liberal politics. Even so, the fact that Turin's parliamentary system survived the reactionary wave that broke over Italy in 1849 meant the Kingdom of Sardinia became a rallying point for Italian patriots.

One of the men elected to the Chamber of Deputies in Turin in 1848 was a thirty-eight-year-old aristocrat named Camillo Benso, the Count of Cavour. His father had been a close friend of Carlo Alberto, but during Camillo's brief stint in the army, the Austrian minister in Turin reported back to Vienna that the young man, though "gifted with much talent," hung out with "wrong-thinking persons" and as a result had become "a very dangerous man."[6] Indeed, Cavour frequented republican circles and expressed in a letter to a friend a desire for "Italy's emancipation from the barbarians who oppress her."[7] In the aftermath of the Carboneria uprisings of 1830 (in which he played no part), Cavour was sent by his father, in a kind of internal exile, to administer the family's estates in southern Piedmont, forty miles south of Turin. Based at the family castle in Grinzane, for whose 350 citizens he served as mayor, he quickly distinguished himself as an agricultural innovator, using fertilizers and implementing new technologies. He began experimenting with nebbiolo—a thin-skinned, high-tannin grape hitherto used to make a sweet red wine—to see if it might produce a dry, robust red. Hence, Barolo, with its garnet color and velvety finish, was born.

Cavour quickly distinguished himself as a politician, serving as a cabinet minister in various departments before, in 1852, he became prime minister. He initiated a series of administrative reforms and promoted free trade, freedom of the press, and laws restricting the power of the Church.

Camillo Benso, Count of Cavour (1810–1861): a "Piedmontese Machiavelli"?

He was, however, a fierce antagonist of Giuseppe Mazzini's revolutionary methods and republican ideals, and he opposed universal suffrage in the belief that the masses were not yet ripe for participation in the political process.

Portly, ruddy-haired, and rosy-cheeked, with a fringe of beard and steel-framed spectacles, Cavour was a cunning strategist blessed with shrewdness, foresight, and superlative political intuitions. Realizing he needed powerful international allies to defeat the Austrians, he courted both the British and the French, sending Piedmontese troops to Crimea in 1855 in support of their war against Russia. This action gave him a seat at the peace congress in Paris in 1856 and ultimately, two years later, a secret meeting at Plombières-les-Bains with Louis-Napoleon Bonaparte, by then Emperor Napoleon III. The emperor was suspicious of Cavour, calling him "a most unprincipled politician" and a "Piedmontese Machiavelli"[8]—a prime example of what the Italians call *il bue che dice cornuto all'asino* ("the ox calling the donkey horned"). Even so, Napoleon was well disposed to listen to him, believing Cavour could help him to advance French interests in Europe at the expense of the Austrians. After receiving verbal assurances of the emperor's support, the Piedmontese mobilized and, in the late spring of 1859, hostilities broke out—the Franco-Austrian War, aka the Second Italian War of Independence—as Austrian troops poured into Lombardy. Napoleon III was true to his word, and the Austrians suffered two rapid and decisive defeats to the combined French and Piedmontese forces, at Magenta (near Milan) and then Solferino (near the bottom of Lake Garda). At the latter battle, the suffering and bayoneting of wounded soldiers on both sides led to the Geneva Convention and the International Red Cross.

What followed the armistice in the summer of 1859 was a territorial swap that would lead, finally, to the unification of large chunks of Italy under Victor Emmanuel. The king handed to the French, in return for their support in the war, both the Duchy of Savoy and the County of Nice—a personal sacrifice for him since these lands were closely linked to the House of Savoy. The kingdom of Sardinia gained Lombardy and then, exploiting the Austrian collapse, annexed the Grand Duchy of Tuscany, the duchies of Parma and of Modena and Reggio, and much of the Papal States. By the spring of 1860, therefore, virtually all of northern and much of central Italy were under the rule of Victor Emmanuel and his prime minister, Cavour. But in the South, the Kingdom of the Two Sicilies was still ruled by a Bourbon king, Francesco II, and Rome by the pope. Cavour accepted this division, but others did not. And so, on the night of May 5, 1860, wearing a red shirt and a poncho, and with a Colt rifle slung over his shoulder, Giuseppe Garibaldi boarded a ship in Genoa with a thousand ragtag volunteers shouting the battle cry *Italia e Vittorio Emanuele!*

In the spring of 1860, Giuseppe Garibaldi, red-haired and blue-eyed, stocky and bearded, was fifty-two years old. A lifetime of adventure already lay behind him. Born in Nice, he was the son of a maritime merchant who had wanted him to become a priest. But young Garibaldi—who regarded the "black brood" of the priesthood as the "pestilent scum of humanity" and "the enemy of the whole human race"— had other ideas.[9] In 1824, still only sixteen, he boarded a ship to Odessa on the Black Sea, and the following year he accompanied his father, who owned a boat named the *Santa Reparata*, on a voyage to Rome with a cargo of wine. Fortunately for Garibaldi, his father was unable to pay the man who owned the team of buffaloes that towed the *Santa Reparata* up the Tiber to the port of Ripetta, necessitating a longer stay. The Eternal City made a vivid impression on him. Its ruins, he later wrote, were the "relics of all that was greatest in the past"[10]—potent symbols that would inflame his imagination and inspire his famous battle cry: *Roma o morte!* ("Rome or death!")

Over the next decade, Garibaldi's shipboard travels took him all over the Mediterranean as well as to Constantinople and the Canary Islands. His shipmates and the expatriates he met ashore confirmed him in the patriotic and republican political ideals of Giuseppe Mazzini—whose Young Italy (as we've seen) he joined in 1832—as well as the humanitarian philosophy of the French social reformer Henri de Saint-Simon, a socialist who believed in a brotherhood of man and the improvement of the conditions of the poorest classes. Garibaldi would thereafter commit his life to democracy, humanitarianism, socialism, and Italian unification.

Garibaldi first put his political ideals into practice not in Italy but in South America. After the military court in Genoa sentenced him to death, he had made his way to Rio de Janeiro, where he assisted the Riograndense Republic in its struggle to secede from the Empire of Brazil. He became a privateer on a twenty-two-ton ship that he christened the *Mazzini*, harassing maritime traffic from states hostile to the breakaway republic. His cutlass-wielding acts of derring-do—surprise attacks, naval clashes, ship boardings, seizures of cargo, the freeing of African slaves—were later breathlessly reported in biographies and popular weekly magazines. In 1843, his thoughts turning homeward, he formed the Italian Legion, whose flag featured an erupting volcano and whose uniform included a red shirt of the sort worn by Rio de Janeiro's slaughterhouse workers.

In April 1848, during the "springtime of the people," Garibaldi returned to Italy on a ship named *Speranza*, or *Hope*. He brought with him his wife, Anna Maria Ribeiro da Silva, who had marched and fought alongside him in the South American jungles, tramping through bamboo swamps with their son in a sling around her neck. Also aboard the *Speranza* were sixty members of the Italian Legion. Their military services spurned by King Carlo Alberto, Garibaldi and his men fought instead for the provisional government of Milan, putting up an energetic defense against superior Austrian might. Then, with his troops swollen to some four thousand men, he marched to Rome to make a similarly vigorous but equally futile defense of the republic against the French. But such was the Garibaldi legend that the mere rumor of his marching to Venice to fight to restore the republic was enough to send jubilant crowds pouring into the city's piazzas.

Another exile beckoned, and in 1850 Garibaldi crossed the Atlantic, this time disembarking in New York City. The *New-York Tribune* described the new arrival as a "man of world fame, hero and defender of Rome."[11] He worked briefly at the Staten Island candle factory of another recent Italian immigrant, Antonio Meucci, before, canvassing for work at the dockyard, he got command of a merchant ship. For the next two years, he sailed around the world, from Peru to Hong Kong, Australia, and New Zealand before—thanks to a modest legacy from his brother—he settled down on Caprera, a ruggedly beautiful island off the coast of Sardinia. Here, suffering badly from rheumatism and depression following the death of his beloved wife, he built a stone house and grew figs and raised cows and goats. His military career appeared to be at an end.

By this time Garibaldi had broken with Mazzini, whose uncompromising political aim—Italy unified as a republic—he judged unrealistic, and whose sporadic revolutionary uprisings during the 1850s had ended in a series of dismal failures. Instead, like Camillo Cavour, he pinned his hopes on a nation unified as a constitutional monarchy under King Victor Emmanuel. That may have appeared a vain and distant hope during much of Garibaldi's shipboard and goat-rearing exile, but the outbreak of war in 1859 changed everything.

The exploits of Garibaldi and his volunteers, the Thousand, are as thrillingly incredible and historically momentous as Hannibal crossing the Alps, Julius Caesar crossing the Rubicon, or Constantine defeating Maxentius at Milvian Bridge. He was already world-famous at the start of 1860, and his stunning series of victories against the Bourbon armies sealed his legend as the greatest protagonist of his age—the mythical *eroe dei due mondi* ("hero of two worlds"). The only figure from his century who compares for the brilliance of his leadership and the magnitude of his victories, Napoleon, was a vainglorious, nepotistic tyrant, whereas Garibaldi fought for freedom and democ-

Giuseppe Garibaldi (1807–1882): "Hero of Two Worlds"

racy. If Napoleon was the jackbooted conqueror, Garibaldi was the rose-garlanded liberator of the people.

Garibaldi and the Thousand landed at Marsala, captured Palermo, crossed the Strait of Messina, marched through Calabria, and entered Naples on September 7—all in the course of four months during which his troops scored one sensational victory after another over the numerically superior Bourbon armies. "Here we either make Italy or we die," Garibaldi told his troops as they appeared before the walls of Palermo, defended by twenty thousand Bourbon soldiers.[12] The latter seemed a far more likely scenario, and it is little wonder that Sicilian peasants, witnessing his triumphs, came to believe in the magical properties of Garibaldi's red shirt. The Thousand (their exact number was in fact 1,089) were mostly Italians: a heterogeneous band of barbers, cobblers, civil servants, students, journalists, and sailors, along with a hundred doctors and 150 lawyers. They included one woman (a washerwoman who was the mistress of one of the lawyers) and an eleven-year-old boy. The Thousand were overwhelmingly men from the North, almost half of them from Lombard cities, but in Sicily their ranks were joined by insurgents who went down in history as the *picciotti* (young guns). By the time they crossed the Strait of Messina to attack on the mainland, the Thousand were probably three-thousand-strong.

On an overcast day at the end of October, Garibaldi, wearing a porkpie hat, met Victor Emmanuel in the village of Teano, some 30 miles (50 km) north of Naples, handing over the conquered territories. The pair then entered Naples together, King Francesco having fled for Gaeta and then, when it fell, for the safety of Rome, where he was given refuge by Pope Pius IX. The Kingdom of Italy was officially proclaimed in Turin on March 17, 1861, with the forty-year-old Victor Emmanuel as the hereditary monarch. A burly, brusque man with a gravity-defying moustache, the new *padre della patria* ("father of the fatherland") came from the oldest ruling dynasty in Europe. Although born at a time when powdered wigs and pigtails were the fashion at the court in Turin, he himself was ill at ease in high society. Uncouth and often vulgar, he was "incapable," according to a biographer, "of writing a single page of literate prose."[13] He preferred his hunting lodges and country estates to the more refined delights of court or city life.

King Victor Emmanuel II (1820–1878): "Father of the Fatherland"

Under Victor Emmanuel, most of the peninsula, along with Sicily and Sardinia, was united. The exceptions were Rome and the surrounding Papal States, protected by the French, as well as Venice and the Veneto, still under Austrian control. Such unfinished business chafed at Garibaldi, who hoped to raise a force of thirty thousand volunteers to complete unification. Cavour was sympathetic, for Rome's historical and religious importance made it a symbol of the national reunification process. He even negotiated with the papacy to have Rome serve as the official capital of Italy despite being outside the territories of the kingdom. The offer was rebuffed by the Holy See, and Cavour, the wily strategist of unification, died that summer from malaria. He was mourned both in Italy—where deputies wept openly in parliament—and abroad: the English newspapers hailed him as "the most remarkable man of our generation" and "the foremost statesman in Europe."[14]

As Cavour had known, any attempt to capture Rome by force would immediately bring Italy into conflict with France. Even so, in 1862, Garibaldi returned to Sicily and then, with his retinue of Redshirts, crossed into Calabria and began marching north, intent, it soon became apparent from his slogan, *Roma o morte*, on attacking the Papal States. Under pressure from Napoleon III and with newspapers headlines around the world proclaiming "Civil War in Italy," Victor Emmanuel sent troops to intercept Garibaldi. A brief battle was joined at Aspromonte, in the hills of southern Calabria. Dozens of Redshirts were arrested, while Garibaldi himself was wounded and forced to surrender, then put on board a frigate and taken to the fort of Varignano, near La Spezia. Here, in his confinement, he was showered by well-wishers from around the world with telegrams, poems, cigars, books, and even a comfortable bed. Garibaldi was released from prison at the end of October, with his wounds—one in the thigh, the other in the ankle—giving him both a limp and pains that, along with his rheumatism, he would bear for the rest of his life.

Venice and the Veneto ultimately proved an easier matter, thanks to help from Otto von Bismarck. In 1866, the Kingdom of Italy formed an alliance with Prussia against Austria. The Italians fared poorly both on the battlefield and, especially, at sea, where their navy was routed by an Austrian fleet. Garibaldi provided some consolation with a victory at Bezzecca, near the top of Lake Garda, albeit reduced because of his wounds to commanding his volunteers from a jolting carriage. However, the overwhelming Prussian victory in the seven-week campaign meant the Kingdom of Italy was able to gain the Veneto—although the Austrians, believing they had bested the Italians, humiliatingly refused to surrender the territory to them: Emperor Franz Josef called them "pickpockets and land thieves."[15] He surrendered it instead to the French, who, in turn, ceded it to Victor Emmanuel.

Only Rome remained, and it, too, became part of the unified kingdom thanks, ultimately, to scorching Prussian firepower and the machinations of Bismarck. In 1870, the French could not come to the rescue of Pius IX: the devastating victory by the Prussians in the Franco-Prussian War led to the collapse of the French Empire, the fall of Napoleon III, and the withdrawal of all French troops from Rome. In September 1870, taking advantage of the sudden power vacuum, fifty thousand Italian troops entered the Papal States and, on the September 20, opened fire outside the Aurelian Walls, near Porta Maggiore. Within hours, a white flag was fluttering above Porta Pia.

The sovereignty of the popes over Italian territories came to an end, and after a plebiscite in October, Rome at last became the capital of the Kingdom of Italy. In July 1871, Victor Emmanuel established his court at the Quirinal Palace, the summer residence of the popes since its completion in 1583. Refusing to leave the Vatican Palace, the pope became, in effect, a prisoner. He excommunicated the king and Italy's other rulers, refusing to recognize either the loss of his temporal powers or the legitimacy of the Kingdom of Italy—a dispute that would prevail for the next six decades.

As for Garibaldi, he lived out his remaining years on Caprera, so crippled by rheumatism and bullet wounds that he was forced to trundle around his small patch of property in a wheelchair. In June 1882, he died in his bed. Given the many dangers he had faced, it was another remarkable, against-the-odds feat.

As Camillo Cavour lay dying in 1861, he told his friends: *Non temete, l'Italia è fatta*. ("Fear not, Italy is made.") To which another politician, Massimo d'Azeglio, supposedly replied: *Fatta l'Italia, bisogna fare gli italiani*. ("Italy is made, now we must make the Italians.")[16]

The task of "making Italians" would not be easy or simple. Unification, led by an elite from the North, had not been a mass movement. The political system of the new kingdom was conspicuously undemocratic: the king appointed a Senate while a vanishingly small electorate voted for parliamentary candidates. Eligibility to vote was extended only to men who were literate (only 31 percent of the population in 1871),[17] aged over twenty-five, and paid a minimum of forty lire in direct taxes. This high bar meant the electorate throughout the 1860s had been a little over four hundred thousand people, or less than 2 percent of the total population.[18] Unpopular measures, such as new taxes and conscription, were introduced. Moreover, many of the new administration's politicians were fiercely anticlerical in a kingdom whose population was overwhelmingly Catholic and devoted to its institutions. It was seemingly impossible to be both a good Catholic and a loyal Italian, for in 1868 the Vatican had called on Italians to boycott all participation in the kingdom's political life, including elections. Ruling Italy, and keeping it together, was obviously going to be as daunting a challenge as ousting the Bourbons and the Habsburgs.

One of the greatest challenges was integrating North and South. Enormous social, cultural, economic, political, and even religious differences separated areas such as Lombardy, the Veneto, and Tuscany from Puglia, Calabria, and Sicily. The economic backwardness, political corruption, and social violence of the South, along with its supposedly unstable, idle, and ignorant populace, became a familiar theme for politicians and journalists from the North. Massimo d'Azeglio, a well-bred aristocrat from Turin who painted as a hobby, wrote novels, and frequented literary salons in Milan (he married Alessandro Manzoni's daughter), expressed the cultural differences—and inherent prejudices—when he remarked: "In every way union with the Neapolitans scares me. It's like getting into bed with someone with smallpox."[19]

The South had suffered decades of economic hardship and political turmoil whose fallout, the miserable condition of the poorest classes, required urgent solutions. However, Garibaldi's stunning victories in 1860 came so quickly that politicians in the North, such as Camillo Cavour (who was not told in advance of Garibaldi's expedition), were caught off guard, with no plan how to govern these vast and politically complex new territories that Cavour (who had never traveled south of Florence) called "the weakest and most corrupt part of Italy."[20] One of Cavour's envoys assured him that it would be possible for the North to "tame and govern" the South thanks to "our greater courage, our superior intelligence and morality, our experience and character."[21] The supposed inferiority of the southerners became a constant refrain among intellectuals in the North. In 1876, one of them, a Tuscan, compared Sicilians to the "savages" of North America.[22]

The new administration did press forward with attempts at reform and modernization. Construction began on roads and railways—the sort of infrastructure projects neglected under the Bourbon rule: by 1860 only 60 miles (100 km) of track had been laid in the entirety of the Kingdom of the Two Sicilies. But after Unification most of these projects proceeded only very slowly because of the same fiscal constraints that troubled the Bourbons. Elementary schooling was made compulsory in 1861, a vital measure given that the rate of illiteracy in Puglia, Calabria, Sicily, and Sardinia was more than 90 percent.[23] Yet parents needed to be convinced that their children should learn to read and write, a particularly daunting task among poor peasants whose children of necessity worked in the fields. The low rate of literacy in the South meant a smaller proportion of its population was eligible to vote and therefore, theoretically at least, to effect change. The lands of the former Kingdom of the Two Sicilies counted 9.2 million people in 1861, or 47 percent of the total population of the new Kingdom of Italy, and yet those in the South made up less than a third of the electorate.

The inability of the government to impose authority on the South, especially in the poor rural areas, was exposed by what became known as the *grande brigantaggio* ("great banditry") that plagued the countryside during and after Unification: armed gangs that kidnapped, robbed and extorted, attacked mail coaches, and murdered policemen and other officials. This breakdown of order in the rural South produced another force in Italian society that lasted far longer and caused infinitely more harm. The word "Mafia" appeared for the first time in popular culture in 1863 in a Sicilian comedy called *I Mafiusi de la Vicaria* set in a Palermo prison. By the mid-1860s, officials in Palermo were using the term—which appears to derive from the Arabic word *marfud*, or rejected[24]—to describe petty criminals and political malcontents. There was also a mafia among the higher classes, a *Mafia in guanti gialli* ("kid-glove Mafia") consisting of landowners and other wealthy citizens who regarded the monarchy's institutions as instruments of restriction and control that detracted from their traditional power and influence. They regarded themselves as "men of honor" who solved political, legal, and territorial problems for themselves and others without resorting to the perennially weak and ineffective organs of the state.

Yet another clandestine society had begun developing by the 1870s, albeit with entirely different motives. In 1864, the Russian anarchist Mikhail Bakunin moved to Florence and founded a secret band of revolutionaries called the Florentine Brotherhood, dedicated to insurrection and revolution. A year later, convinced that the South's impoverished and unruly peasants were a promising fuse with which to ignite the revolution, Bakunin relocated to Sorrento, near Naples.

Here he found enthusiastic followers among those disillusioned with both the Risorgimento and authority in general. Two of his disciples were a medical school dropout named Errico Malatesta and a young man from a family of wealthy landowners in Puglia, Carlo Cafiero.

Like many anarchists, Malatesta and Cafiero subscribed to "propaganda by the deed," a belief that acts of insurrection were the most effective tools of propaganda. To that end, in April 1877 they attempted to stage an uprising in the rugged bandit country of the Matese mountains some 40 miles (60 km) northeast of Naples, among the tough peasants whom the government authorities, perennially struggling to control them, called "descendants of the Samnites."[25] Their revolt was quickly suppressed thanks to the rapid descent on the region of twelve thousand soldiers, a large force that indicated how the authorities genuinely feared the anarchists might succeed in triggering a widespread rebellion. As for the young anarchists, they were philosophical about their failure. "If we did not succeed this time," one of them shrugged to an interrogator after he and his comrades were arrested, "we will succeed the next."[26]

Italian anarchists would indeed remain undaunted in the years that followed, despite government roundups and crackdowns. In later years, they would therefore turn from fomenting uprisings to carrying out acts of terror, sometimes with spectacular and shocking results.

Unification made the language question all the more urgent because, after 1860, the Kingdom of Italy needed to communicate—for a host of bureaucratic, diplomatic, and pedagogical reasons—across previously disparate territories, each with its own dialect. The linguistic quandary was highlighted by the fact that three of the greatest protagonists of the Risorgimento were not native speakers of Italian. Garibaldi grew up in Nice speaking the Ligurian dialect as his mother tongue, with French as his second language. French was Camillo Cavour's first language (his first name was actually Camille). According to a friend, he was *impacciato* (clumsy) whenever he spoke or wrote in Italian.[27] King Victor Emmanuel was likewise fluent in French but preferred the Piedmontese dialect of his native Turin. His famous phrase on entering Rome in 1871, *Ci siamo e ci resteremo* ("Here we are and here we shall stay"), was actually expressed in Piedmontese: *Finalment i suma* ("Here we are at last"). This phrase most likely expressed not a momentous fulfillment of historical destiny but relief that his train from Florence—which was running late—had finally arrived at the station in Rome.

Education was clearly the key to establishing the Italian language as a cohesive force. The Casati Law, first passed in the Kingdom of Sardinia in 1859 and then, after Unification, extended across all of Italy, affirmed the role of the state in providing education alongside, or in place of, the Catholic Church, which for centuries had taken sole charge of schooling. Primary education was made compulsory for the first two years (and then, after 1877, for three years). Italian was to be the most important lesson in primary schools. In January 1868, the minister of Public Education, Emilio Broglio, put together a special commission—headed by none other than Alessandro Manzoni, then eighty-two years old—to investigate how to teach proper grammar, spelling, and pronunciation, or what became known as "Florentine usage." One of the commission's recommendations (which proved logistically difficult to implement) was to make special use of teachers from Tuscany who would fan out across the country to spread the use of Florentine. It also recommended the compilation of a vocabulary: what eventually became the four-volume *Novo Vocabolario della Lingua Italiana Secondo l'Uso di Firenze* ("New Vocabulary of the Italian Language According to the Usage of Florence"), published between 1870 and 1897.

The *Novo Vocabolario* was a weighty tome more than a quarter of a century in the making. In July 1881, a rather slighter and more accessible volume, written in the Florentine tongue and aimed specifically at schoolchildren, began appearing in installments in the *Giornale per Bambini* (one of Italy's first periodicals for children, itself an indication that children were becoming readers). The novel was composed by a Florentine journalist and follower of Giuseppe Mazzini named Carlo Lorenzini, who was working on a series of children's books that taught—by means of lively language and humorous narratives—subjects such as mathematics, grammar, and geography. Published in book form in 1883 under the pen name Carlo Collodi, the novel rapidly became the biggest selling and most translated book in the world after the Bible.[28] *Le Avventure di Pinocchio: Storia di un Burattino* told the story of a lively and mischievous wooden puppet who, endowed with life and after numerous scrapes and adventures, becomes a real boy. Given that the book was read throughout the nineteenth and twentieth centuries by more Italians than any other work, Pinocchio no less than Dante or Alessandro Manzoni deserves to be seen as one of the fathers of the Italian language, and as someone who helped make the Italians.

CHAPTER 10

"Dov'è la Vittoria?"
The Kingdom of Italy

At 8:20 on the evening of July 29, 1900, a thirty-year-old man, fair-haired and handsome, made his way through the teeming crowds at a gymnastics event in Monza, 10 miles (16 km) northeast of Milan. Gaetano Bresci was from a village near Florence where, from the age of fifteen, he had worked in a textile factory. Only recently had he returned to Italy. Early in 1898, he boarded a ship to the United States, following in the wake of, quite literally, millions of Italians: almost four million men and women had left Italy over the previous twenty-five years. More than a million and a half settled in Brazil and the Republic of Argentina, while at least another million went, like Bresci, to the United States.[1]

Many Italian immigrants to America settled in New York City: some 225,000 by the time Bresci disembarked. Bresci, however, had moved to Paterson, New Jersey, America's "Silk City," likewise home to a large Italian community (by the middle of the twentieth century more than half of Paterson's population would be of Italian descent).[2] Most of the Italian immigrants to Paterson were, like Bresci, textile workers from the North, and like so many of them, he began work at one of the silk mills. He was paid twenty dollars per week, more than five times what he could have earned in Italy. Even so, America was not necessarily a Promised Land for Italian immigrants.

Many encountered prejudice: they were Catholics in an overwhelmingly Protestant country, many were poor and spoke little English, and often they were forced to take low-paying jobs and live in impoverished and sometimes crime-ridden neighborhoods. It was unclear to many Americans if these new arrivals were to be regarded as "black" or "white," and indeed the epithet *guinea*, a racist slur originally applied to African slaves and their descendants, became by the turn of the twentieth century a derogatory name for Italians.[3] Italian immigrants, furthermore, were often seen as gangsters, thanks to the arrival of the Mafia on American shores. In a notorious incident in 1891, eleven Sicilians were lynched by a mob in New Orleans after they were suspected—despite having been acquitted in a trial—of belonging to the Mafia. Such prejudices and negative stereotypes would prove deeply ironic in view of the tremendous contributions, both cultural and economic, made by Italians to American life over the following century.

Italian immigrants were also seen as exponents, often violent, of radical politics, in particular anarchism. In the last years of the nineteenth century, Italian anarchists had struck a series of deadly blows against heads of state: one stabbed the French president to death in 1894, another assassinated the Spanish prime minister with a pistol in 1897, and in September 1898 a third plunged a homemade stiletto into the heart of Empress Elisabeth of Austria, wife of Franz Josef, as she left the Hôtel Beau-Rivage in Geneva. As an American newspaper reported: "No matter where one hears of the life of some ruler or royal personage being attempted, one may always be certain to find that the assassin bears an Italian name."[4]

Gaetano Bresci was, in fact, an anarchist and aspiring assassin. He had served several short stints in Italian prisons for left-wing political agitation. In 1895, he had been shipped off to the island of Lampedusa, used by the government as a penal colony for anarchists. When he arrived in Paterson, he found himself among an even greater number of anarchists.[5] They hosted picnics, dances, and harvest festivals, and even formed an anarchist mandolin orchestra. They published newspapers, founded a library, and grouped into little societies, such as Pensiero ed Azione (Thought and Action) and Gruppo Verità (Truth Group). On one memorable occasion at a particularly heated meeting in 1899, Errico Malatesta—a hero of the Matese uprising who had recently escaped from Lampedusa and ended up in Paterson—was attacked by another anarchist. The assailant was quickly disarmed by none other than Gaetano Bresci.

Bresci abruptly left Paterson in May 1900 and by early June he was back in his home village in Tuscany. Here he spent his time practicing his aim with a pistol in the fields behind the family home. On July 24, he turned up in Milan, and a few days later, in Monza, where, on the 29th, he rose early, put on an elegant suit, had his fingernails done, and then wandered aimlessly around the shops. To the astonishment of the proprietor of a local cafe, he ate five ice creams in rapid succession. Then, as evening fell, he made his way to the gymnastics ceremony in the park alongside Via Matteo da Campione, not far from Villa Reale, the favorite residence of the King of Italy.

King Victor Emmanuel II had died from a fever in Rome in January 1878, at the age of fifty-seven. He was survived by numerous offspring since his first wife, Adelaide of Austria, gave birth to eight children before she died at the age of thirty-two. A half dozen mistresses added at least another seven children to the royal tally, while his second wife, Rosa Vercellana, known in Piedmontese as "La Bela Rosin," gave him two more. (He took seriously indeed his role as *Padre della Patria*. His heir and successor was, however, his eldest son, the thirty-three-year-old Umberto. King Umberto I made for a less than regal figure. Clumsy and awkward, he had staring eyes and a drooping lower lip. His most distinctive features were a walrus moustache and closely cropped hair, a style that became known as *capelli all'umberta*. He spoke little, and when he did, his perpetually inflamed larynx made him sound huffy and agitated. He was happy to stand aside in favor of his beautiful and charismatic wife, his first cousin, Margherita. It was for her, according to legend, that in 1889 a pizza-maker in Naples created the "Pizza Margherita" with its patriotic toppings of tomato (red), mozzarella (white), and basil (green).

Umberto's reign had been a troubled one. An aggressive foreign policy intended to make the new kingdom a great power with overseas holdings had ended disastrously. In 1890, a royal decree established the Italian colony of Eritrea on the western shore of the Red Sea, strategically located for refueling ships passing through the Suez Canal (completed in 1869). Italy soon went to war with the neighboring

King Umberto I (1844–1900): a troubled reign

power, Menelik II, the emperor of Ethiopia whose troops—wearing lion's-mane headdresses but heavily armed with modern weapons—destroyed the Italian forces in battle at Adwa in 1896. Six thousand Italian soldiers were killed and many more taken prisoner.

Italy scarcely fared any better domestically during the 1880s and 1890s. Some economic success stories could be found, such as Alessandro Rossi's huge textile factory in Schio, near Vicenza, founded in 1861 and employing five thousand workers by the time Umberto came to the throne. Another triumph came when, in 1880, the Buitoni family, who had been pasta-makers in Sansepolcro since 1827, built a steam-powered factory in Perugia with machines specially invented for making dried pasta, thereby turning an artisanal product into one manufactured on an industrial level. The family later branched out into chocolate, founding Perugina, famous for its Baci chocolates. Other famous Italian brands that appeared or else became internationally successful in the decades following Unification included Peroni (beer), Talmone (chocolate), Citterio (sausages), Pirelli (rubber), two vermouth producers (Cinzano and Martini & Rossi), and makers of liqueurs such as Campari, whose distinctive red color was achieved by using the dye from crushed cochineals.

Even so, the Italian economy remained largely agricultural, with production, apart from in the Po Valley, still primitive compared to that of other European countries—a sad irony given that protagonists of the Risorgimento such as Camillo Cavour had enthusiastically promoted modern improvements in agriculture. At various points, two of the largest industries were damaged by disease: silk production by *pebrina*, a disease of silkworms, and wine by phylloxera, which first appeared in Lombardy and Sicily in the early 1880s. The lack of leadership and foresight in business and industry was signaled by the fate of a young aristocrat from Bologna during the 1890s. During experiments at his father's villa, Guglielmo Marconi—the latest in a long succession of brilliant Italian engineers and inventors stretching back to Brunelleschi and Leonardo da Vinci—developed a way to send and receive radio waves over great distances without recourse to conducting wires. According to legend, Marconi asked for development funding from the Italian Ministry of Post and Telegraphs, only to have his application tossed by the minister with the phrase *alla Lungara*—that is, "to via della Lungara," the location of one of Rome's insane asylums. The story has been disputed, but the fact is that in February 1896, sensing better opportunities abroad, the twenty-one-year-old Marconi left Italy and settled in London, where, a year later, after finding support from the General Post Office, he founded his Wireless Telegraph & Signal Company.

The 1890s brought economic difficulties as one of Italy's largest credit institutions, the Banca Romana, collapsed amid financial shenanigans that involved the prime minister, Giovanni Giolitti (who was forced to resign) and members of the royal family. Amid the economic turmoil, Umberto's reputation, never especially buoyant, dipped sharply. The sentiments of many of his subjects were expressed in March 1893 by Luigi Berardi, a thirty-three-year-old drifter who, like Bresci, had lived for a time in America: he tossed a bag of excrement into Umberto's carriage as it left the Quirinal Palace.

The Italian government faced even greater problems in 1898 when bad wheat harvests and the Spanish-American

War (which made importing American grain difficult) led to food shortages and, within the space of a few months, a 50 percent increase in the price of bread. In early May 1898, protests in Milan were pitilessly suppressed by General Fiorenzo Bava Beccaris, whose troops deployed grapeshot, cavalry charges, and finally cannons against the demonstrators. According to official sources, at least eighty people were killed, but the number was almost certainly higher. For his "great service . . . to civilization," King Umberto appointed General Bava Beccaris to the Senate and decorated him with various medals.[6] Others commemorated the occasion in a different fashion. The phrase *i cannoni di Bava Beccaris* became proverbial to describe senseless and bloody overkill, while an anarchist protest song went:

> *Alle grida strazianti e dolenti*
> *Di una folla che pan domandava*
> *Il feroce monarchico Bava*
> *Gli affamati col piombo sfamò.*

> "To the harrowing and painful cries
> Of a crowd that asked for bread
> The ferocious monarchist Bava
> Fed the starving people with lead."

The cannons of Bava Beccaris inspired yet another act of commemoration. Gaetano Bresci had been in the United States for some three months by the time the protestors were killed in Milan, but that event, he later claimed, was what led him to board the ship back to Europe and make his way to his appointment with destiny in Monza.

Gaetano Bresci is apprehended by onlookers, including a pair of gymnasts in their striped jerseys.

The prize-giving ceremony in Monza, hosted by the local gymnastics club, went off without a hitch, ending punctually at 10:30 in the evening. The crowd was large and enthusiastic because gymnastics was the most popular sport in Italy and the local team had come out on top. King Umberto was in a good mood, hoping to walk the 600 yards (550 m) to Villa Reale, his favorite residence because through a gate in the grounds he could access the adjacent home of his longtime mistress, Eugenia, Duchess Litta. He was dissuaded from walking, and by the time he climbed into his two-horse carriage, the cordons had been removed, allowing the crowd to press close to the vehicle. Gaetano Bresci stepped forward and discharged three shots from close range. Umberto collapsed and Bresci was quickly disarmed and then pummeled by some of the gymnasts. Rushed in the carriage to Villa Reale, Umberto survived another forty minutes. "It is the greatest crime of the century!" cried Queen Margherita.[7] That much was no doubt true, although the century was barely more than six months old and so there was plenty of time for many more terrible crimes to be committed.

Bresci's trial began and ended in Milan on August 29, 1900. He was found guilty with no extenuating circumstances and—because Italy had abolished the death penalty in 1892—sentenced to life imprisonment. He was sent to the grim and forbidding prison built by the Bourbons on Santo Stefano, a volcanic island some 50 miles (80 km) from Naples to which, exactly 1,898 years earlier, Emperor Augustus had exiled his promiscuous and high-spirited daughter Julia.

Here, in May 1901, in circumstances later deemed suspicious, Bresci was found hanging from the window bar in his cell. An autopsy determined that he died from suffocation rather than, as one would expect from a hanging, fracture of the second cervical vertebra.[8]

The new king of Italy was Umberto's son, thirty-year-old Victor Emmanuel III. With him the nation took its first faltering steps into a new century.

In the same year that King Umberto was assassinated, a factory opened in Corso Dante on the southern outskirts of Turin. Covering 100,000 square feet (9,300 sq m) and employing fifty workers, it was called Fabbrica Italiana Automobili Torino, better known as FIAT. Led by one of its investors, a former cavalry officer named Giovanni Agnelli, FIAT was destined to become one of Italy's greatest industrial successes. By

1905, its profits exceeded four million lire, leading to an expansion of the factory to almost 450,000 square feet (42,000 sq m)—the size of some six soccer fields—and the opening of a ball bearing factory in Agnelli's home village of Villar Perosa, 25 miles (40 km) southwest of Turin. Other automobile manufacturers also appeared in the North: Lancia in 1906, likewise in Turin; Alfa Romeo in Milan in 1910; and Maserati, originally started in Bologna in 1914

An 1899 lithograph advertising FIAT, which began production that year

by four brothers. A fifth brother, Mario Maserati, a painter, came up with the company's distinctive trademark: a trident based on that in the Fountain of Neptune in Bologna.

The first two decades of the twentieth century also witnessed successful flourishes in the Italian fashion industry. In 1910, a twelve-year-old prodigy whose seven older siblings had all immigrated to America began turning out twenty-five pairs of shoes per week from a room in his house in the village of Bonito, 50 miles (80 km) east of Naples. Five years later, Salvatore Ferragamo would move to the United States and become the "shoemaker of dreams," outfitting Hollywood stars such as Mary Pickford, Douglas Fairbanks Jr., and Rudolph Valentino (another recent immigrant from southern

Italy). Twelve years later, following his return to Italy, he based his operation in Florence, inspired by "this beautiful city, with its centuries of wealth in art."[9]

Florence was in the process of becoming Italy's fashion capital: it was here, in 1921, that Guccio Gucci, a former bellhop in London's Savoy Hotel, opened an upscale leather goods store. The success of such companies was made possible thanks to both skilled craftsmanship and individual creative flair (always in rich supply in Italy) and favorable economic conditions (far scarcer).

Much of the South remained impoverished, so much so that, in the first decade of the twentieth century, 2.3 million Italians, the vast majority (86 percent) from the South, immigrated to the United States—the largest wave of migrants in American history.[10] But elsewhere in Italy, the early 1900s were a time of tremendous and unprecedented expansion. Industrial growth rose almost 8 percent each year, and Italy's overall economic growth was three times greater than Britain's.[11] The reorganization of the banking system following the Banca Romana scandal had made industrial start-ups possible, thanks to the availability of long-term investment capital. Meanwhile, Italian factories made up for the country's lack of coal with *carbone bianco*, or "white coal"—the electricity generated by dams and power stations in the Alps, such as the Bertini plant completed in 1898 in Cornate d'Adda, 20 miles (30 km) northeast of Milan. The most powerful in Europe, it powered the streetlights and electric tramlines in Milan, as well as the 2,800 lamps in La Scala opera house. By 1905, Italy led all of Europe in hydroelectric power. As one politician enthused in that same year, electricity offered a "new, grand horizon to Italian life."[12]

This new Italy of electricity and motor cars found its most strident cultural expression in the bombastic writings of the poet Filippo Marinetti, who became the leader of an avant-garde artistic movement known as Futurism. Among his publications we find such revealing titles as *Elettricità Sessuale* ("Sexual Electricity") and *Lussuria-Velocità* ("Lust-Speed"). Marinetti's 1909 manifesto for Futurism hailed the "reign of divine Electric Light" and enthusiastically celebrated the "racing car with a hood that glistens with large pipes resembling a serpent."[13] This document was what Marinetti called "a manifesto of burning and overwhelming violence"—a blustering and provocative anthem that saluted the danger, courage, progress, dynamism, and speed epitomized by "man at the steering wheel." The modern world was to be celebrated in all its furious velocity, and everything from the past so thoroughly rejected that libraries were to be torched and ancient monuments demolished. Marinetti and his friends called for a revolution in art that would involve both subject matter taken from modern life and visual style using distortions, force lines, and violent colors to reflect the gaudy intensity of the modern world. The movement was meant to change the way people thought and behaved: the way they wrote, dressed, danced, made plays and films, and performed music. There

Futurist sculpture: Boccioni's Unique Forms of Continuity in Space *(1913)*

was even to be a "Futurist cuisine," heavy on preservatives, processed food, kitchen gadgets, and mass production (an all too prophetic vision of the food of the future).

As an art movement, Futurism may have been harmless enough, and some of Marinetti's friends, especially the sculptor Umberto Boccioni in works such as *Unique Forms of Continuity in Space*—a statue of a distorted figure striding forward in a robust bronze swirl—created brilliant works of art. But Marinetti also had a political agenda. One purpose of Futurism was frankly nationalistic: the exaltation and glorification of Italy. And the glory of Italy could best be achieved, according to the manifesto, by means of the ultimate expression of modern industrial and mechanized ferocity. As Marinetti declared in his manifesto: "We intend to glorify war—the only hygiene of the world—militarism, patriotism, the destructive gesture of anarchists, beautiful ideas worth dying for."

Marinetti was not alone in calling for a war. In 1910, a group of intellectuals gathering in Florence formed the Associazione Nazionalista Italiana, aimed at enhancing Italy's power and prestige in the world. Many members were "irredentists" who favored expanding Italy's national borders to encompass regions with large Italian populations—the so-called *terre irredente* ("unredeemed lands") such as Istria, Dalmatia, and South Tyrol—that were subject to powers such as Austria. Other groups of similar persuasion soon arose with names including La Grande Italia (formed in Milan) and Italia Nostra (Turin). Nationalistic sentiments were whipped up by literary productions, such as Gabriele D'Annunzio's play *La Nave* ("The Ship"), whose story of sixth-century Venetians shaking off Byzantine control resounded with an unmistakable contemporary relevance. First performed in Rome in 1908, it attracted as much attention and applause for its vision of an Italian power gaining control of the Adriatic and Mediterranean as it did for its scene in which the female lead performed a striptease and danced naked onstage.

In the middle of June in 1914, D'Annunzio deplored the present state of Italy to a French ambassador. "The genius of the Latin people has never fallen so low," he lamented, explaining that the Italians had lost all of their heroic virtues. But for D'Annunzio, as for Marinetti, there was a solution: "A war, a national war, is the last remaining hope of salvation. It is only through war that peoples who have been turned into brutes can halt their decline."[14] D'Annunzio, Marinetti, and other nationalists would get their wish soon enough.

Italy did not enter the Great War as, in the famous words of Sir Edward Grey, the lights went out "all over Europe." Italy had been part of the Triple Alliance with Germany and Austria-Hungary since 1882. However, Italy declared its neutrality when, in 1914, the Austrians went to war against the Triple Entente (France, Britain, and Russia). The Italian government pointed out that not only had the Austrians been the aggressors, but they had failed to consult their Italian allies before declaring war on Serbia, rendering the pact null and void. Cue much agitation and debate in the weeks and months that followed as the nationalists and interventionists called for Italy to enter the war, not on the side of the Triple Alliance but (in order to "redeem" the "lost" territories) against Austria.

The Italian government was content to sit on the sidelines not least because a recent military adventure had not proved an unqualified success. Following Unification, Italy had become one of the "Great Powers," an exclusive club that included Britain, France, Germany, and the Austro-Hungarian Empire. However, as one historian has pointed out, Italy's shaky national cohesion, economic debility, and lack of both industrial and military might made it the "least of the Great Powers."[15] To assert and maintain their precarious status on the world stage, Italian politicians had therefore pursued a policy of slippery diplomacy and occasional attempts at colonial expansion—the latter sorely beyond their limited means, as the ill-starred adventures in the Horn of Africa betrayed all too clearly. But in 1911, the fiftieth anniversary of Unification, the time seemed ripe for further aggressive exploits on foreign soil.

In September of that year, an Italian expeditionary force invaded Libya, in part to thwart French designs on North Africa and control the Mediterranean, but also (as one politician admitted with striking candor) to avenge Italy's "shameful history" of invasion and oppression by foreign powers by securing "a virile victory of its people over an enemy—no matter who."[16]

The invasion force that ultimately numbered one hundred thousand men captured Tripoli, Benghazi, and Homs from the Ottomans, and in November 1911 King Victor Emmanuel III proclaimed the annexation of "Italian Tripolitania" and "Italian Cyrenaica." As an Italian writer exulted: "No longer are we 'nothing': We are an ancient people that has found its youth and its strength. We are a great nation."[17] However, the Italians had drastically overestimated the local support for their invasion, and soon they found themselves fighting not the Ottomans—with whom they signed a peace treaty in October 1912—but the indigenous Arab population. The war would drag on for decades as Italy struggled to maintain control over its recalcitrant African colony.

Italy had profited territorially from the Franco-Austrian War of 1859 and the Austro-Prussian War of 1866. By early 1915, the prime minister, Antonio Salandra, and his foreign secretary, Sidney Sonnino, decided on their own that, in order to extend its borders in similarly opportunistic fashion, Italy should choose sides and enter this latest European conflict. They parleyed with both sides in such secrecy that neither parliament nor the king was aware of their negotiations. Eventually, in April 1915, siding with the Triple Entente, they signed the Treaty of London, a secret pact with which the British and French tantalized their new allies with the prospect of the "unredeemed" territories of South Tyrol, Trentino, Trieste, Istria, and much of Dalmatia. When the terms were disclosed and Italy officially declared war on Austria, Salandra described in a rousing speech on the Capitol how the war would represent the "sublime task of realizing the ideal of a great Italy that the heroes of the Risorgimento were not able to see finished."[18] Both Italy's gobbled-up lands and its much-trampled honor were to be redeemed.

These ambitions were dramatically and tragically shattered in the autumn of 1917 at the Battle of Caporetto, fought in what is today Kobarid in Slovenia, some 50 miles (80 km) north of Trieste. If the trenches of the Western Front were dug in the green fields of France and Belgium, the Italians were forced to fight the Austrians along the Karst Plateau, a disheveled mountainscape of jagged rocks, caverns, sinkholes, perilous roads, and, as the war progressed, shattered villages with the all-pervasive stench of cadavers. The valley of the Isonzo, carving its way through the Julian Alps, represented Italy's best hopes for an offensive breakthrough into Austrian territories. They enjoyed only limited success in eleven consecutive assaults across the river before, in October 1917, the Austrians launched a massive counteroffensive with the help of German stormtroopers wielding flamethrowers and unleashing poison gas. The Italian troops were forced into a panicky and chaotic retreat. Their casualties were staggering: 40,000 dead and 300,000 taken prisoner, while another 350,000 soldiers simply deserted. The shame of defeat was made worse due to looting and vandalism by the soldiers as they retreated through the towns and villages of northeast Italy. The locals denounced them as *camorristi* (that is, mafiosi) because of their pillaging (and no doubt because many of these fleeing conscripts were peasants from the South). Caporetto soon became a byword for incompetence, cowardice, surrender, and defeat. Twelve years later, the catastrophic episode was described so unsparingly by Ernest Hemingway in *A Farewell to Arms* that the novel would be banned in Italy for the morale-shattering influence of such an embarrassing reminder.

Italy's participation in the Great War—not to mention its six hundred thousand dead—gave the new prime minister, Vittorio Emanuele Orlando, born in Palermo in 1860 (hence his patriotic name), a seat at the Peace Conference in Paris. But Orlando was rebuffed by the Americans, French, and British in his demands for the "unredeemed" lands on the eastern shore of the Adriatic promised by the 1915 Treaty of London. The Great Powers felt the Italians had drastically underperformed during the war (Georges Clemenceau spoke scathingly of "the boys who scampered away from Caporetto").[19] Italy had borrowed seven hundred million British pounds from the Allies, not all of which was spent, as intended, on the war effort. Meanwhile, Italy's navy, the Regia Marina, had barely nudged into open water.

Opinions about the Italians were not improved when, as a late addition to the territorial wish list, Orlando demanded the deep-water port city of Fiume (or Rijeka) on the Adriatic coast. From the Middle Ages through the eighteenth century, Fiume had enjoyed economic prosperity and a strong measure of political independence, with a distinctive Italian dialect (Fiumano, related to Venetian) and culture (its church of San Vito was built in imitation of Santa Maria della Salute in Venice). Fiume had been annexed in the fifteenth century by the Austrian Habsburgs, but over the next four centuries its language and institutions were generally respected as it passed back and forth among Austria, Hungary, France (in Napoleonic times), and Croatia. Its one constant was its Italian-speaking inhabitants, who at the outbreak of the war made up almost half of the fifty-thousand-strong population (though the surrounding hinterland was almost entirely Slavic).

The American president, Woodrow Wilson ("very anti-Italian," according to a British official),[20] refused to accept Italian sovereignty over Fiume, which quickly became the flashpoint for what Italian nationalists condemned as the *vittoria mutilata* (mutilated victory). Orlando and Sidney Sonnino found themselves in an impossible situation from which their petulance and intransigence did little to extract them. Meanwhile, in Turin the sign for the Corso Wilson, recently named for the American president, was torn down and replaced by one reading "Corso Fiume." Graffiti appeared on the walls in Rome demanding the annexation of Fiume, and the Italian press began reporting stories of Slavs murdering Italian women and children in Istria and Dalmatia. And it was at this delicate moment of volatile politics and tense international negotiations that Gabriele D'Annunzio launched himself into the fray.

D'Annunzio had enjoyed a good war, which he used as a stage for his latest artistic performances. Born in Pescara in 1863, he was a boisterously charismatic showman who first demonstrated his flair for self-promotion when he launched his career as a poet at the age of seventeen by faking his death and publishing obituaries tearfully lamenting the loss of such a young genius. He soon became famous, indeed notorious, for poems and novels celebrating both the cult of beauty and the *superuomo*—the Nietzschean superman who scorns traditional rules and morality in favor of a heedless pursuit of both heroic deeds and erotic pleasure. D'Annunzio's masculine ideal, which he did his best to emulate, was a strange mashup of the swashbuckling action hero and the orchid-sniffing aristocratic dandy.

Gabriele D'Annunzio (1873–1938): poet, playwright, soldier, and madcap showman

D'Annunzio had been one of the loudest voices in Italy calling for a war, and when it finally arrived, he embraced it with such reckless and daring enthusiasm that he emerged from it, at the age of fifty-five, as Italy's most highly decorated soldier. He served on the sea—on both motorboats and submarines—and in the air, losing an eye in an airplane crash in 1916. In 1918, he participated in madcap raids that made him a national hero, such as the *volo su Vienna* (flight over Vienna), in which his Ansaldo biplane led seven others into the sky above the imperial capital, which they showered with four hundred thousand leaflets decorated with the Italian tricolor and insults about the Austrian government. Of no military value, the flight was nevertheless a huge morale-booster for the Italians following the disgrace of Caporetto.

D'Annunzio's next daredevil performance was even more audacious. Humiliatingly for the Italian government, Fiume was ultimately declared a neutral city under the protection of the League of Nations, while Dalmatia went to Yugo-slavia. D'Annunzio therefore decided to take international law into his own hands. In September 1919, he and 287 volunteers set off from Ronchi (today known in tribute as Ronchi dei Legionari) for their 60-mile (100 km) overland expedition. Their slogan (deliberately echoing Garibaldi) was "Fiume or Death." The numbers of legionaries swelled as they approached Fiume, which they captured (from, ironically, the small Italian military contingent guarding the city) without a shot being fired.

What followed for the next fifteen months was interna-tional consternation and outrage, dithering on the part of the Italian government (which hesitated to send in troops lest they defect to D'Annunzio's side), and, in Fiume itself, D'Annunzio's jaw-dropping displays of political theater. He took to addressing the masses from the balcony of the town hall, declaring that Fiume had been restored to "mother Italy." There were banners and flags, parades, balls and spec-tacles, elaborate ceremonies and pageants, cocaine-fueled orgies and rampant syphilis. D'Annunzio uttered his famous battle cry (*Eia, eia! Alalà!*) and adopted a raised-arm salute that he and the director Giovanni Pastrone had used in their 1914 sword-and-sandal epic, *Cabiria*, about the Second Punic War.[21] Celebrities soon began arriving in Fiume. In September

1920, hoping to settle the matter, the Italian government dispatched Guglielmo Marconi to negotiate D'Annunzio's surrender. But after D'Annunzio lauded him as "the magic hero" and "genius of Italy," and after the adoring crowd began shouting, *Viva Italia! Viva Marconi! Viva D'Annunzio!*, the great inventor was converted to the cause.[22] Two months later, Arturo Toscanini arrived to conduct a concert at the Garibaldi Theatre, followed by a more informal performance of patriotic hymns at the nearby Bettola dell'Ornitorinco (Platypus Tavern).

This comic opera finally came to an end with the *Natale di Sangue* (Bloody Christmas) in December 1920. The *Andrea Doria* arrived in the harbor on Christmas Eve, giving an ultimatum for surrender. When D'Annunzio refused, shells began falling on Fiume, one scoring a direct hit on D'Annunzio's palazzo and showering him with debris as he was eating his lunch. "They will not have my head!" he declared. "I intend to keep it for my implacable and inevitable vengeance."[23] But his defiance was short-lived. Regular Italian troops poured into the city, bloody battles were joined, and two days later D'Annunzio surrendered. Fiume became, under the terms of the Treaty of Rapallo, signed by Italy and Yugoslavia the previous month, a free and independent state linked by a slim strip of land to Italy (which gained most of the Istrian peninsula and a few islands in the Adriatic).

As for D'Annunzio, he retired to a villa overlooking Lake Garda. But his incendiary nationalism, narcissistic posturing, personality cult, black-clad followers, balcony speeches, ululating war cries, and raised-armed salutes all caught the envious eye of a former schoolmaster, erstwhile firebrand socialist, and anti-war protester named Benito Mussolini.

CHAPTER 11

The "Putrid Corpse" of Liberty
Italy under Fascism

In 1920 Benito Mussolini was thirty-seven years old and beginning to move inward from the fringes of Italian politics. He had started his political life as a socialist, working as secretary and agitator for local clubs in the small towns in northern Italy, where he briefly taught school in the early 1900s. He himself had been a rambunctious bully as a pupil, expelled from one school for slashing a fellow student with a penknife. Despite his violence and lack of discipline, he had been an able student, raised by a mother who taught school in his hometown, Predappio, 50 miles (80 km) southeast of Bologna, and a father, a blacksmith who treated him to nightly chunks of Karl Marx's *Das Kapital*. Like his father, young Benito (named for the Mexican republican leader Benito Juárez) was vehemently left-wing and anticlerical, opposed to nationalism and militarism, though not to violence: he served a three-month stint in prison in 1908 for uttering threats, then five more months in 1911 for inciting the masses to violence during a general strike.

Articulate and self-assured, a quick study if not a deep thinker, Mussolini soon turned to journalism, rising through the ranks of left-wing newspapers in the years before the Great War. He became editor of the socialist *L'Avvenire del Lavoro* in 1909 and then *Avanti!* in 1912, increasing the latter's circulation over the next two years from twenty thousand to one hundred thousand. A charismatic hardliner, he became, by 1914, the most powerful figure within the Italian Socialist Party (PSI). But his career within the PSI imploded with the outbreak of war. At first favoring neutrality, he quickly came to the opinion that Italy should participate in a conflict that he foresaw (as it happened, with great prescience) could create ideal conditions for a workers' revolution. His fellow members in the PSI disagreed, leading to his expulsion from the party, his resignation from *Avanti!* and his launch of a new organ, *Il Popolo d'Italia*. In his maiden issue, Mussolini addressed "the young people of Italy," exhorting them to action with "a fearful and fascinating word: war!"[1]

Despite his expulsion from the PSI, Mussolini remained a devoted socialist. At the end of 1914, in order to "reaffirm socialist ideals,"[2] he began what he called a *movimento fascista*. He took the name from the ancient Roman *fasces*—the bundle of elm or birch rods, bound together with straps, that featured an axe inserted in the middle. Carried aloft in procession by the lictors, the bodyguards of the Roman magistrates, the *fasces* had been a sign of coercive authority: the rods symbolic of beatings, the axe of beheadings. It was an appropriate emblem for a man, such as Mussolini, bewitched by power and violence.

The *movimento fascista* was paused for the two years that Mussolini spent in the army after Italy declared war in 1915. After serving on the harrowing Karst Plateau, he was discharged in June 1917 following an injury caused in a mortar explosion that killed five of his comrades and left him with forty shrapnel wounds. He resumed his journalism, penning bloodthirsty articles calling for strict discipline in the army in the wake of Caporetto. The disaster had a shattering effect on him, causing him to change his political stripes as he became stridently nationalistic, dedicated to the idea of a strong and united Italy. In March 1919, in Milan, he revived his idea of a fascist movement, forming the Fasci Italiani di Combattimento, dedicated to regaining Italy's "unredeemed" territories. It was also violently opposed to the socialists: one of the first deeds of the Fascists was to ransack the headquarters of Mussolini's former newspaper *Avanti!*. It marked the beginning of the Fascists' campaign of unrestrained violence against their enemies.

Overshadowed by the antics of Gabriele D'Annunzio, the Fascists performed poorly at the elections in November 1919, failing to get a single deputy elected. Even Arturo Toscanini (who the following year would give his performance in Fiume) went down in defeat. Over the next year, following D'Annunzio's surrender at Fiume, and with the country deeply polarized and the central government weak and ineffective, Mussolini's Fascists began asserting themselves more aggressively on the national scene. The years 1919 and 1920 became known as the *biennio rosso*, the "two red years," because of a wave of strikes and other disputes, including between peasants and landowners. At their national congress in Milan in May 1920, the Fascists presented themselves as the bulwark against socialism and bolshevism, gaining support from the middle classes, conservatives, and wealthy landowners—anyone with a horror of socialism. Among the ranks of the Fascists were many army veterans, especially the Arditi, the crack assault troops formed after Caporetto with a black flame as their symbol, a black fez as their headgear, and bloodthirsty company names such as Esploratori della Morte (Explorers of Death).

By the end of 1920, many of these veterans and their turbulent young hangers-on formed armed "action squads" as a tool of political struggle against the left. Groups of blackshirted thugs known as *squadristi* violently attacked socialist officials, workers' groups, trade unions, and newspaper offices. As a police inspector in the Veneto wrote about the local Fascist squads in a report in the spring of 1921, "Not a day goes by in which they do not chase, confront, beat, and abuse those who belong to socialist organizations." He described how they broke into homes, set them alight, shot through windows and conducted menacing patrols aimed at keeping the people "in a perpetual state of intimidation."[3] One of their favorite forms of humiliation was to force-feed castor oil to their victims; another was to make them swallow live toads. Their weapon of choice was a wooden club they called a *santo manganello* (holy cudgel). *Squadristi* in Ferrara took to beating their victims with dried cod.

Membership in the movement skyrocketed from only 20,165 in December 1920 to 187,588 in May 1921, and then surpassed 200,000 before the end of the summer. In the national election of May 1921, marred by violent clashes in which at least forty people were killed, the Fascists elected thirty-five deputies (out of 535 in the Chamber). Mussolini himself was elected with a tally of more than three hundred thousand votes a few weeks after making a speech in Bologna in which he declared it necessary "to beat refractory skulls with resounding blows."[4] This electoral success enhanced Mussolini's prestige and ambitions, and by the spring of 1922 the newly branded Partito Nazionale Fascista (National Fascist Party) could boast more than three hundred thousand members. Mussolini's ascent to power looked inevitable.

The ascent came with the March on Rome in October 1922. On October 24, a mass rally of *squadristi* in Naples called for a march—long discussed and desired in Fascist circles—to oust the government and seize power. The operation began a few days later, with twenty thousand *squadristi* pushing north and, on the way, seizing various prefectures, telephone exchanges, and post offices. By October 27 and 28, the first of the *squadristi* had begun to swarm into Rome, although they were fiercely resisted by the Arditi del Popolo, an anti-Fascist group recently formed to resist the *squadristi* (its logo was an axe splitting a *fasces*). Early on the morning of October 28, the Italian prime minister, Luigi Facta, proclaimed a state of siege, but Victor Emmanuel III—for reasons still unknown and much debated—refused to sign a decree that would have allowed the army to open fire on the *squadristi*. On October 29, with violence spreading to other cities, the king sent a telegram summoning Mussolini. He had not been part of the march but, rather, remained

Benito Mussolini (center) marches in Rome with medal-wearing Fascists, October 1922.

safely ensconced in Milan, pacing up and down in his news-paper office, prepared to flee north of the Alps if events turned against him. A day later, he arrived in Rome by train. Dressed in a black shirt—his luggage had been misplaced en route—he had his audience with the king and became, at the age of thirty-nine, the new prime minister. Italy's Fascist era had begun.

The Fascist state born in 1922 was not yet an autocratic regime. Two weeks after taking power, Mussolini delivered a bellicose and threatening speech in the Chamber of Deputies: "I could make this deaf and gloomy hall into a bivouac of soldiers," he told his fellow deputies. "I could bolt the door of parliament and set up a government exclusively of Fascists. I could, but I choose not to, at least in this first phase."[5] Despite this bluster, the constitution and parliamentary system remained intact, deputies from other parties held cabinet posts, and Mussolini was merely the prime minister. Victor Emmanuel III remained the head of state and commander of the armed forces, and, having appointed Mussolini, could in theory depose him.

This "first phase" ended within a few years as Mussolini began dismantling the parliamentary system and concentrating maximum power in his own person as "Duce," a term he took from the Latin *dux*, an honorary title given by the Roman emperors to a victorious military or distinguished civic leader (and then taken over, as we've seen, by the heads of the Lombard clans). Boasting that liberty was nothing but "a putrid corpse,"[6] he pushed through dictatorial powers for himself, banning all opposition parties, tightening censorship on newspapers, and giving wide-ranging powers to the police. Political opponents received the harshest of treatments. In the summer of 1924, the leading socialist politician Giacomo Matteotti was bundled into a car in Rome, stabbed to death, and buried in a shallow grave north of the city. A year later, the journalist and politician Giovanni Amendola, another vocal critic, was beaten so brutally by *squadristi* who ambushed him on a road north of Florence—one of them wielding a "holy cudgel" equipped at its business end with a nail—that he died nine months later.[7]

Many writers and intellectuals were imprisoned or sent into "internal exile"—dispatched to Italian islands or to remote and desolate villages in the South (the latter fate evocatively described in Carlo Levi's 1945 autobiography, *Christ Stopped at Eboli*). One of the people deprived of his liberty was the founder of the Italian Communist Party, the Sardinian-born journalist and intellectual Antonio Gramsci. Arrested in November 1926, he was sentenced to twenty years in prison. Here he composed what later became famous as his *Prison Notebooks* before dying in 1937, due to the harsh conditions of his confinement, at the age of forty-six. Italy's most influential thinker of the twentieth century, Gramsci developed the political theory of "hegemony" (from the Greek *hēgemonia*, "dominance over"). He argued that governments ruled not merely by force—by beating "refractory skulls"—but also through ideas: the rulers fostered allegiance and consensus among the ruled by disseminating and popularizing their own self-serving worldview by means of schools, churches, newspapers, magazines, books, films, and a whole range of other cultural products and institutions.

Just such a hegemony was, of course, vividly on display in Mussolini's Italy. Amendola coined a new term to describe the Fascist state, *totalitario* (totalitarian), by which he meant a complete and uncontrolled domination of politics and culture.[8] In fact, Mussolini's control was rather less than this term suggested. The Church and the monarchy offered alternative spheres of power and influence, and resistance likewise came from forces within Italian society, such as landowners, industry, lingering regional and class identities, and from within the Fascist party itself (ever prone to bickering). Even so, Mussolini readily embraced the term, declaring in a speech in 1925: "That which has been defined as our ferocious totalitarianism shall be pursued with even greater ferocity." He went on to describe how he wanted to *fascistizzare* (fascistify) the nation, "so that tomorrow Italian and Fascist, much like Italian and Catholic, will be the same thing."[9] If the founders of the Risorgimento had been concerned with "making Italy," Mussolini wished to make Italy Fascist. He would attempt to do so not only by means of beating skulls with truncheons but also (as Gramsci realized) through art, architecture, and language—all of which, Mussolini believed, were in urgent need of fascistification.

Rome was as symbolically important for Mussolini as it had been for architects of the Risorgimento, such as Mazzini, Cavour, and Garibaldi. Like so many before him, Mussolini wished to restore the grandeur that was Rome, in his case the imperial Rome of marching legions, territorial conquests, and grandiose architecture. A few weeks before coming to power, he presented Fascism as the rebirth of the martial and moral values of imperial Rome: "We dream of a Roman Italy that is wise and strong, disciplined and imperial. Much of what was the immortal spirit of Rome resurges in Fascism."[10] A visible sign of this resurgent spirit was to be the cityscape of

Rome and other Italian cities. As *The New York Times* pointed out in 1924, with his ambitious architectural projects, Mussolini planned "to outdo the dreams of the Caesars."[11]

The first of Mussolini's grand architectural gestures was announced in September 1924: the world's tallest skyscraper. Rising 88 stories and 1,080 feet (330 m) into the sky above Rome, the building, to be named L'Eternale, would, its architect Mario Palanti promised, "externalize for the centuries the work of the Fascist government in the Eternal City."[12] Although nothing came of this project, Fascism left its mark in other ways. More recent buildings redolent of less illustrious eras were knocked down to make way both for Fascist contributions to the skyline and for the more effective exposure of excavated Roman ruins. Particularly dear to Mussolini's heart was the restoration of the semi-derelict Mausoleum of Augustus and the excavation, reconstruction, and relocation (next to the Mausoleum of Augustus) of the Ara Pacis, the Augustan Temple of Peace originally inaugurated in 9 BCE. A nearby inscription offered fulsome praise to Mussolini for having demolished "the old narrow alleys" and embellished "with even more splendid streets" this place where "the shade of Augustus hovers in the air."[13] Mussolini began his demolitions enthusiastically wielding a pickaxe for the ritualistic *primo colpo di piccone* (first blow of the pickax). The grunting effort earned him the nickname *Il Piccone*.

One of the most conspicuous demolitions took place in the ancient, historic neighborhood facing the Basilica of St. Peter through which Mussolini ploughed the grandiose Via della Conciliazione. The conciliation referenced in the name was that between the Kingdom of Italy and the Vatican, whose troubled relations went back to Unification. In

1929, Mussolini healed the rift by signing the Lateran Pacts with the Vatican. In return for the Holy See finally recognizing the existence of the Kingdom of Italy and relinquishing any legal claim on Roman territory, the Kingdom of Italy declared Catholicism the state religion and compensated the Church for the material damages suffered through the loss of its temporal possessions.

Mussolini's demolitions extended to language, for he was determined to purge Italy of the various dialects that had so vexed Alessandro Manzoni and other leaders of the Risorgimento, and that many Italians, more than fifty years after Unification, still spoke and wrote. In 1934, the use of dialect was banned not only in schools—for which standard textbooks were issued for the entire kingdom—but also in theaters, cinemas, and publications, such as books, magazines, and newspapers. He also hoped to rid the Italian language of what he saw as unsightly accretions and additions, taking measures to uproot foreign words and expressions. He believed that words imported from French or English such as "chauffeur," "mannequin," "omelette," "sandwich," "garage," "manager," and "croissant" were indications of "a deficiency of Italian spirit and sentiment."[14] The Italian vocabulary was therefore carefully sifted for any imports while arbiters such as the Reale Accademia d'Italia produced suitable replacements. Newspapers also helped out: in 1932, *La Tribuna* asked its readers to suggest Italian words for fifty of these unwelcome linguistic border-crossers. As a result of these efforts, a "shock" became *un urto di nervi*; a "ferryboat," *un ferribotto*; and a "mannequin," *una indossatrice*. A "cocktail" became *un arlecchino*, and a "bar" was transformed into *una mescita* or *liquoreria*. Some of the newly coined words did actually catch on: *autista* instead of *chauffeur*, *regista* instead of *régisseur* (director), *manifesto* instead of *affiche* (poster), and even *cornetto* instead of *croissant*. A sandwich became, and remains, *un tramezzino*, first served under that name in 1925 in the Caffè Mulassano in Turin.

If Fascism was truly to be the rebirth of "the immortal spirit of Rome," then Italy, like Ancient Rome, needed not only architecture but also an empire. It could count its Libyan colonies, Tripolitania and Cyrenaica, which by 1934 had been merged to become "Libia Italiana." This North African domain was finally under control following a long and ferocious decade of "pacification" that witnessed executions, mass killings, and the use of both mustard gas and concentration camps. Italy also had Eritrea and Italian Somaliland, its colonies in East Africa. But Mussolini's African ambitions extended beyond these slivers of coastline. While virtually all of Africa had already been carved up by other European powers during the "Scramble for Africa," the vast Empire of Ethiopia still remained independent, ruled by Emperor Haile Selassie.

Ethiopia had been the object of the Italian designs so spectacularly crushed in 1896 at the Battle of Adwa, at a cost of more than five thousand Italian lives. In October 1935, to redeem this ignominious episode and expand Italian possessions, Mussolini ordered the invasion of Ethiopia. The campaign proceeded fitfully until the end of the year, when the Italian commander, Pietro Badoglio, dropped mustard gas on the Ethiopians. After Haile Selassie fled to England and Badoglio entered Addis Ababa in triumph in May 1936, Mussolini proclaimed the "Italian Empire" and added to his official title *Fondatore dell'Impero* (Founder of the Empire).

Mussolini believed his invasion of Ethiopia enjoyed the tacit consent of France and Great Britain. Instead, amid international outrage, both powers condemned his aggression while the League of Nations announced sanctions. One of the few countries to disregard these sanctions was Nazi Germany, whose leader since 1933, Adolf Hitler, had revered Mussolini as a political model. In October 1936, the pair formed the Rome-Berlin Axis, which Mussolini claimed was "animated by a desire for collaboration and peace."[15] The pact was animated, in fact, by their deep grudge against Britain and France, and by a shared belief that their countries had both been victimized after the Great War. Drawing ever closer in his fatal embrace with the Nazis, Mussolini enacted racial laws in 1938, ushering in state-sponsored anti-Semitism that removed Jews from government jobs, newspapers, and the armed forces, and banned marriages between Jews and non-Jews. This despite the fact that one of his longtime mistresses, Margherita Sarfatti, was Jewish. Sarfatti, a sophisticated patron of the arts and Mussolini's first biographer, departed for South America soon after the laws were passed.

Italy's fortunes were definitively linked to those of Germany with the signing in May 1939 of the Pact of Steel (which Mussolini had wanted to be called, more gruesomely, the Pact of Blood). This agreement committed each nation to the military defense of the other. However, Hitler had little confidence in what he called "the natural boundaries of Italian capabilities."[16] Indeed, despite Mussolini spending almost 12 percent of the nation's budget on the military, the ill-equipped and poorly trained Italian armed forces were anything but imposing. Their deficiencies were blatantly exposed after Mussolini committed huge resources to support Francisco Franco in the Spanish Civil War, only to have four of his divisions routed in March 1937 in a fierce counterattack by Republican forces at Guadalajara. The British press dubbed this dismal performance the "new Caporetto," while David Lloyd George, one of the architects of the "mutilated victory," wrote an article mocking what he called "the Italian skedaddle."[17]

Mussolini stressed to the Germans that Italy would be unprepared for war for at least three years. Hitler paid scant heed, and so after the Nazis invaded Poland in September 1939, Italy lingered on the sidelines. Mussolini declared war on Britain and France only in June 1940 in a purely opportunistic move when, with the fall of France to the Nazis, it appeared as if Fascism was about to triumph and great advantages were to be gained by rallying faithfully to Hitler's side.

Fears about Italy's lack of preparedness for battle immediately proved well founded. An invasion of Greece in the autumn of 1940—intended to enhance Italian power in the Adriatic and Mediterranean—met with unexpectedly tenacious resistance and then, as the Greeks pushed the Italians back into Albania, bitter humiliation. The Italian campaign against the British in North Africa went even worse. After invading Egypt from their Libyan colony in September 1940, the Italian 10th Army was chased 500 miles (800 km) back across the desert into Libya by Britain's much smaller Western Desert Force. The British cornered and destroyed the 10th Army at El Agheila, captured hundreds of tanks and airplanes, and took almost 140,000 Italian soldiers prisoner.

The abysmal performance of Mussolini's armed forces meant that Winston Churchill, who famously described Italy as the "soft underbelly" of Europe, began making plans for an Allied invasion that would knock Italy out of the war and divert German troops from France. Operation Husky, the invasion of Sicily, began in July 1943 with a massive amphibious assault by British, American, and Canadian troops. Within a month the island was taken, along with more than a hundred thousand Italian prisoners of war. Within a few days of the invasion, on July 25, following ferocious Allied aerial bombardment of Rome, Victor Emmanuel used a vote of no confidence in the Duce by the Fascist Grand Council to depose Mussolini, who was then arrested and sent to Campo Imperatore, a ski lodge high in the Gran Sasso mountains, 100 miles (160 km) northeast of Rome. The building was D-shaped, with two other structures, never built, supposed to have been constructed in the shape of a V and an X, thus spelling out a triumphant "DVX" (Latin for *duce*, or leader).

The king appointed as Mussolini's replacement Pietro Badoglio, who planned to hand over the Duce to the Allies, with whom he concluded a separate peace, signed in secret on September 3 and made public five days later. However, another act was in store: Mussolini was dramatically freed from his mountaintop prison and whisked away to Germany following a daring special operations raid by German paratroopers acting on Hitler's orders. Hitler put him in place as the head of a new puppet regime, the Italian Social Republic (sometimes known as the Republic of Salò after the town where it was based on the western shore of Lake Garda). Italy was effectively partitioned: the South was run by the Italian government under the watchful supervision of the Allied Control Commission, while the Republic of Salò encompassed much of northern and central Italy (apart from Trentino, Alto-Adige, Friuli, Venezia Giulia, and Istria, all of which had been annexed by the Third Reich). Vigorously anti-Semitic and brutally repressive, the Republic of Salò was largely subordinate to the occupying Nazis. It did, however, give Mussolini a few last opportunities for bombastic posturing on balconies in front of wildly cheering crowds.

Hitler had sent six army divisions into Italy following Operation Husky and the Allied invasion of Italy, initially to support the Italians and then, after the armistice, to fight the Allies, who in September 1943 landed at Salerno, south of Naples. If Churchill had regarded Italy as a soft underbelly, the American general Mark Clark later reflected that, thanks to the rough terrain and fierce German resistance, it proved to be "one tough gut." The Allies captured Naples in early October, thanks in large part to the "Four Days of Naples," a Neapolitan uprising against the occupying Nazis. But northward progress slowed due to heavy fortifications along the Gustav Line—a formidable array of gun pits, concrete bunkers, barbed wire, machine-gun emplacements, and minefields—that barred the way to Rome. The Allies eventually broke through in May 1944 after the five-month-long Battle of Montecassino, in which American bombers (acting on intelligence reports of Nazis using the site as an observation post) destroyed the historic abbey, founded by St. Benedict of Nursia in 529. In fact, no Germans had been in the abbey and the only casualties were the Italian civilians who had fled inside for shelter.

The destruction of Montecassino in February 1944 came less than two months after General Dwight D. Eisenhower, the commanding general, issued an order to all Allied generals in Italy. "Today we are fighting in a country which has contributed a great deal to our cultural inheritance," he wrote, "a country rich in monuments which by their creation helped and now in their old age illustrate the growth of the civilization which is ours. We are bound to respect those monuments so far as war allows." However, he noted that if the commanders needed to choose between destroying a "famous building" and sacrificing their own men, "then our men's lives count infinitely more and the buildings must go."[18]

Montecassino was the highest-profile casualty of this "buildings must go" policy that claimed other victims such as the beautifully frescoed Camposanto in Pisa and the Ovetari Chapel in Padua, where a fresco by Andrea Mantegna was pulverized. Many masterpieces were saved due to precautions taken in late 1942 and into the summer of 1943 when thousands of paintings and statues, as well as entire libraries of books and manuscripts, were crated up and transported away from the cities to villas, fortresses, and monasteries in the countryside. Michelangelo's *David*, too big to be moved, was encased in a brick silo in its niche in the Accademia, while the facades of many buildings in Florence, as in other cities, were packed with sandbags to await the firestorm.

There were many close calls and near misses, including Leonardo da Vinci's *Last Supper*, which miraculously survived a stray bomb that fell on the convent of Santa Maria delle Grazie in August 1943. In a small Tuscan town some 60 miles (95 km) southeast of Florence, Piero della Francesca's *Resurrection of Christ* survived when the name of Sansepolcro rang a bell with Anthony Clarke, the British commander about to shell the town. Suddenly remembering an essay by Aldous Huxley extolling the work as "the greatest painting in the world," Clarke stopped his men from firing and the painting was saved. Huxley may well have been right about Piero's work. Found in Sansepolcro's Museo Civico, the fresco shows a somber but triumphant Christ, as ripped as an athlete and as stoic as a philosopher, stepping from his sepulcher against a landscape background that transitions from winter to spring. It offers an image of both human dignity and a regeneration that is deeply and intensely spiritual, but also—because its original setting was on the outside wall of the palace that served as the city's

A miraculous survivor: Piero della Francesca's Resurrection of Christ *(1465) in Sansepolcro*

seat of government—civic and communal, concerned (like Donatello's statues at Orsanmichele) as much with lessons about the here and now as with the hereafter. With its theme of resurrection and renewal, the fresco is an emblem of the Italian Renaissance, of the awakening from a centuries-long slumber into a splendor infused by the spirit of a magnificent past. It is an emblem, too, that epitomizes Italy itself, whose history is so often punctuated by remarkable moments of resilience and renewal after tragedy and disaster.

Rome was liberated by the Allies on June 4, 1944, two days before the D-Day landings in Normandy. After eleven more months of fighting, the rest of Italy was liberated by the 15th Army Group, a multinational force composed of not only British and American soldiers but also ones from Brazil, Canada, Greece, India, Poland, South Africa, and New

Zealand (both whites and Maoris). Taking part in the liberation, too, were hundreds of thousands of Italians—not just members of the armed forces, but also resistance fighters in the Garibaldi Brigades, the Matteotti Brigades, and the Partito d'Azione (Action Party). Many members of these groups came from preexisting Catholic, socialist, communist, and anti-Fascist groups. A prominent member of the Action Party was the Turin-based chemist (and later writer) Primo Levi, who was arrested at the end of 1943 and then deported to Auschwitz, an experience that, miraculously, he survived to write about in his 1947 book *If This Is a Man*. In the autumn of 1943, the Germans had begun rounding up and then deporting thousands of Italian as well as Libyan Jews to Auschwitz, Bergen-Belsen, Ravensbrück, and other concentration camps. Only a few hundred survived. Thousands of Jews were sheltered both by other Italians and by the Catholic Church, including three thousand at the pope's summer residence at Castel Gandolfo. Pope Pius XII has been accused by detractors of having done too little to save the Jews, but it's worth noting that in 1942 Josef Goebbels printed ten million pamphlets denouncing him as a "pro-Jewish pope." In the 1960s, an Israeli journalist and diplomat estimated that Pius was responsible, either directly or indirectly, for saving as many as 860,000 Jewish lives across Europe.[19]

At least seventy thousand women took part in the resistance movement against the Fascists and Nazis. Initially they offered logistical support to the male fighters, sheltering them and carrying messages and weapons (as shown through the character of Pina, played by Anna Magnani in Roberto Rossellini's 1945 film about the Nazi occupation, *Roma Città Aperta*). But by the end of the war, half of them came to serve as what the National Association of Italian Partisans recognized as *partigiani combattenti* (fighting partisans). The role was a remarkable one for women raised in Mussolini's Italy. The duty of women under Fascism was to have children—"as many children as possible," as Mussolini urged them in 1937—and to raise them to become defenders of the Empire.[20] Valuing them only as wives and mothers, the Fascist state had refused women the right to vote, to serve as principals of schools, and even to teach certain subjects. By 1938, the female staff in public and private workplaces was limited to 10 percent of the labor force, with women banned from many jobs for reasons of supposed physical unsuitability or the nature of the employment.

The heroic contribution of Italy's female resistance fighters is reflected in the fact that more than a thousand were killed in combat, almost 5,000 arrested, and another 2,812 executed by the Nazis and Italian Fascists.[21] Many of the survivors would go on to have distinguished careers as intellectuals and social justice campaigners as well as—when women in Italy finally got the right to vote and hold office in 1946—politicians.

Italian resistance fighters from the 52nd Garibaldi Brigade captured Mussolini on April 27, 1945. Hidden in a truck of retreating Luftwaffe personnel and wearing the helmet and greatcoat of a German private, he had been fleeing north in a convoy along Lake Como, heading for Switzerland. He was recognized by the partisans despite the German uniform. *Gh'é che el crapun!* ("We've got Big-Head!") one of them exclaimed in—such was the mockery of fate—the local dialect.[22] Mussolini and his mistress, thirty-three-year-old Claretta Petacci, were held in a farmhouse near Giulino

Some of the 70,000 Italian women who took part in the resistance against Fascism

di Mezzegra and, a day later, put up against a wall and shot. The following day, April 29, their corpses were taken to Piazzale Loreto in Milan, to the spot where fifteen resistance fighters had been executed and strung up by the Nazis the previous August (a grim spectacle that, ironically, Mussolini himself had deplored).[23] After being insulted and brutalized by the crowd, the corpses of Mussolini and Claretta were hung upside down from a girder in the forecourt of an Esso gas station next to other executed members of the Fascist regime. Carefully choreographed by the partisans, it was the Duce's last public performance and marked a suitably gruesome closing scene to Italy's Fascist era.

CHAPTER 12

Andrà tutto bene
Italy since the War

King Victor Emmanuel III, who came to the throne after the assassination of his father in 1900, proved to be one of Europe's longest-reigning monarchs. He was also one of its least effective and, in many ways, most unfortunate. The son of first cousins, he was shy and introverted, with watery blue eyes, a toothbrush moustache, and spindly legs resulting from a childhood bout of rickets. Standing only 5 feet, 3.5 inches tall, he tried various guises to conceal his lack of height: a tall cap, a long cloak to hide his short legs, and even a booster seat in the royal limousine. He was dwarfed by his statuesque, 6-foot-tall wife, Queen Elena, a black-haired, deep-voiced Montenegrin princess. Time and again he had acquiesced to Mussolini's demands, whether for the invasion of Ethiopia, the implementation of laws against the Jews, or the alliance with Adolf Hitler. In 1940, an American journalist called him "a diminutive, pathetic marionette flung about by a move of the great Mussolini's fingers." Yet the writer also pointed out that this "scrawny, elderly little man" was revered by the Italian people up and down the peninsula.[1]

That reverence had dimmed considerably by the end of World War II. The king had shown great bravery and leadership during World War I, touring the front in a battered

FIAT, sleeping under canvas, and doling out cigars and cheese to the soldiers. But his behavior in World War II was less heroic and endearing. After the armistice was announced in September 1943, he fled Rome for Brindisi in the middle of the night. Once Rome was liberated in 1944, he remained king in name only, handing over his powers—with great reluctance, since he regarded him as unfit to rule—to his forty-year-old son, Umberto; he then retired to a villa near Naples. The crown prince was tall and handsome but soon showed himself less than inspiring as a leader. The diplomat and statesman Count Carlo Sforza called him "a stupid young man who knew nothing of the real Italy." Count Sforza also dismissed him as "a degenerate"—an allusion to Umberto's rumored homosexuality.[2]

The fate of the House of Savoy was determined at the ballot box. On June 2, 1946, a plebiscite was held to decide whether Italy should remain a constitutional monarchy under the House of Savoy or become a republic. Hoping to salvage the situation, Victor Emmanuel abdicated on May 9 in favor of his son, who then ruled for only a few weeks as King Umberto II—the last King of Italy, known as *Il Re di Maggio* (the May King). The vote was relatively close, with 12.7 million casting ballots in favor of a republic against 10.7 million for the monarchy. The ballots revealed a strong North-South divide: the North voted by a large majority for a republic (more than 80 percent in Emilia-Romagna, the region around Bologna) and the South overwhelmingly for the monarchy (nearly 80 percent in Naples). Father and son went voluntarily into exile, Victor Emmanuel to Alexandria in Egypt (where he died the following year) and Umberto to the Portuguese seaside resort of Cascais, near Lisbon. He lived until 1983.

On the same day the plebiscite was held, voters elected—for the first time in Italy, by universal suffrage—556 deputies for a constituent assembly. The results were similar to those that came to characterize Italian politics for the next few decades. The country was sharply divided between the centrist Christian Democrats (who won 207 seats) and two left-wing parties, the Italian Socialist Party and the Italian Communist Party, who between them polled 219 seats. A half-dozen other parties (including monarchists) scooped up the remaining 130 seats. The Christian Democrats were to prove one of the most successful electoral machines of the second half of the twentieth century, serving as the largest party in the Italian parliament for the best part of the next fifty years. Sometimes known as the "party of God," they were supported by—but independent from—the Catholic Church, upholding its moral and family values but maintaining a resolutely secular vision of politics. They could boast a broad-spectrum appeal and, not least, served as a bulwark during the Cold War for those who feared the socialism and communism flourishing in the cities of the North.

Despite their dominance, the Christian Democrats only once won an outright majority. This election, in April 1948, fought at the height of the Cold War, proved a bitter contest that pitted the Christian Democrats against a coalition of socialists and communists who put aside their doctrinal differences and came together as the Popular Democratic Front. Given the pro-Soviet stance of this left-wing coalition, which opinion polls early in 1948 predicted would win the April election, the United States government under Harry S. Truman undertook covert operations, pouring millions into the campaign to support the Christian Democrats and other anti-communist parties. American propaganda efforts included heartfelt radio appeals by Italian-American celebrities, such as Frank Sinatra, Joe DiMaggio, and the boxer Rocky Graziano. In the end, the Christian Democrats triumphed under their leader, Alcide De Gasperi, winning 305 of the 574 seats. The following year, Italy became one of the founding members of NATO.

Unable to repeat their success in later elections, the Christian Democrats were obliged to form governments by entering into coalitions with other, smaller parties. The politically delicate equilibrium was easily disturbed by conflicting interests and personalities, including disputes between and among Christian Democrats themselves. The upshot was that each Italian government since World War II lasted, on average, only thirteen months. De Gasperi proved to be Italy's longest-serving prime minister in the second half of the twentieth century, but his seven consecutive years in office witnessed him forming eight separate governments, one of which lasted only thirty-two days. The shortest government of all came in 1954, when one of De Gasperi's successors, Amintore Fanfani, survived a mere twenty-two days. Fanfani would go on to serve as prime minister four more times, with his longest stint, in the early 1960s, lasting almost three years—impressive longevity in the ephemeral world of postwar Italian politics.

After the mid-1950s, the political uncertainty inherent in the cobbling together of these shaky coalitions was offset by *il miracolo economico*, the Italian "economic miracle." The recovery marked an incredible turnaround in the country's economic fortunes. The heavy Allied bombing meant that, in 1945, the country's economic infrastructure had been, to say the least, severely impaired: 70 percent of its roads had been damaged, and almost half the railroad network, with the tracks twisted into pretzels, was unusable. The wreckage of the transportation network left firms unable to get raw material from suppliers. Industrial production plunged to less than a third of its prewar level, and wages in 1945 fell to half of what they had been in 1939. Little wonder that a journalist called the years immediately after 1945 the "heroic" years of reconstruction—a time of energetic reform and renewal when the Italians would grapple with the psychological effects of military defeat, as well as with the devastating economic consequences of Allied bombing and German looting.[3]

The economic hardships caused by the war were one of the reasons for the rise in popularity of the socialist and communist parties. Determined to keep Italy out of communist hands, during the late 1940s and early 1950s, the United States, via the Marshall Plan, ploughed huge amounts of aid into Italy. By the early 1950s, thanks also to the discovery of gas and oil fields in Val Padana, both the infrastructure and the economy had begun recovering. In the peak years of the economic miracle, between 1956 and 1963, Italy's GDP grew at an average rate of 6.3 percent per year, catapulting the country—for so long an economic sluggard compared to its European neighbors—into the ranks of the major industrialized nations. Italians could afford televisions and seaside holidays, while men realized their dream of achieving the "three Ms": *macchina, mestiere, moglie* (car, job, wife). The fate of women, meanwhile, changed very little during these years: as late as 1970, Italian women made up only 18.6 percent of the total workforce.[4]

This newfound affluence had wide-ranging repercussions as Italy was transformed from a predominantly rural and agricultural country into an urban and industrial one. As the industrial workforce expanded at the expense of the agricultural sector, many farm workers from the South moved to the North to find jobs in the factories of Milan and Turin. Among the most successful firms were Olivetti, makers of precision mechanical and electronic products as well as, famously, typewriters. FIAT became the most prolific and successful car manufacturer in Europe, out-selling even Volkswagen. Two of the greatest icons of the economic boom—and of Italian postwar manufacture and design—were scooters, the Lambretta and the Vespa, which quite literally rose from the wreckage of the Allied bombing. The Lambretta was manufactured by Ferdinando Innocenti, who since the early 1930s had operated a factory for metal tubing in Lambrate, an eastern suburb of Milan. With his factory damaged by Allied bombing, he came up with a new product inspired by the sight of the Cushman scooters used by the Americans to navigate Italy's bombed-out roads. The Lambretta Model A was launched in 1947, quickly becoming popular with young people who used it to escape their parents' neighborhoods and socialize more widely and distantly. Advertising campaigns in the 1950s extolled the Lambretta as *Felicità su due ruote* ("happiness on two wheels").

While the Lambretta was manufactured in Milan, a competitor, the Vespa, took shape in Pontedera near Pisa. It was made by Piaggio, a company originally founded in Genoa by Rinaldo Piaggio in 1884 to produce woodwork and other furnishings for ships before, in the twentieth century, it branched out into aeronautics and railways. In the aftermath of World War II, Rinaldo's son Enrico was left, like Ferdinando Innocenti, with devastated factories and an ambition to make a low-cost and convenient form of transport for mass consumption. The prototype, the MP5, became known because of its ungainly shape as "Paperino" (Donald Duck). The next version, patented in 1946, was a sleeker model whose buzzing engine, according to legend, caused Enrico Piaggio to remark that it sounded like *una vespa* (a wasp). The first models left the factory in Pontedera in 1948, capable of speeds of about 40 miles per hour (60 km/h).

It was on a Vespa that Gregory Peck and Audrey Hepburn made their chaotic circuit of Roman streets in the 1953 film *Roman Holiday*. The movie was a product of what in 1950 *Time* magazine dubbed "Hollywood on the Tiber." Big-budget American films, both historical epics such as *Quo Vadis?* (1951) and *Ben-Hur* (1959) as well as romantic comedies, including *Three Coins in the Fountain* and *The Barefoot Contessa* (both 1954), were shot in Rome's huge Cinecittà studio complex, first opened under Mussolini in 1937. However, by the 1950s, Italian-produced films had become world-famous thanks to an approach completely different from that of Hollywood. During and just after the war, directors such as Roberto Rossellini, Vittorio De Sica, and Luchino Visconti began taking grittier and more realistic material for their subjects. This new movement, known as *neorealismo* (neorealism), explored the harsh and challenging lives of ordinary people such as peasants, fishermen, slum-dwelling working people, or, as in Rossellini's *Roma Città Aperta*, resistance fighters. The masterpiece of neorealism—and a

Audrey Hepburn and Gregory Peck ride a Vespa in Roman Holiday *(1953).*

film widely regarded as among the greatest of all time—was De Sica's *Ladri di Biciclette* ("Bicycle Thieves"), released in 1948. Telling the story of a poor Roman billposter whose job depends on the bicycle that he redeems from a pawnshop only to lose to a thief, it offers an unsentimental but deeply moving study of a social reality cruelly indifferent to human needs and suffering.

If neorealism depicted the poverty and fraught social climate in the aftermath of Fascism and the war, another film, released twelve years after *Ladri di Biciclette*, captured the spirit of Italy's economic boom and its resurgence as an intellectual and artistic capital. Federico Fellini's *La Dolce Vita* was filmed from March through September in 1959, appearing the following year and immediately attracting worldwide attention that included the Palme d'Or at the Cannes Film Festival and six Oscar nominations, as well as a good deal of outrage and various attempts at censorship.

Its opening scene offers an aerial tour of Rome, past and present, as a helicopter transporting a statue of Christ crosses the city. It first passes above the ancient ruins of the Aqua Claudia, then over a modern ruin—a crane-and-scaffold landscape of building projects from which a pair of scaffolders cheerily wave—before whirring past an apartment on whose roof terrace four young women sunbathe in bikinis. To the tolling of bells, it finally hovers over St. Peter and the Vatican, where Christ's outstretched arms offer a benediction to the tourists and pilgrims in the square below. The sequence is as ironic as the title, for what has come to Rome is not a spiritual redemption through Christ but, Fellini suggests, a dissolute and wasteful life of parties and casual, fleeting encounters devoid of depth and meaning. *La Dolce Vita* depicts a Rome very different from the desperate portrait offered by *Roma Città Aperta* or *Ladri di Biciclette*: a place that was affluent, secular, and perhaps morally dubious.

The economic miracle had much less purchase in the South, from which emigrated so many of the workers whose low wages, long hours, and harsh conditions powered the boom in the factories of the North—a scenario graphically depicted in Luchino Visconti's 1960 film *Rocco and His Brothers*. The disparities that concerned the protagonists of the Risorgimento had grown more pronounced as the North industrialized and the agricultural communities of the South continued to languish, offering its young people few opportunities apart from emigration, which they took, quite literally, in their millions. It was largely the result of the impoverished South that, as the war ended, Italy had the highest rate of illiteracy, the lowest rate of industrialization, and the lowest per-capita income of any country in Western Europe apart from Fascist Spain and Portugal.[5]

The reasons for this poverty were manifold and longstanding. Indeed, one historian writing in the mid-1960s claimed that the problems went back to Hannibal's devastation of the South's rural landscape, where the marks of the Carthaginian general's destructive presence "were still discernible."[6] A decade earlier, an American political scientist named Edward Banfield had tried to put his finger on the major problem. On the basis of his study of an impoverished village in Basilicata, he argued that the people in the South were dominated by "amoral familialism." By this he meant the villagers were loyal to family members but otherwise, unless monitored by coercive powers such as the police, acted exclusively out of short-term self-interest in order to further the fortunes of their immediate families at the expense of everyone else. Recognizing no moral obligations beyond the nuclear family, they utterly failed, or refused, to act in the interests of any common good. They lacked, in other words, the kind of civic consciousness that writers of the Florentine Renaissance had celebrated and advocated. The result was that the economy of the South suffered because the mutual trust and cooperation necessary for a fair and flourishing market—the willingness to deal openly and fairly with strangers—was completely lacking.[7]

Attempts were made to rectify the dire economic situation by flooding the region with capital. In 1950, Alcide De Gasperi's government formed a special fund, the Cassa per il Mezzogiorno, with the plan of boosting the economic and social fortunes of the South by means of land reclamation and infrastructure projects, such as aqueducts, sewers, and roads. However, the Mafia quickly came to control the land reclamation agencies and most of the public works contracts, soon spreading its tentacles into the regional government thanks to, in the words of one journalist, "the protection, collusion, and complicity of . . . government personalities, not only in Sicily but probably in Rome as well."[8] The Mafia certainly remained a malevolent presence. Although its "men of honor" (as irony-free members call themselves) purported to provide stability, safety, and justice, that argument broke down spectacularly in the last few decades of the twentieth century, when Sicily suffered a series of violent and bloody wars as the ruthless leaders of a clan from Corleone, 30 miles (50 km) south of Palermo, fought and ultimately defeated the Palermo families. The death toll in the early 1980s rose into the hundreds. A dozen separate murders took place in Palermo on one day alone in November 1982. The Corleonesi targeted not only rival mafiosi but also judges, politicians, and policemen, as well as women and children. The law enforcement authorities reacted by rounding up hundreds of alleged mafiosi and prosecuting them in the *Maxiprocesso* (or Maxi Trial) that took place between 1986 and 1992. More than five hundred of them were corralled in a purpose-built bunker beneath a prison in Palermo, the majority of them convicted and given long sentences. The Mafia took its revenge, but caused unprecedented popular outrage, with the murders in 1992 of two of the judges, Paolo Borsellino and Giovanni Falcone, and the bombing in 1993 of the Uffizi Gallery in Florence, where among the five dead were two children, including a two-month-old baby.

The Mafia were not the only architects of violence in Italy in the last decades of the twentieth century. By the late 1960s, the economic miracle had ended and another age, tragically, was dawning: the *anni di piombo*, or "years of lead," a twenty-year period of fierce ideological divisions, political unrest, and terrorist attacks, kidnappings, and assassinations. It's sometimes said that May 1968, with its civil unrest caused by strikes and protests, lasted a month in France but a decade in Italy. The mass protests by students and wildcat strikes by workers in 1968 and 1969 resulted in a right-wing backlash known as the "strategy of tension," a policy perpetrated by a sinister matrix of neo-Fascist groups, Freemasons, and shadowy elements within the Italian security services. Their violent and random mayhem was intended to wreak havoc and sow terror, thereby triggering repressive measures by the state. The first atrocity took place in Milan in December 1969, when seventeen people were killed and almost one hundred injured after members of the neo-Fascist Ordine Nuovo (New Order) detonated a bomb in Piazza Fontana. Others followed, including a bombing by far-right militants in Brescia's Piazza della Loggia in May 1974 and, two months later, an express train in the Apennines. They culminated with the outrage on August 2, 1980, when at the height of the holiday season a fifty-pound (23 kg) bomb was detonated in the second-class waiting room of the train station in Bologna, killing eighty-five (including fifteen children) and wounding more than two hundred.

To the destruction and horror of right-wing terrorism was added the violence of the Red Brigades, a Marxist-Leninist group founded in the aftermath of the Piazza Fontana bombing. Their campaign of kidnappings, beatings, and kneecappings reached its gruesome climax in the spring of 1978 with the kidnapping and, fifty-five days later, the murder of Aldo Moro, the prominent Christian Democrat statesman and former prime minister. Moro had been one of the main architects of the *Compromesso Storico* (Historical Compromise) between the Christian Democrats and the Italian Communist Party. The latter, the largest Communist party in Western Europe, had reached the brink of power by the mid-1970s with more than a third of the electoral tally. The collaboration with the Christian Democrats, intended to create a center-left political affiliation capable of delivering social change against more conservative forces, enraged extreme left and extreme right in equal measure. A massive search for Moro as well as a televised appeal by Pope Paul VI for clemency both proved unavailing. Moro's body, riddled with ten bullets, was found in the trunk of a red Renault 4 on Via Michelangelo Caetani—symbolically, midway between the headquarters of the Christian Democrats and the Italian Communist Party.

The scene in Via Fani of the ambush and kidnapping of Aldo Moro: All five bodyguards were killed.

The murky circumstances of Moro's death fueled conspiracy theories that attributed the security services' inability to find him not to incompetence but rather to their opposition, as ultraconservatives, to the Historic Compromise.

The existence of baleful forces at work in Italian political society was revealed after the discovery in March 1981, in the safe in a factory near Arezzo owned by a Tuscan entrepreneur named Licio Gelli, of a list of 962 members of a secretive masonic lodge named Propaganda Due (P2). The members were dedicated to preventing a communist takeover by subverting Italy's democratic order through the strategy of tension and, if necessary, a political coup and authoritarian government. The list encompassed politicians, industrialists, journalists, and, most numerously, members of the Italian military and security services. "We were like a sentinel," an unrepentant Gelli later boasted, "carefully ensuring that the Communist party should never emerge."[9]

A more pervasive and old-fashioned kind of political misconduct came to light with the arrest in 1992 of a would-be politician named Mario Chiesa, the director of a nursing home in Milan. A candidate for mayor of Milan, Chiesa had close links to the Italian Socialist Party and its leader, Bettino Craxi, the prime minister between 1983 and 1987. After Chiesa was caught pocketing a seven-million-lire ($5,000) bribe from the owner of the cleaning company hoping to secure a contract at the nursing home, Craxi denounced him as a *mariuolo* (rogue). Chiesa took his revenge by cooperating with investigators, who quickly began uncovering a widespread system of kickbacks in the awarding of government contracts.

The investigation became known as *Mani Pulite* (Clean Hands), a reference to a 1983 speech by Sandro Pertini, the Italian president, claiming that "politics must be done with clean hands." The corruption scandal witnessed lawyers, judges, and a hundred officials at the Guardia di Finanza arrested for taking bribes. In Milan alone, some five thousand people, including two hundred members of parliament and four former prime ministers, Craxi included, came under investigation. High-profile casualties included Gabriele Cagliari, the president of Italy's largest company, the energy giant Eni, whose iconic logo—a six-legged, fire-breathing black dog—has adorned Italian gas stations since the 1950s. He died by suicide in prison in 1993. As for Craxi, he was pelted with coins by an outraged mob outside the luxury hotel where he lived in Rome. Sentenced to twenty-seven years in prison, he fled to his villa in Tunisia, a fugitive from justice, dying in self-imposed exile in January 2000.

The scale of the corruption horrified the public, not least because it seemed to be centered not in the Mafia-ridden South but rather in Milan, formerly the "moral capital" of Italy but suddenly christened *Tangentopoli* (Bribesville). (In fairness to Milan, the kickbacks were countrywide.) The *Mani Pulite* investigations overlapped with a series of sensational trials after prosecutors in Palermo in 1993 accused the seven-time prime minister Giulio Andreotti—for decades a pillar of the Christian Democrats, of which he was one of the founders—of involvement with the Sicilian Mafia. A Mafia informer testified that, at the start of a 3.5-hour meeting in Palermo in September 1988, Andreotti, as a sign of respect, exchanged a "kiss of honor" with the Sicilian boss of bosses, Salvatore Riina.[10] Andreotti was also indicted on a charge of having instigated the 1979 murder of the journalist Mino Pecorelli, editor of a journal, *Osservatore*

Giulio Andreotti (1919–2013): Christian Democrat and "Beelzebub"

Politico, that had begun publishing evidence of Andreotti's financial misdeeds. He was acquitted in both cases after a decade-long process of trials and appeals that reached the Supreme Court. Acquittals notwithstanding, the whiff of sulfur lingered around the man who was the subject of more than twenty parliamentary investigations, and who Craxi once dubbed *Belzebù* (Beelzebub). Andreotti retained his wry humor throughout. "Apart from the Punic Wars, for which I was too young," he once said, "I have been blamed for everything."[11]

The old Italian political class could hardly survive such scandal and corruption. The trials and investigations led to the disintegration, in the 1990s, of two of the parties that had dominated Italian politics since the war, Andreotti's Christian Democrats and Craxi's Socialist Party. New parties filled the political void, including Umberto Bossi's Lega Nord, which advocated the secession from Italy of the state of "Padania"—the prosperous regions of Piedmont, Lombardy, and the Veneto. Bossi and his fellow Lega Nord MPs advocated scrapping the Italian *tricolore* and took to booing "Fratelli d'Italia," the Italian national anthem. Instead, they advocated Verdi's "Va, pensiero" as their anthem. It was an ironic choice, given Verdi's support for Italian unification.

The dominant figure in Italian politics over the following two decades was to be Bossi's frequent political bedfellow, Silvio Berlusconi. Known as Il Cavaliere (The Knight), he was equally adored and reviled. An impresario who once sold vacuum cleaners and sang on cruise ships, Berlusconi parlayed his undoubted charm and ability into a successful property career, creating leafy, pedestrian- and cycle-friendly suburbs in Milan in the 1970s and '80s. He soon built up a vast media empire of television stations, publishing houses, newspapers, and film distribution companies, to which he added various banks and, in 1986, the soccer club AC Milan. In January 1994, in the wake of Tangentopoli, Berlusconi launched his own center-right political party, Forza Italia (named for a chant by AC Milan fans). Its populist agenda promised, among other things, a second economic miracle and a million new jobs. When the party won 21 percent of the vote in the March election, Berlusconi gained power by forming a coalition with two other parties, including Bossi's Lega Nord.

Berlusconi's first stint as prime minister proved short-lived as Bossi pulled the plug the following December. Further electoral success appeared unlikely during the second half of the 1990s due to both reservations about a media mogul holding high political office and the numerous judicial investigations into his labyrinthine financial activities. Yet Berlusconi returned to power between 2001 and 2006, and then again from 2008 to 2011. By the time he resigned in November 2011, he was Italy's longest-serving postwar prime minister. But he was also, for many, an increasingly ridiculous and toxic figure, given to casual expressions of homophobia ("It is better to have a passion for beautiful women than to be gay"), racism, (describing Barack Obama as "suntanned"), and misogyny (reportedly calling Angela Merkel an "an unfuckable lard-arse"). He was dogged by legal troubles such as accusations that he bribed senators and—most fatally for his political career—that during one of his infamous *bunga bunga* parties he paid for sex with an underage nightclub dancer known as Ruby Rubacuori (Ruby the Heartstealer).

In January 2013, Berlusconi caused further controversy when, at a speech in Milan on Holocaust Memorial Day, he claimed that Italy did not have "the same responsibilities" as Germany for the war, and that, apart from the 1938 racial laws, Mussolini "in so many other ways did well."[12]

Berlusconi was far from alone in entertaining such opinions. Whereas Angela Merkel on that very same day said that Germans had an "everlasting responsibility" for the crimes of the Nazis,[13] Italians have often been accused of failing to own up to the country's responsibilities for, and actions taken during, World War II, as well as for Mussolini's murderous campaigns in Ethiopia and North Africa—two decades when the Fascist dictatorship caused the premature deaths of, in one estimate, at least a million people.[14] A powerful and consoling myth known as *Italiani, brava gente* ("Italians, the good people") took shape in the decades after the war, offering a heartening vision of the Italians, in contrast to the Nazis, as compassionate and humane, as *brava gente* caught in a bad situation of someone else's making.

This myth was perpetuated in films such as Gabriele Salvatores's 1991 feel-good comedy, *Mediterraneo*, in which eight endearingly inept Italian soldiers land on an Aegean island in 1941. Instead of making war, they befriend the Greeks, who come out of hiding when they realize their invaders are Italians rather than Germans. The Italians take to drinking ouzo, painting frescoes, kicking around a soccer ball with children, and pursuing amorous adventures with a shepherdess and the local prostitute. While *Mediterraneo* was rewarded with an Oscar for its happy clichés of fun-loving Italians, ten years earlier, the Syrian-American director Moustapha Akkad's *Lion of the Desert* (1981), dealing with Mussolini's ruthless pacification of Libya, went virtually unseen in Italy (despite stars such as Anthony Quinn, Oliver Reed, and Sir John Gielgud) because no Italian distributor would purchase its rights. A politician named Raffaele Costa attacked it as "detrimental to the honor of the Italian Army." One of its few screenings, at a film festival in Trento in 1987, was stopped by the police on orders from Giulio Andreotti.[15]

Italy is by no means alone in having a troubled relationship with the murkier aspects of its past. Its plight is mirrored by many other Western democracies attempting to come to terms with legacies of war, colonialism, and slavery. Many Italians, to be sure, have attacked the *brava gente* myth as well as the historical amnesia and silence that have enabled it. In 2021, Mario Draghi, then the serving prime minister, offered a positive foil to Andreotti when he delivered a speech criticizing "reductive and misleading revisionisms" in Italian history. When looking back at the past, he argued, "we must also remember that we Italians were not all 'good people.'"[16]

As for Berlusconi, he died at the age of eighty-six in June 2023. A full panoply of honors followed, including a day of national mourning, flags at half-mast for three days, and a state funeral in Milan's cathedral. The archbishop, Mario Delfini, delivered a homily of dazzling (and highly diplomatic) oratory. Outside the cathedral, massed behind barriers, some ten thousand people gathered to watch on big-screen TVs and pay their respects, some with stadium chants and AC Milan flags. A smaller contingent staged protests, with a woman in a T-shirt reading *Io non sono in lutto* ("I'm not in mourning") hastily bundled away by security for her own protection. "He has supporters and opponents," intoned Archbishop Delfini. "There are those who exalt him and those who detest him." But the life and career of Il Cavaliere were perhaps best summed up by a placard held aloft by an onlooker in the piazza: *Il più italiano degli italiani* ("the most Italian of the Italians").

Berlusconi's second economic miracle failed to take place. In the first two decades of the twenty-first century, the annual GDP never once increased by more than 2 percent per annum, while unemployment hovered steadily around 10 percent. Yet there were, as ever, great successes. Italy has the third largest economy in the European Union and the eighth largest in the world. It has long been a world leader in creative industries such as fashion and luxury goods, with "Made in Italy" a reliable marker of elegant style and quality craftsmanship. Milan has supplanted Florence (still, however, headquarters of Ferragamo and Gucci) as Italy's fashion capital. Milan's longstanding importance in the textile industry is indicated by the fact that the English word "milliner" comes from *Milaner*: someone who sold wares from Milan. Since the 1970s, the city's catwalks and boutiques have been the launching pad for some of the greatest protagonists of Italian fashion and design. In 1975, Giorgio Armani (from nearby Piacenza) launched his label from a shop in Corso Venezia. Three years later, Gianni Versace (from faraway Reggio Calabria) opened a showroom in Via della Spiga. Versace soon caused a sensation with unusual combinations of

Miuccia Prada transformed a small family firm into one of the world's most successful fashion businesses.

materials—leather and silk, rubber with metal—and the use of a mesh-like metallic fabric, Oroton. Also in 1978, a thirty-year-old trained mime with a PhD in political science named Miuccia Prada took over the running of the leather-goods company founded in 1913 by her grandfather Mario and his brother Martino. Women such as Prada have been at the forefront of the fashion business in Italy for decades, with Giuliana Benetton, Wanda Ferragamo, Laudomia Pucci, and Donatella Versace all at various times directly involved in the running of family brands.

Italian businesses are often kept in the family. Of the ten oldest surviving family-run business in the world, six are in Italy, including Pontificia Fonderia Marinelli, makers of bells for more than a thousand years, as well as the winemakers Barone Ricasoli (founded in 1141) and Marchesi Antinori (1385). Family businesses are the driving force behind the Italian economy, accounting for 85 percent of the GDP.[17] Yet the Italian family has changed drastically in the century since Mussolini urged women to have "as many children as possible." Italy has one of the world's lowest birth rates, at 1.2 children per woman. In 2021, fewer than four hundred thousand children were born in Italy, the lowest number since Unification. The lack of *bambini* is one of the reasons why Italy's population dropped by a million people in the five years between 2014 and 2019, slipping to just over fifty-nine million. This decline can also be attributed to Italy's age-old emigration problem. Between 2012 and 2018, some 980,000 Italians left the country, many of them young (the mean age was thirty-three for men, thirty for women) and well educated.[18] Meanwhile, Italy ranks third (behind Monaco and Japan) for having the largest percentage of the population (24 percent) over the age of 65, and fifth in the world for the highest median age (46.5).

On a positive note, the aging population is a tribute to Italy's sixth-place ranking for life expectancy (eighty-four years for women). The healthy Mediterranean diet, cities and towns that encourage walking (including the essential *passeggiata* in the evening), close family bonds that involve the participation of older people in social events, and a moderate consumption of alcohol in comparison to many other Western countries all make for the enviably healthy lifestyle that other cultures have tried (too often in vain) to emulate. While Americans, Canadians, and the British get 50 percent of their daily caloric intake from processed foods, for Italians the total is less than 20 percent.[19] In 2016, the seaside village of Acciaroli, 75 miles (120 km) south of Naples, attracted much media attention when a third of its 1,000 residents were reportedly over the age of 100, with possibly as many as sixty over 110.[20] Researchers speculated that this longevity may have something to do with a diet heavy in anchovies and rosemary, along with regular sexual intercourse. "Sexual activity among the elderly appears to be rampant," gasped one astonished researcher.[21]

Older people may still have sex, but they don't have babies. Immigration is one way to shore up a population, and by 2020 Italy had the second-lowest ratio of immigrants to inhabitants in the EU, at 4.2 per 1,000 inhabitants. Its population losses coincided with the European migrant crisis in the years after 2015. However, attempts to advance immigration as a solution to the demographic problem ran into resistance from some Italians who, like those in many other European countries, feared competition from immigrants for limited jobs and basic public services. Such objections, ironically, reflected those voiced against Italian immigrants to America a century earlier. The migrant crisis led to the rise of parties stridently opposed to immigration such as the populist Five Star Movement and the far-right Brothers of Italy. In October 2022, on the eve of the hundredth anniversary of the March on Rome, the leader of the latter, Giorgia Meloni—whose background includes active membership in neo-Fascist political parties—became Italy's first woman prime minister with 26 percent of the popular vote.

If Italy has been at the center of the migrant crisis, it was also, tragically, a focal point for the COVID-19 pandemic.

La notte dell'Italia: *Bergamo, March 18, 2020*

On March 9, 2020, it became the first country in the world to impose a nationwide lockdown. Images of famous piazzas standing eerily empty became one of the enduring images of the pandemic. Some of the most chastening footage showed a procession of camouflaged army trucks transporting loads of coffins through the dark streets of Bergamo—among the cities most devastated—because its crematoria were unable to cope with the numbers of dead. Seared into the national soul, March 18, 2020, became known as *la notte dell'Italia* (Italy's night).

But after the night came Italy's dawn, for Italian history has always been about resilience and rebirth. The nation featured powerfully in more uplifting images from the darkest days of the pandemic, from Italians up and down the country singing on their balconies, to the signs appearing in windows, often with a rainbow and inscribed in a child's hand, declaring hopefully: *Andrà tutto bene* ("Everything will be all right"). Then, on Easter Sunday in 2020, the tenor Andrea Bocelli sang, live and alone, in Milan's magnificent cathedral.

Easter Sunday, April 12, 2020: Andrea Bocelli sings "Amazing Grace" in front of Milan's cathedral.

It was only fitting that a signal of heroic resurgence in the face of worldwide tragedy should have come from a country that for so many centuries has offered up visions of the wonders to which we humans, at our very best, can aspire.

THE SHORTEST HISTORY OF ITALY

Notes

1. "That People in Togas": Ancient Italy and the Roman Republic

1. Virgil, *Aeneid*, trans. Frederick Ahl (Oxford: Oxford University Press, 2007), ll. 171–2. *Aeneid*, l. 282.

2. Dante, *Inferno*, canto XXXIII, l. 80; Petrarch, *Canzoniere*, CXLVI, ll. 13–14; Dionysius of Halicarnassus, *Roman Antiquities*, Book 1, XXXVII.

3. Cosimo Posth et al., "The Origin and Legacy of the Etruscans through a 2000-year Archeogenomic Time Transect," *Science Advances*, vol. 7, issue 39 (September 2021).

4. On political graffiti and other electoral issues, Matthew Dillon and Lynda Garland, *Ancient Rome: From the Early Republic to the Assassination of Julius Caesar* (Abingdon: Routledge, 2005), pp. 78–80.

2. "Let the Die Be Cast": The Crisis of the Roman Republic

1. Aulus Gellius, *Attic Nights*, vol. 2, books 6–13, trans. J. C. Rolfe, Loeb Classical Library 200 (Cambridge, MA: Harvard University Press, 1927), p. 299. For the Sanskrit origin, see Carl Darling Buck, *A Grammar of Oscan and Umbrian* (Boston: Ginn & Co., 1904), p. 33.

2. Cicero, *Pro Caelio. De Provinciis Consularibus. Pro Balbo*, trans. R. Gardner, Loeb Classical Library 447 (Cambridge, MA: Harvard University Press, 1958), p. 665

3. Plutarch, *Lives*, vol. VII, trans. Bernadotte Perrin, Loeb Classical Library 99 (Cambridge, MA: Harvard University Press, 1919), p. 589.

4. Suetonius, *Lives of the Caesars*, vol. I, trans. K.R. Bradley, Loeb Classical Library 31 (Cambridge, MA: Harvard University Press, 1914), p. 141.

3. "Masters of all in Existence": The Roman Empire

1. *Lives of the Caesars*, p. 193.

2. The speech is reproduced in Tacitus, *Annals*, Book 11, trans. John Jackson, Loeb Classical Library 312 (Cambridge, MA: Harvard University Press, 1937), pp. 285–91.

3. Quoted in Aude Chatelard, "Women as Legal Minors and Their Citizenship in Republican Rome," trans. Anne Stevens, *Clio: Women, Gender, History*, no. 43 (2016), p. 24.

4. Werner Riess, "*Rari Exempla Femina*: Female Virtues on Roman Funerary Inscriptions," in Sharon L. James and Sheila Dillon, eds., *A Companion to Women in the Ancient World* (Chichester, 2012), p. 493.

5. Appian, *Roman History*, vol. 5, ed. and trans. Brian McGing, Loeb Classical Library 543 (Cambridge, MA: Harvard University Press, 2020), pp. 245–7.

6. Tacitus, *Annals*, p. 281.

7. Tacitus, *Annals*, p. 283.

8. For Tacitus's description of the persecutions, see *Annals*, p. 285.

9. Suetonius, *Lives of the Caesars*, vol. II, trans. J.C. Rolfe, Loeb Classical Library 38 (Cambridge, MA: Harvard University Press, 1914). p. 171.

4. "From a Kingdom of Gold to One of Iron and Rust": Decline and Fall of the Empire

1. Tacitus, *Agricola. Germania. Dialogue on Oratory*, trans. M. Hutton and W. Peterson, revised by R.M. Ogilvie, E.H. Warmington and Michael Winterbottom, Loeb Classical Library 35 (Cambridge, MA: Harvard University Press, 1914), p. 81.

2. Pliny the Younger, *Letters, Volume II: Books 8–10. Panegyricus*, p. 325.

3. H.M.D. Parker, *A History of the Roman World from A.D. 138 to 337* (London: Methuen, 1935), p. 20.

4. Dio Cassius, *Roman History*, trans. Earnest Cary, Loeb Classical Library 177 (Cambridge: Harvard University Press, 1927), p. 69.

5. Alexander Demandt, *Der Fall Roms: Die Auflösung der Römischen Reiches im Urteil der Nachwelt* (Munich: C.H. Beck, 1984).

6. Augustus J. C. Hare, *Walks in Rome* (London: George Allen, 1893), vol. 1, p. 235.

7. Tenney Frank, "Race Mixture in the Roman Empire," *The American Historical Review*, vol. 21 (July 1916), p. 690.

8. "Satire 13," l. 30, in *Juvenal and Persius*, ed. and trans. Susanna Morton Braund, Loeb Classical Library 91 (Cambridge, MA: Harvard University Press, 2004).

9. See the website Pharos (https//pharso.vassarspaces.net); and for a good discussion of many issues involved in the disputes, see Jamie Mackay, "The Whitewashing of Rome," *Aeon*, June 25, 2021, available online.

10. Carl-Johan Dalgaard et al., "Roman Roads to Prosperity: Persistence and Non-Persistence of Public Infrastructure," in *Journal of Comparative Economics*, vol. 50 (December 2022), pp. 896–916.

5. Goths, Longbeards, Franks, Saracens, and Normans: Italy Under the "Barbarians"

1. See Peter Heather, *The Fall of the Roman Empire: A New History of Rome and the Barbarians* (Oxford: Oxford University Press, 2006); and Bryan Ward-Perkins, *The Fall of Rome and the End of Civilization* (Oxford: Oxford University Press, 2005).

2. Quoted in Jonathan J. Arnold, *Theoderic and the Roman Imperial Restoration* (Cambridge: Cambridge University Press, 2014), p. 1.

3. Between the first and the fifth centuries, the population of Europe may have dropped from 33 million to 18 million: Alexander B. Murphy et al., *The European Culture Area: A Systematic Geography* (Lanham, MD: Rowman & Littlefield, 2009), p. 72. For the depopulation of Rome, see Gino Luzzatto, *An Economic History of Italy from the Fall of the Roman Empire to the Beginning of the Sixteenth Century*, trans. Philip Jones (London: Routledge, 1961), p. 48.

4. Estimates vary widely, and one scholar has even given a number as high as 300,000: Gabriella Piccinni, *I Mille Anni del Medioevo* (Milano: Mondadori), p. 44.

5. Ferdinand Gregorovius, *History of the City of Rome in the Middle Ages*, trans. Annie Hamilton, vol. 2 (London: George Bell, 1894), p. 17.

6. Quoted in Francesco Cognasso, "Carlomagno, Re dei Franchi e dei Longobardi, Imperatore Romano," *Enciclopedia Italiana* (1931), online edition; my translation.

7. David J. Hay, *The Military Leadership of Matilda of Canossa* (Manchester: Manchester University Press, 2008), p. 40.

8. See Giuseppe Perta, "Fragile Borders beyond the Strait: Saracen Raids on the Italian Peninsula (8th–11th century A.D.)," in Giuseppe d'Angelo and Jorge Martins Ribeiro, eds., *Borders and Conflicts in the Mediterranean Basin* (Fisciano, IT: ICSR Mediterranean Knowledge), p. 150; my translation. For the possibility that Sawdan came from sub-Saharan Africa, see Alex Metcalfe, *The Muslims of Medieval Italy* (Edinburgh: Edinburgh University Press, 2009), p. 21.

9. Amatus of Montecassino, *The History of the Normans*, trans. Prescott N. Dunbar (Woodbridge, Suffolk: Boydell Press, 2004), pp. 50–1.

10. *The Alexiad of the Princess Anna Comnena*, trans. Elizabeth A.S. Dawes (London: Kegan, Paul, Trench & Trübner, 1928), p. 27.

6. "All the Cities of Italy": The Middle Ages

1. *The Itinerary of Benjamin of Tudela*, ed. M.N. Adler (London: Henry Frowde, 1907), p. 5.

2. For this estimate, see Daniel Waley, *The Italian City-Republics* (London: Longman, 1978), p. xvii.

3. Michele Renee Salzman, *Crises, Resilience and Resurgence in Late Antiquity* (Cambridge: Cambridge University Press, 2021), p. 158.

4. Michelet, *La Sorcière* (Paris, 1862), p. 110.

5. Pierre Toubert, *Les Structures du Latium Médiéval* (Rome: École Français de Rome, 1973).

6. Werner Rösener, *Peasants in the Middle Ages*, trans. Alexander Stützer (Urbana and Chicago: University of Illinois Press, 1992), pp. 43, 117.

7. E.A. Weiss, *Spice Crops* (Abingdon, Oxon: CABI Publishing, 2002), p. 156.

8. Lauro Martines, *Power and Imagination: City-States in Renaissance Italy* (Baltimore: Johns Hopkins University Press, 1979), p. 34.

9. Dante, "Purgatorio," VI, ll. 107–8, in *The Divine Comedy*, trans. C.H. Sisson (Oxford: Oxford University Press, 1993).

10. Dante, "Purgatorio," VI, ll. 124–5.

11. *The Opus Major of Roger Bacon*, trans. Robert Belle Burke (Philadelphia: University of Pennsylvania Press, 1928), vol. 1, p. 233.

12. *Mornings in Florence*, in *The Complete Works of John Ruskin, LLD* (Philadelphia: Reuwee, Wattley & Walsh, 1891), vol. 14, p. 36.

13. Millard Meiss, *Painting in Florence and Siena after the Black Death* (Princeton: Princeton University Press, 1951).

14. Edwin S. Hunt, *The Medieval Super-Companies: A Study of the Peruzzi Company of Florence* (Cambridge: Cambridge University Press, 1994).

15. Barbara Tuchman, *A Distant Mirror: The Calamitous 14th Century* (New York: Alfred A. Knopf, 1978).

7. Italy's Age of Gold: The Renaissance

1. Marsilio Ficino, *Opera Omnia* (Turin: Bottega d'Erasmo, 1959), p. 944.

2. Robert S. Lopez, "Hard Times and Investment in Culture," in *The Renaissance: A Symposium* (New York: Metropolitan Museum of Art, 1953), pp. 19–34.

3. David Herlihy and Christiane Klapisch-Zuber, *Tuscans and Their Families: A Study of the Florentine Catasto of 1427* (New Haven: Yale University Press, 1985).

4. Richard A. Goldthwaite, *The Building of Renaissance Florence: An Economic and Social History* (Baltimore and London: The Johns Hopkins University Press, 1980).

5. See Hans Baron, *The Crisis of the Early Italian Renaissance: Civic Humanism and Republican Liberty in an Age of Classicism and Tyranny*, 2 vols. (Princeton: Princeton University Press, 1955).

6. See Frederick Hartt, "Art and Freedom in Quattrocento Florence," in Lucy F. Sandler, ed., *Essays in Memory of Karl Lehmann* (Locust Valley, NY: New York University Institute of Fine Arts, 1964), pp. 114–31.

7. Giorgio Vasari, *Lives of the Artists*, trans. George Bull (London: Penguin, 1965), vol. 1, p. 175.

8. Niccolò Machiavelli, *The Prince*, trans. Peter Bondanella (Oxford: Oxford University Press, 2005), p. 87.

9. Quoted in Marino Sanuto, *I Diarii di Marino Sanuto*, ed. Federico Stefani et al. (Venice: Visentini, 1896), vol. 45, p. 219.

10. Robert Bonfil, *Jewish Life in Renaissance Italy*, trans. Anthony Oldcorn (Berkeley: University of California Press, 1994).

11. William Eamon and Françoise Paheau, "The Accademia Segreta of Girolamo Ruscelli: A Sixteenth-Century Italian Scientific Society," *Isis*, vol. 75 (June 1984), pp. 327–42.

12. Quoted in *Palladio's Rome: A Translation of Andrea Palladio's Two Guidebooks to Rome*, ed. and trans. Vaughan Hart and Peter Hicks (New Haven: Yale University Press, 2006), p. xxv.

13. Margaret Rose, "The First Italian Actresses, Isabella Andreini, and the *Commedia dell'Arte*," in *The Palgrave Handbook of the History of Women on the Stage*, eds. Jan Sewell and Clare Smout (London: Palgrave Macmillan, 2020), p. 110.

14. Quoted in Rose, "The First Italian Actresses," pp. 108–9.

15. Quoted in Iain Fenlon, "The Mantean 'Orfeo,'" in John Whenham, ed., *Claudio Monteverdi: Orfeo* (Cambridge: Cambridge University Press, 1986), p. 1.

16. Quoted in Ellen Rosand, *Opera in Seventeenth-Century Venice: The Creation of a Genre* (Berkeley: University of California Press, 1991), p. 9.

17. Vincenzo Galilei, *Discorso Intorno all'Opere de M. Gioseffo Zarlino* (Venice, 1589), p. 120.

18. Galileo Galilei, *Sidereus Nuncius, or, The Sidereal Messenger*, trans. with introduction, conclusion and notes by Albert Van Helden (Chicago: University of Chicago Press, 1989), p. xviii.

8. "Go, Thought, on Golden Wings": Italy in the *Illuminismo*

1. Quoted in *Early Modern Spain: A Documentary History*, ed. Jan Cowans (Philadelphia: University of Pennsylvania Press, 2003), p. 189.

2. "Il Caffè," in *Articoli Tratti dal Caffè* (Milan: Nicolò Bettoni, 1829), p. 9.

3. Arthur Young, *Travels During the Years 1787, 1788 and 1789* (Dublin, 1793), p. 471.

4. Antonio Genovesi, *Opere Scelte* (Milan, 1828), p. 73.

5. Quoted in Marianna Prampolini, *La Duchessa Maria Luigia: Vita Familiare alla Corte di Parma: Diari, Carteggi Inediti, Ricami* (Bergamo: Bergamo: Istituto Italiano Arti Grafiche, 1942), p. 112.

6. Quoted in Leonardo Farinelli, *Maria Luigia, Duchessa di Parma* (Milan: Rusconi, 1983), p. 45.

7. Quoted in *The Foreign Quarterly Review* (October 1835), p. 48.

9. "Here We Make Italy": The Risorgimento

1. Klemens Wenzel von Metternich, *Mémoires, Documents et Écrits Divers Laissés par le Prince de Metternich Chancelier de Court et d'État*, 8 vols. (Paris, 1881–84), vol. 7, p. 393.

2. *The Foreign Quarterly Review* (London, 1830), p. 158.

3. Quoted in Claudio Povolo, *The Novelist and the Archivist: Fiction and History in Alessandro Manzoni's "The Betrothed,"* trans. Peter Mazur (Basingstoke: Palgrave Macmillan, 2014), p. 7.

4. Verdi, *Lettere*, ed. Eduardo Rescigno (Turin: Giulio Einaudi, 2012), p. 199.

5. Quoted in Mariachiara Fugazza and Karoline Rörig, eds., *La Prima Donna d'Italia: Cristina Trivulzio di Belgiojoso tra Politica e Giornalismo* (Milan: FrancoAngeli, 2010), p. 7.

6. Quoted in Harry Hearder, *Cavour* (Abingdon, Oxon.: Routledge, 2013), p. 19.

7. Quoted in Hearder, *Cavour*, p. 43.

8. Quoted in Denis Mack Smith, *Cavour* (London: Weidenfeld and Nicolson, 1985), p. 139.

9. Quoted in Christopher Hibbert, *Garibaldi: Hero of Italian Unification* (Basingstoke: Palgrave Macmillan, 2008), p. 4.

10. Quoted in Alfonso Scirocco, *Garibaldi: Citizen of the World*, trans. Allan Cameron (Princeton: Princeton University Press, 2007), p. 6.

11. *New-York Tribune*, July 30, 1850.

12. Quoted in Denis Mack Smith, *Garibaldi* (London: Hutchinson, 1957), p. 97.

13. Denis Mack Smith, *Italy and Its Monarchy* (New Haven and London: Yale University Press, 1989), p. 5.

14. Quoted in Mack Smith, *Cavour*, p. 274.

15. Quoted in Joseph Redlich, *Emperor Francis Joseph of Austria: A Biography* (Hamden, CT: Archon Books, 1965), p. 273.

16. A discussion of this famous phrase—which the authors suggest d'Azeglio never actually uttered—is found in Simonetta Soldani and Gabriele Turi, eds., *Fare Gli Italiani: Scuola e Cultura nell'Italia Contemporanea* (Bologna: Mulino, 1993), vol. 1, p. 17.

17. Armando Petrucci, "Alfabetismo," *Enciclopedia Italiana*, vol. 5, *Appendice* (1991), online edition.

18. John Gooch, *The Unification of Italy* (London: Methuen, 1986), p. 33.

19. Quoted in Nelson Moe, "Altro che Italia!" Il Sud dei Piemontesi (1860–1861), *Meridiana* (September 1992), p. 68.

20. Quoted in Lucy Riall, *Politica Liberale e Potere Locale, 1815–1866* (Torino: Einaudi, 2004), p. 143. For these North–South problems I am indebted to the discussion in Riall's "Il Sud e i Conflitti Sociali," in Giovanni Sabbatucci and Vittorio Vidotto, eds., *L'Unificazione Nazionale* (Rome: Treccani, 2011), pp. 129–49.

21. Quoted in Moe, "Altro che Italia!" p. 67.

22. Leopoldo Franchetti, quoted in Jane Schneider and Peter Schneider, "Mafia, Antimafia, and the Plural Cultures of Sicily," *Current Anthropology*, vol. 46 (August/October 2005), p. 504.

23. Luciano de Pascalis and Diego de Castro, "Analfabetismo," in *Enciclopedia Italiana*, vol. 2, *Appendice* (1948), online edition.

24. Diego Gambetta, "'In the Beginning Was the Word . . .' The Symbols of the Mafia," *European Journal of Sociology / Archives Européennes de Sociologie / Europäisches Archiv für Soziologie*, vol. 32 (1991), p. 64.

25. Quoted in Nunzio Pernicone, *Italian Anarchism, 1864–1892* (Princeton: Princeton University Press, 1993), p. 120.

26. Quoted in Pernicone, *Italian Anarchism*, p. 127.

27. Quoted in Tullio de Mauro, *Storia Linguistica dell'Italia Unita* (Rome and Bari: Laterza, 1972), pp. 287–88.

28. For this claim, see Domenico Proietti, "Lorenzini, Carlo," *Dizionario Biografico degli Italiani*, volume 66 (2006), online edition.

10. "Dov'è La Vittoria?": The Kingdom of Italy

1. Gianfausto Rosoli, ed., *Un Secolo di Emigrazione Italiana, 1876–1976* (Rome: CSER, 1978), pp. 350 ff. For details about Gaetano Bresci, see Gian Domenico Zucca, "Appunti per una Biografia su Gaetano Bresci a Cento Anni dalla Morte" (Brescia: Fondazione Biblioteca Archivio Luigi Micheletti, 2001), pp. 1–19.

2. Patrick J. Gallo, *Ethnic Alienation: The Italian-Americans* (Rutherford, NJ: Fairleigh Dickinson University Press, 1974), p. 26.

3. On these issues, see Jennifer Guglielmo and Salvatore Salerno, eds., *Are Italians White? How Race Is Made in America* (Abingdon, Oxon.: Routledge, 2003). Guglielmo discusses the use of *guinea* on p. 11.

4. Quoted in Nunzio Pernicone, "The Case of Pietro Acciarito: Accomplices, Psychological Torture, and *Raison d'État*," *Journal for the Study of Radicalism*, vol. 5 (Spring 2011), p. 67.

5. For the anarchists in Paterson, see Kenyon Zimmer, *Immigrants Against the State: Yiddish and Italian Anarchism in America* (Urbana: University of Illinois Press, 2015), pp. 62–3.

6. Quoted in Alfredo Canavero, *Milano e la Crisi di Fine Secolo (1896–1900)* (Milan: Unicopli, 1998), pp. 256–7.

7. *The Times of London*, July 31, 1900.

8. See Zucca, "Appunti per una Biografia su Gaetano Bresci a Cento Anni dalla Morte," p. 14.

9. Salvatore Ferragamo, *Shoemaker of Dreams: The Autobiography of Salvatore Ferragamo* (London: George Harrap & Co., 1957), p. 144.

10. Patrick J. Gallo, *Ethnic Alienation*, p. 25.

11. Ivan T. Berend, *An Economic History of Nineteenth-Century Europe: Diversity and Industrialization* (Cambridge: Cambridge University Press, 2013), p. 227.

12. Francesco Saverio Nitti, *La Conquista della Forza* (Turin: Casa editrice nazionale, 1905), p. 231.

13. *Futurism: An Anthology*, eds. Lawrence Rainey, Christine Poggi and Laura Wittman (New Haven and London: Yale University Press, 2009), pp. 49, 67.

14. Quoted in Christopher Duggan, *The Force of Destiny: A History of Italy Since 1796* (Boston: Houghton Mifflin, 2008), pp. 376–77.

15. R.J.B. Bosworth, *Italy, the Least of the Great Powers: Italian Foreign Policy before the First World War* (London and New York: Cambridge University Press, 1979).

16. Quoted in Duggan, *The Force of Destiny*, p. 384.

17. Cesare Causa, *La Guerra Italo-Turca e la Conquista della Tripolitania e della Cirenaica*, 2nd ed. (Florence: Salani, 1913), p. 805.

18. Quoted in Duggan, *The Force of Destiny*, p. 389.

19. Quoted in Margaret MacMillan, *Paris 1919: Six Months That Changed the World* (New York: Random House, 2001), p. 296.

20. Quoted in MacMillan, *Paris 1919*, p. 287.

21. For the history of this salute, see Martin M. Winkler, *The Roman Salute: Cinema, History, Ideology* (Columbus: Ohio State University Press, 2009).

22. See Marc Raboy, *Marconi: The Man Who Networked the World* (Oxford: Oxford University Press, 2016), pp. 449–50.

23. Quoted in Federico Nardelli and Arthur Livingstone, *Gabriel the Archangel: Gabriele D'Annunzio* (New York: Harcourt, Brace, 1931), p. 315.

11. The "Putrid Corpse" of Liberty: Italy under Fascism

1. Quoted in Emilio Gentile, "Mussolini, Benito," *Dizionario Biografico degli Italiani*, vol. 77 (2012), online edition.

2. *Opera Omnia di Benito Mussolini*, eds. Edoardo and Duilio Susmel, 36 vols. (Florence: La Fenice, 1951–63), vol. 7, p. 71.

3. Quoted in Michael R. Ebner, *Ordinary Violence in Mussolini's Italy* (Cambridge: Cambridge University Press, 2011), p. 23.

4. Quoted in Mark Robson, *Italy: Liberalism and Fascism, 1870–1945* (London: Hodder & Stoughton, 1992), p. 51.

5. *Opera Omnia di Benito Mussolini*, vol. 19, p. 17.

6. Quoted in Cosimo Ceccuti, *Mussolini nel Giudizio dei Primi Antifascisti* (Milan: Mondadori, 1983), p. 147.

7. See R.J.B. Bosworth, *Politics, Murder and Love in an Italian Family: The Amendolas in the Age of Totalitarianism* (Cambridge: Cambridge University Press, 2023).

8. For a history of the term, see Bruno Bongiovanni and John Rugman, "Totalitarianism: The Word and the Thing," *Journal of Modern European History / Zeitschrift für Moderne Europäische Geschichte / Revue d'Histoire Européenne Contemporaine*, vol. 3 (2005), pp. 5–17.

9. *Opera Omnia di Benito Mussolini*, vol. 21, p. 362.

10. Quoted in Jan Nelis, "Constructing Fascist Identity: Benito Mussolini and the Myth of 'Romanità,'" *The Classical World*, vol. 100 (Summer 2007), p. 403.

11. Quoted in Dietrich Neumann, "A Skyscraper for Mussolini," *AA Files* (2014), p. 141.

12. Quoted in Neumann, "A Skyscraper for Mussolini," p. 143.

13. Quoted in Aristotle Kallis, " 'Framing' *Romanità*: The Celebrations for the Bimillenario Augusteo and the Augusteo-Ara Pacis Project," *Journal of Contemporary History*, vol. 46 (October 2011), p. 831, n. 83.

14. Quoted in Sergio Raffaelli, *Le Parole Proibite: Purismo di Stato e Regolamentazione della Pubblicità in Italia* (Bologna: Il Mulino, 1983), p. 128.

15. Quoted in Augusto Torre, "Asse," in *Enciclopedia Italiana*, Appendice (1948), online edition.

16. Quoted in MacGregor Knox, *Mussolini Unleashed: Politics and Strategy in Fascist Italy's Last War* (Cambridge: Cambridge University Press, 1982), p. 1.

17. Quoted in Knox, *Mussolini Unleashed*, p. 6.

18. Eisenhower's Protection of Cultural Monuments Order, 29 December 1943, National Archives, File: CAD 000.4 (3-25-43) (1), Sec. 2, Security Classified General Correspondence, 1943–July 1949, General Records, Civil Affairs Division, Records of the War Department General and Special Staffs, RG 165.

19. Detractors include John Cornwell, *Hitler's Pope: The Secret History of Pius XII* (New York: Viking, 1999); and Susan Zucotti, *Under His Very Windows: The Vatican and the Holocaust in Italy* (New Haven: Yale University Press, 2001). For the defense: Ronald J. Rychlak, *Hitler, the War, and the Pope* (Huntington, IN: Our Sunday Visitor, 2000); David G. Dalin, "Pius XII and the Jews," *Rivista di Studi Politici Internazionali*, vol. 69 (October–November 2002), pp. 614–28; and idem., *The Myth of Hitler's Pope: How Pope Pius XII Rescued Jews from the Nazis* (Washington DC: Regnery Publishing, 2005). Dalin discusses Goebbels's pamphlet in "Pius XII and the Jews," p. 622.

20. Quoted in Stefania Costa and Anne Noon-Luminari, "Forced Motherhood in Italy," *Frontiers: A Journal of Women Studies*, vol. 2 (Spring, 1977), p. 51.

21. See Laura Gnocchi, "Donne, Resistenza e Voto," *Atlante* (May 22, 2022), available online.

22. Quoted in R.J.B. Bosworth, *Mussolini* (London: Bloomsbury Academic, 2010), p. 31.

23. Bosworth, *Mussolini*, p. 25.

12. *Andrà Tutto Bene*: Italy since the War

1. Frederic Sondern, Jr., "The Little King," *Life*, May 27, 1940, p. 94.

2. Quoted in Denis Mack Smith, *Italy and Its Monarchy* (New Haven: Yale University Press, 1989), p. 325.

3. Piero Barucci, quoted in John Lamberton Harper, *America and the Reconstruction of Italy, 1945–1948* (Cambridge: Cambridge University Press, 1986), p. 4.

4. Costa and Noon-Luminari, "Forced Motherhood in Italy," p. 43.

5. Mark Gilbert and Sara Lamberti, *Historical Dictionary of Modern Italy*, 3rd ed. (Lanham, MD: Rowman & Littlefield, 2020), p. 17.

6. Arnold J. Toynbee, *Hannibal's Legacy: The Hannibalic War's Effects on Roman Life*, 2 vols. (London: Oxford University Press, 1965), vol. 2, p. 35.

7. Edward C. Banfield, *The Moral Basis of a Backward Society* (Glencoe, IL: Free Press, 1958). His theory was widely attacked and revised in the decade after publication: see Frank Cancian, "The Southern Italian Peasant: World View and Political Behavior," *Anthropological Quarterly*, vol. 34 (1972), pp. 1–18; Gilberto A. Marselli, "American Sociologists and American Peasant Society," *Sociologia Ruralis*, vol. 3 (1963), pp. 319–38; and Sydel F. Silverman, "Agricultural Organization, Social Structure, and Values in Italy: Amoral Familialism Reconsidered," *American Anthropologist*, vol. 70 (1968), pp. 1–20.

8. Quoted in Judith Chubb, *Patronage, Power, and Poverty in Southern Italy: A Tale of Two Cities* (Cambridge: Cambridge University Press, 1982), p. 139.

9. Quoted in James Politi, "Licio Gelli, Fascist and Masonic Chief," *Financial Times*, December 17, 2015.

10. "Quel Bacio di Riina ad Andreotti," *La Repubblica*, April 21, 1993.

11. John Tagliabue, "Giulio Andreotti, Premier of Italy 7 Times, Dies at 94," *New York Times*, May 6, 2013.

12. Quoted in Josephine Mckenna, "Silvio Berlusconi Under Fire for Defending Benito Mussolini," *Daily Telegraph*, January 27, 2013.

13. Josephine Mckenna, "Silvio Berlusconi under fire for defending Benito Mussolini."

14. Bosworth, *Mussolini*, pp. 2, 32.

15. See Maria Francesca Piredda, "Rovine e Macerie: Permanenze e Rimozioni dell'Identità Coloniale nel Cinema Italiano dal Secondo Dopoguerra alle Migrazioni Contemporanee," in *Cinema e Identità Italiana: Cultura Visuale e Immaginario Nazionale fra Radizione e Contemporaneità*, ed. Stefania Parigi, Christian Uva and Vito Zagarrio (Rome: Roma-TrE, 2019), pp. 633–4.

16. "Il Discorso di Draghi: 'Non Fummo Tutti Brava Gente,'" *Domani*, April 25, 2021.

17. Maria Brizi, Debora Ercoli and Catia Trinari, "An Overview of the Environment for Family Businesses in Italy: National Report," Family Business Successful Succession, Project number: 2016-3-EL02-KA205-002673 (June 2017), p. 9.

18. "Registration and Deregistration of the Resident Population: Year 2018," Istituto Nazionale di Statistica, December 16, 2019, https://www.istat.it/it/files//2020/05/Migrazioni_EN.pdf.

19. Mariavittoria Savini, "Tumori, dalla Dieta un Aiuto Concreto per la Prevenzione," *Rai News*, February 4, 2023.

20. "In One Italian Village, Nearly 300 Residents Are Over 100 Years Old," *All Things Considered*, NPR, March 30, 2016.

21. Quoted in Harry Cockburn, "Scientists 'Find Key to Longevity' in Italian Village Where One in 100 People Live Beyond 100 Years," *The Independent*, September 8, 2016.

Acknowledgments

I am grateful, first of all, to Chris Feik, who in the summer of 2021 made an offer I could not refuse: the chance to write about Italy for Black Inc.'s Shortest History series. I also thank the rest of the wonderful and supportive team at Black Inc., including Jo Rosenberg, Sophy Williams, Amelia Willis, and (for her attentive copyediting) Kate Morgan. Likewise the team at The Experiment, especially Anna Bliss and Zach Pace, for their hard work on my behalf.

I am also deeply indebted to a number of scholars and experts from whose expertise I benefited, and on whose generosity and good natures I depended. Paul Erdkamp, Scott Perry, William Cook, Alberto Mario Banti, and Richard Bosworth all read significant chunks of the work in manuscript, offering excellent advice and saving me from various errors. Richard and Scott, in particular, read long sections: Richard the final three chapters and Scott the manuscript in its entirety.

Other people responded to my queries or cast their eyes over various sections. Dava Sobel and Nuno Castel-Branco read and improved my passages on Galileo, and Adam Fix helped me with Galileo's father. Paola Stanzione read my sections on Italian fashion, and Alexandra Ares provided information about the Romanian anthem and Romania's

Roman connections. Despite all of this wise and patient guidance, I must take responsibility for whatever muddles inevitably remain.

I am grateful to John Gilkes for creating the maps and Diane Lowther for the index.

I must also thank, as always, the two people who have been such constants in both my writing career and in my life for more than twenty years: my wife, Melanie, and my agent, Christopher Sinclair-Stevenson. This book is dedicated to my beloved sister-in-law, good friend, and frequent traveling companion in Italy and elsewhere, Destine Bradshaw.

Image Credits

Maps and illustrations on pages 5, 33, and 75 by Alan Laver.

Maps on pages 51, 118, and 139 by John Gilkes.

p. 8: *Wenceslaus Hollar*, from a design by Giulio Romano for Stucco Medallions at the Palazzo Te, Joseph Pulitzer Bequest, 1917, Metropolitan Museum of Art.

p. 9: Nicolas Poussin, *Abduction of the Sabine Women*, Harris Brisbane Dick Fund, 1946, Metropolitan Museum of Art.

p. 18: © The Trustees of the British Museum.

p. 25: Collection of Walters Art Museum, Baltimore. Image via the museum, CC.0.

p. 29: © The Trustees of the British Museum.

p. 30: Photograph by the author.

p. 35: *Marble Portrait Bust of the Emperor Gaius, known as Caligula*, 37–41 CE, Rogers Fund, 1914, Metropolitan Museum of Art.

p. 47: nickgavluk/ iStock.

p. 52: Photograph by the author.

p. 55: Photograph by the author.

p. 58: *Marble Portrait of the Emperor Caracalla*, Roman, 212–217 CE, Samuel D. Lee Fund, 1940, Metropolitan Museum of Art.

p. 95: Mrkit99 / iStock.

p. 100: Giotto, *St. Francis at the Crib at Greccio*, 1295, Upper Basilica of San Francesco, Assisi. Image via Wikimedia Commons.

p. 103: Giotto, *Crucifix*, 1290, Santa Maria Novella, Florence. Image via Wikimedia Commons.

p. 110: Masaccio, *Holy Trinity*, c. 1426–1428, Basilica of Santa Maria Novella, Florence. Image via Wikimedia Commons.

p. 113: Photograph by the author.

p. 115: aluxum / iStock.

p. 125: Sofonisba Anguissola, *Self-Portrait*, 1554. Collection of Museo Poldi Pezzoli, Milan. Photograph by the author.

p. 128: Photograph by the author.

p. 138: Jean-François Bosio, *Portrait of Cesare Bonesana, Marchese di Beccaria*, The Elisha Whittelsey Fund, 1949, Metropolitan Museum of Art.

p. 142: Jacques-Louis David, *Napoleon Crossing the Alps*, 1805, collection of the Château de Malmaison. Image via Wikimedia Commons.

p. 144: Jean-Baptiste Paulin Guérin (after François Gérard), *Empress Marie Louise of the French* (1791–1847), c. 1812, collection of the Château de Versailles, France. Image via Wikimedia Commons.

p. 146: Robineau, "Vente de Carbonari," 1820, p. 106, col. 1; public domain.

p. 149: 19th-century engraving after a portrait by Pietro Ermini; public domain.

p. 152: Image via State Library of Victoria.

p. 157: Image via State Library of Victoria.

p. 162: Unknown author, c. 1861, Photograph from Library of Congress, Washington, DC. Image via Wikimedia Commons.

p. 163: Photograph by André-Adolphe-Eugène Disdéri, 1861. Image via Tim Ross, Wikimedia Commons.

p. 176: Sophus Williams, *King Umberto*, 1878. Collection of Wartenberg Trust. Image via Wikimedia Commons.

p. 180: Edward Sylvester Ellis and Charles F. Horne, *The Story of the Greatest Nations: From the Dawn of History to the Twentieth Century*, F.R. Niglutsch, New York, 1900, p. 239. Image via www.ilgiornale.it

p. 182: Giovanni Battista Carpanetto, *F.I.A.T. Società Anonyma Torino Fabbrica Italiana d'Automobili*, 1899. Image via Wikimedia Commons.

p. 184: Umberto Boccioni, *Unique Forms of Continuity in Space*, 1989. Bequest of Lydia Winston Malbin, Metropolitan Museum of Art.

p. 191: Photographer unknown; public domain. Image via Geelong Regional Libraries.

p. 198: Photographer unknown, 28 October 1922; public domain. Image via Encyclopedia Britannica.

p. 210: Piero della Francesca, *The Resurrection of Christ*, 1463, Museo Civico di Sansepolcro. Image via Wikimedia Commons.

p. 213: Photograph by Sueddeutsche Zeitung Photo, 1945. Image via Dress Is More.

p. 221: Trailer, *Roman Holiday*, dir. William Wyler, Paramount Pictures, 1953. Image via Wikimedia Commons.

p. 226: Ur Cameras/Flickr.

p. 229: Photographer unknown via www.moondo.info

p. 234: Andrea Raffin/Alamy Stock Photo.

p. 237: Photo © Sergio Agazz, Sipa USA/Alamy Stock Photo.

p. 238: LM/Daniele Cifalà/Alamy Live News.

Index

Page numbers in *italics* refer to illustrations, maps, and photos.

About the Author

ROSS KING is the author of many bestselling books on Italian history and art, including *Michelangelo and the Pope's Ceiling, Brunelleschi's Dome,* and *The Bookseller of Florence.* He lectures widely on Renaissance art at museums including the Art Institute of Chicago, the Frick Collection, and the National Gallery, and is a regular participant in Italian Renaissance seminars at the Aspen Institute. He lives in the historic town of Woodstock, near Oxford, England.

rosskingbooks.com

Also available in the Shortest History series

978-1-61519-569-5   978-1-61519-820-7   978-1-61519-814-6   978-1-61519-896-2

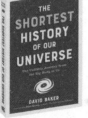

978-1-61519-930-3   978-1-61519-914-3   978-1-61519-948-8   978-1-61519-950-1

978-1-61519-973-0   978-1-61519-997-6   978-1-891011-34-4